CHRISTOPHER MOORE

THE LOYALISTS

REVOLUTION, EXILE, SETTLEMENT

M&S

First published in hardcover by Macmillan of Canada in 1984.
First published in paperback by McClelland & Stewart in 1994.

Canadian Cataloguing in Publication Data

Moore, Christopher
The Loyalists: revolution, exile, settlement

Includes bibliographical references and index.

ISBN 0-7710-6093-9

1. United Empire Loyalists. 2. United States – History –
Revolution, 1775-1783. 3. Canada – History – 1763-1867.
I. Title.

FC426.M66 1994 971.02'4 C94-930040-3
E277.M76 1994

Typesetting by M&S
Printed and bound in Canada

McClelland & Stewart Inc.
The Canadian Publishers
481 University Avenue
Toronto, Ontario
M5G 2E9

1 2 3 4 5 98 97 96 95 94

Contents

Map: The Loyalists in Canada / 5-6

Preface • The Loyalists Themselves / 7

PART ONE • REVOLUTION

The Eve of Revolution, 1774-1775 / 13

The Language of Liberty, 1763-1776 / 39

The Crisis of Loyalty, 1775-1776 / 65

PART TWO • EXILE

The King's War, 1776-1781 / 85

The Loyalists' War, 1775-1781 / 107

Refugee Routes, 1777-1783 / 124

PART THREE • SETTLEMENT

Preparing the Way, 1783 / 157

Edward Winslow's New Brunswick, 1783-1800 / 183

Gideon White's Nova Scotia, 1783-1800 / 203

Samuel Farrington's Upper Canada, 1784-1800 / 224

Taking Root / 248

Notes / 255

Bibliography / 267

Index / 273

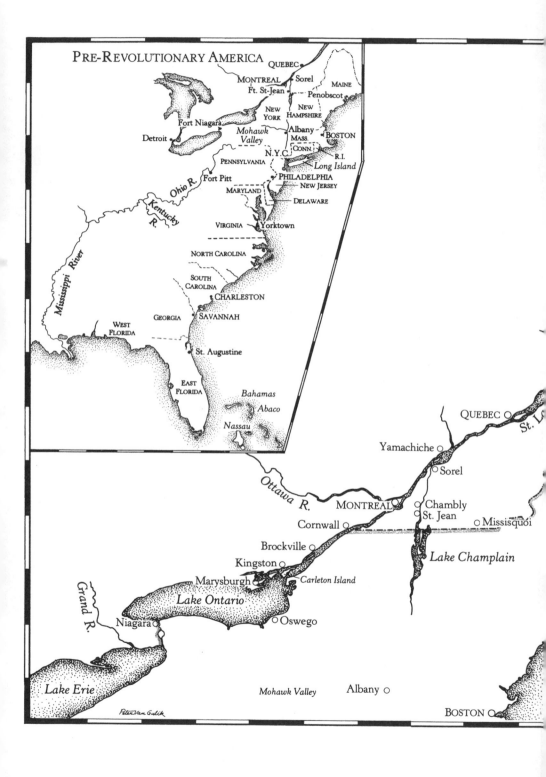

PRE-REVOLUTIONARY AMERICA

QUEBEC
MONTREAL • Sorel
Ft. St-Jean
MAINE
Penobscot
NEW YORK
NEW HAMPSHIRE
Fort Niagara
Mohawk Valley
Albany
MASS.
BOSTON
Detroit
N.Y.C.
CONN.
R.I.
Ohio R.
PENNSYLVANIA
Long Island
Fort Pitt
PHILADELPHIA
MARYLAND
NEW JERSEY
Kentucky R.
DELAWARE
VIRGINIA
Yorktown
Mississippi River
NORTH CAROLINA
SOUTH CAROLINA
CHARLESTON
GEORGIA
SAVANNAH
WEST FLORIDA
St. Augustine
EAST FLORIDA
Bahamas
Abaco
Nassau

QUEBEC ○
St. L
Yamachiche ○
Sorel ○
Ottawa R.
MONTREAL ○
Chambly
St. Jean
Missisquoi ○
Cornwall ○
Lake Champlain
Brockville ○
Kingston ○
Marysburgh ○
Carleton Island
Grand R.
Lake Ontario
Niagara ○
Oswego ○
Lake Erie
Mohawk Valley
Albany ○
Peter Van Gulik
BOSTON ○

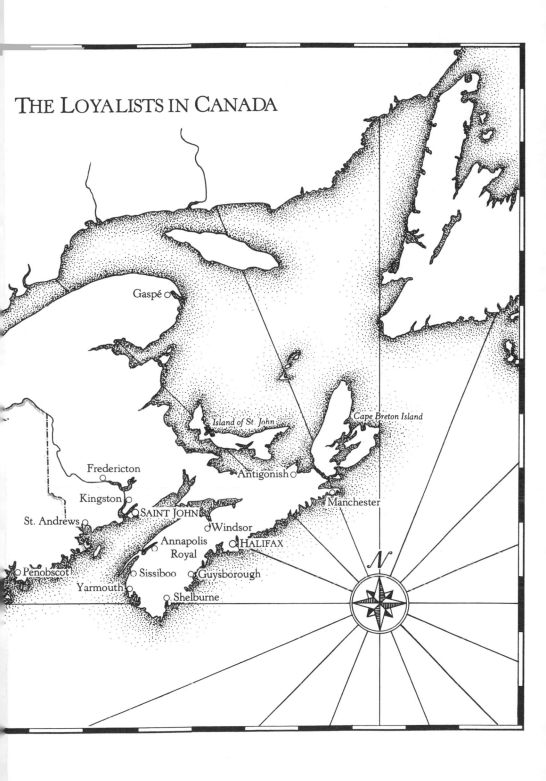

THE LOYALISTS IN CANADA

Gaspé

Island of St. John

Cape Breton Island

Fredericton

Kingston

Antigonish

SAINT JOHN

Manchester

St. Andrews

Windsor

Annapolis
Royal

HALIFAX

Penobscot

Sissiboo

Guysborough

Yarmouth

Shelburne

N

Preface

The Loyalists Themselves

FOR TWO HUNDRED YEARS THE LOYALISTS HAVE BEEN turning into bronze. Statues and plaques stand in half the cities and towns of eastern Canada to affirm their contribution to the country, but we seem to resist letting the loyalists be anything but statues and plaques. Hardly sure who they were or what they did, we have remembered them as ancestors, but even more as symbols and abstractions – of monarchy, of empire, of tradition, of tory power. Honoured or shunned according to current enthusiasms, they are rarely considered for their own flesh-and-blood concerns.

Perhaps this is natural, for it is easy to reduce history to politics and historical characters to labels. But the loyalists themselves have also seemed to resist a more personal attention. As many historians have observed, pioneers rarely enjoyed the luxury of documenting themselves extensively, and so in places the historical record has been thin. More important, perhaps, when they did leave record of themselves, the loyalists did not always say what we might want them to say. Frequently they present the most violent and emotional experiences of their lives in the emotionally reticent, unsentimental style of the late eighteenth century. The loyalists and their contemporaries could speak readily of large concepts like duty, honour, principle – and of course loyalty – that tend to make us uncomfortable. Few of them easily expressed fear, sorrow, joy, or ambition in the ways that we expect personalities to be revealed. "When we push beyond the surface of most eighteenth century sources and ask questions about the character of individuals' lives," says American historian Pauline Maier, "we are often asking what our subjects had no intention of telling us."

To bridge that gap and to approach the personal experience of the loyalists, I have attempted to place them in the American societies that shaped them and the Canadian ones to which they came and contributed. Instead of following loyalist traditions into the nineteenth and twentieth centuries, I have tried to present careers and voices that do manage to speak to us from the loyalists themselves, whether in a Scottish-American soldier's pungent letters or in the private diary of a peaceable Massachusetts merchant. Even if the loyalist in question did not eventually settle in Canada, I have followed testimonies that seemed to illuminate the loyalist experience in revolution, exile, and settlement.

To reach beyond those few who wrote a lot and had their writings preserved, I have followed another, extraordinary source, the Loyalist Claims. After the American war, the British government announced it would hear claims and offer compensation to colonists who had suffered for their loyalty. Many of those who claimed had no particular wealth, fame, or position; those encountered in the extensive records of the Claims Commission include a barrelmaker's widow trying to make ends meet in the newly founded city of Shelburne, Nova Scotia, a tenant farmer uprooted from the western frontier, and a war-ruined merchant trying to support himself as a household servant.

Some of the claimants merely presented an inventory of losses and their instructions for payment. Some wanted to tell war stories. And some used the commissioners' time for an intricate examination of why they were loyal when their neighbours were not. All hoped to win financial compensation from a sometimes miserly commission. Their claims omitted much and distorted some of the loyalists' experience, and most were composed in the formal, third-person style that the claimants believed or were told the officials preferred. Yet, in thousands of statements, the great array of individuals who claimed could hardly avoid presenting much about themselves, and I have quoted their petitions extensively.

The war that created the United States drove at least fifty thousand colonial Americans into exile for the sake of their beliefs. Most of those refugees came to Canada. They assimilated into local societies, and became Nova Scotian or Upper Canadian, but they often preserved specific loyalist traditions too. In Nova Scotia and New Brunswick, in parts of Quebec, and in most of early settled Ontario, towns and communities founded in the loyalist migration have grown into cities – or have persisted quietly in the rural fabric of the country. By numbers alone the loyalists command attention: conscious of it or not, many thousands of Canadians in every part of the country have loyalists in their family tree or loyalist communities in their background.

Still they have maintained their distance. Two hundred years after their arrival in Canada, every statement about the loyalists seems to begin with the announcement that they were "not just" wealthy and aristocratic Harvard graduates driven from Boston as tory tyrants. Indeed they were not, but rather than simply restating the negative, *The Loyalists* tries to reach those diverse loyalists of 1783 and 1784, and to follow their intricate routes to loyalty – and to Canada.

Many individuals and institutions have assisted the research and writing of this book. Specific contributions are acknowledged in the endnotes, but I am particularly grateful to the Explorations Program of the Canada Council and to the Ontario Arts Council for grants in aid of my research, to my editor, Patricia Kennedy, and to my wife, Louise Brophy.

Note on the paperback edition: I have taken advantage of this new edition to make a few small additions and revisions to the 1984 text.

PART ONE

Revolution

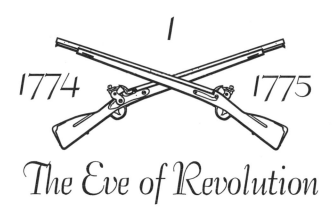

1

1774 ✕ 1775

The Eve of Revolution

EXILE CAME EARLY FOR THOMAS HUTCHINSON.

Son of a long-established and well-connected family of Massachusetts merchants, and himself a youthful success in Boston's lively commerce, Thomas Hutchinson had entered colonial politics early and had risen rapidly. The people repeatedly elected him to Massachusetts' colonial assembly, the Assembly placed him on the Governor's Council, and the Governor made him a judge and then Chief Justice. Respected for his hard-headed financial management, valued for his political ability, supported by an expanding network of allies and relatives, Hutchinson rose steadily, for he seemed able to serve both the local interests of the elected representatives and the imperial policies of the royal government. Before he was fifty, he was virtually a colonial prime minister, key advisor to a royal governor dependent on local counsel.

In 1770 Thomas Hutchinson reached the pinnacle of power and prestige in colonial America. The king named him royal governor of the Massachusetts colony. A baronetcy seemed likely, patronage for his family and clan was assured, his pre-eminence in society was certain. It seemed that Hutchinson had gained all the rewards of eighteenth-century political success.

Instead, the result was disaster. To secure the confidence of the royal officials and parliamentarians in Britain, Hutchinson had worked hard demonstrating his ability to expedite royal policies, and he had given up elective office to take the Crown appointments. Manoeuvring like-minded relatives and friends into supporting jobs, he had vigorously supported both royal policies and the Crown's authority in America. For Hutchinson accepted Massachusetts' colonial situation. He knew the empire and its need for central authority, but he also knew the colonial political system and believed he could make it work for his colony. A practical politician, unimpressed with the rhetoric of political opponents he had frequently bested, Hutchinson believed the empire could work for Massachusetts, and his personal successes reinforced his commitment.

But while Hutchinson was rising above elective politics to take on his royal offices, the political trend turned in Massachusetts. As colonial politicians expressed a growing resistance to all forms of imperial authority, it became impossible for any American to be an effective servant of the Crown and still win colonial acceptance, at least in Boston. When Hutchinson promoted royal measures and accepted ever higher appointments from the king, Bostonians began to call him a traitor, a native son sold out for pay and preferment. Mobs attacked his home and political gatherings began to burn him in effigy. When Hutchinson became governor, the elected assembly refused to co-operate with him, and old allies had to renounce him or risk their own safety. Instead of being flattered by a fellow colonial's rise to high imperial office, Bostonians were enraged, and they vilified Thomas Hutchinson as a conspirator against his own people.

Hutchinson endured four difficult years as royal governor of Massachusetts, employing all his formidable talents one day to sway the British government, the next day to rein in the rising anger of the Boston populace. With the Crown he could feel he had some success, but almost daily he discovered how completely he had lost his hold over the people and their representatives. Finally, with all his policies subverted, his name denounced, and his personal safety at risk, Hutchinson accepted defeat. A British general replaced him as governor of Massachusetts and Thomas Hutchinson became one of the first Americans exiled from his native land.

It was only June 1774 when Thomas Hutchinson boarded ship in Boston harbour to leave America for ever. The first gunshots of revolution would not be fired for another year, the American Declaration of Independence was more than two years ahead, and already one of the most distinguished and successful Americans of his day had been destroyed by the struggles that would provoke the war and the declaration.

A prominent and powerful advocate of the royal cause in America, Hutchinson had naturally been an early target for the Crown's adversaries, but one did not need Hutchinson's prominence or political commitment to become embroiled. All over, colonial men and women were facing crises that paralleled Hutchinson's.

Bartholomew Stavers of New Hampshire had never in his life sought or held any royal office higher than postman. No merchant and no politician, Bart Stavers had earned a living carrying mail and official papers between Boston and Portsmouth, New Hampshire, and after he lost that job he kept a little shop in Portsmouth. His world was that of a simple New England workingman, not even a particularly successful one, and there seemed no reason for political wrangles to intrude on that world in 1774.

And yet at the same time that Governor Hutchinson's

career was being wrecked by popular resentment and political violence, Bartholomew Stavers was discovering that "by steady adherence to government and opposing the lawless conduct of the Americans", a simple postman-turned-shopkeeper could become as hated in Portsmouth as Hutchinson was in Boston. Stavers had apparently gone out of his way to express unpopular political ideas, such as obedience to lawful royal authority, since the first political storms in 1765. As his community's questioning of British authority grew in fervour during the 1770s, Stavers became increasingly "obnoxious", and as an ordinary workingman he had little protection from the wrath of his neighbours. His exposed situation did not silence him. He remained as outspoken as ever, and in the summer of 1774 a Portsmouth mob attacked his house and dragged him out for a beating.

The crowd did not kill Stavers and he seems to have avoided the traditional tar and feathers of the community scapegoat. After much of his furniture had been smashed, "some persons of note" in the town stepped in to quell the disturbance. For Stavers, the help could only be temporary: civil leaders who protected unpopular men like him would find their own authority in jeopardy. Stavers seized the moment of safety he had been granted and made what he called a timely retreat, "until affairs in that part of the world wore a better aspect." Just five months after Governor Hutchinson sailed from Boston, Bartholomew Stavers, too, left America. He intended to make only a temporary retreat, and so his wife and children stayed behind. But, like Governor Hutchinson, Bart Stavers would find his exile permanent.

The fate of Hutchinson and Stavers supports a verdict made nearly fifty years later by one of their adversaries, the second American president, John Adams. According to Adams, the American Revolution took place in the hearts and minds of the American people, and that revolution, he said, had been won before the fighting ever started.

Won, and lost, for if the revolution was won before the fighting started, then the thousands and thousands of Americans who would fight against the revolution and eventually leave the independent United States must already have been defeated. If Adams was right about his revolution, then in some sense the refugees' America, their loyal colonial and monarchical society, must have already been shattered before the war, without their realization, against their will, or despite their efforts.

Considering their number and diversity, and the tenacity with which they fought for their cause, the American loyalists would have found it difficult to accept that their cause was lost and their society dismantled. Yet it seems true that their worlds were shaking on the eve of American independence. For Bart Stavers and Thomas Hutchinson in 1774, loss was already total and obvious, but many other Americans who would not join them in exile for as much as a decade could feel the ground trembling under their feet. They might even then have been wondering if they were not already spiritual exiles in their own homes.

By 1774 Alexander MacDonald had already known three worlds, first that of a young gentleman in the Scottish Highlands, next that of a professional soldier fighting Britain's imperial wars, and only third the world of a settled colonial farmer on rural Staten Island near New York City.

MacDonald never expressed much nostalgia over his early life in Scotland. He was probably young when he left home in 1746 to begin two decades of service in the British army. Here he found a congenial home. He enjoyed the messroom company of "a fine bunch of fellows for officers who loves a drink of Madeira", and he was proud to command Highland soldiers he regularly proclaimed "as good as any to be found in the service". Lacking influential relatives or a knack for self-advancement, he only slowly won army promotion, but he was never just a parade-ground soldier. Between 1746 and 1763 he saw a great deal of active service in Britain, Europe, North America, and the Caribbean, and the extent of his battlefield experience made his survival through those years something extraordinary in itself.

MacDonald gained his first commission in a British army regiment called the Earl of Loudon's Loyal Highlanders, raised to fight against Bonnie Prince Charlie's Highland troops in the Jacobite Rebellion of 1745-46. The Jacobite rising was soon followed by service against the French in Europe, and in 1757 the Seven Years War took him to North America as a lieutenant in another Highland infantry regiment, Montgomery's 77th Regiment of Foot. The Highlanders saw action in every campaign against New France, and MacDonald was seriously wounded in an unsuccessful action near Fort Duquesne in 1758. Recovered, he was transferred south to participate in the attack on the French West Indies, where he fought in the seizure of Dominica and the campaign for Martinique. Spain entered the war, and MacDonald's company went to the bloody midsummer siege of Havana, where the Highlanders again distinguished themselves by bravery and heavy losses. When the 77th returned to North America, the war against France was over, but a massive native uprising on the western frontier sent MacDonald into more action at the savage wilderness battle of Bushy Run in western Pennsylvania.

Finally the wars were over. Though MacDonald had risen no higher than a senior lieutenancy, he had survived, only to find that the peacetime army had no room for him. In 1763, the 77th and many other war-service regiments were disbanded. MacDonald elected to stay in America and embarked on his third career, as a settler in colonial America.

New York had been the scene of much of MacDonald's wartime service, and its diversity was probably an attraction to a settler with no clear direction to his ambition. New York ranked only seventh among the Thirteen Colonies in population, but, from the start, its interests had been varied. Its unique asset was the Hudson, the largest navigable river in the colonies. While most of the colonies remained bound to the coast, the Hudson had since the early 1600s been offering New York an important avenue into the interior. Along its banks had grown a prosperous and long-settled agricultural society. Around the river's upper reaches, northwestern New York had remained a frontier where Indian trade and wilderness pioneering still went on, and at the river's mouth the best major harbour in the colonies sheltered a port with a diverse commerce. Lieutenant MacDonald soon found introductions to all these aspects of New York society.

MacDonald married soon after settling in New York, and through his young wife, Suzanna, he came into contact with her relations the Livingstons, one of the great landowning dynasties of New York. Unlike egalitarian New England, New York had given out enormous tracts of riverfront land to well-connected early settlers, and the successful ones had grown wealthy renting land to scores of tenant farmers. This rather old-world form of landholding gave New York a conservative, almost aristocratic, elite of closely knit landed families, whose social standing and style of life might have recalled to MacDonald his own background among the Scottish landowning gentry. His new in-laws the Livingstons were among the most prominent of the New York elite, not only as major landowners but as leaders of an important faction in the colony's politics. Marriage, even into Suzanna's minor and not notably wealthy branch of the family, gave the ex-soldier an important step upward in New York society.

At the same time, MacDonald kept up his own connections.

Some officers and many ordinary soldiers of the disbanded 77th Regiment had settled further upriver, on the frontier settlements of the Mohawk Valley above Albany, and in the 1770s new waves of Highlanders came directly out from Scotland to join them. Many of these Scots, both the army veterans and the new families coming from Scotland, settled under the supervision of Mohawk Valley patriarch Sir William Johnson. As the Indian agent to the nearby Iroquois nation, Johnson persuaded the Indians to accept this inrush of settlers. As a large landowner in his own right, he simultaneously profited from his rapidly increasing roll of rent-paying tenants. MacDonald had both relatives and former soldiers among the Mohawk Valley settlements, and he kept in contact with his kinsmen.

Despite his upriver connections, MacDonald settled neither on Livingston land nor among the Mohawk Valley Scots. Instead he settled at Decker's Ferry on Staten Island. This was a rural and agricultural community where his wife had inherited property, but it was located close to New York City, the second-largest city in America, with a population of twenty-five thousand people. Many Livingston families maintained town houses in the city, and MacDonald surely had contacts of his own at army headquarters and among the governor's administrative corps, but he may have been equally interested in New York's merchant community, for his landowning background and officer's rank had not raised him above trade. His sister in Britain was married to a merchant in the Portuguese wine trade, who may have been the link by which MacDonald was able to dabble in trading ventures. From New York port, with its well-developed shipping connections, MacDonald could maintain wide-ranging links with Glasgow and London, with old army friends wherever they served, and with Scottish immigrants to North Carolina, who included his kinsman Allan MacDonald, the husband of Flora MacDonald, Bonnie Prince Charlie's famous rescuer.

With all his ties to colonial society, MacDonald should have been content enough during his decade of peaceful enterprise in New York, but he had not forgotten the army. Like most regular officers, he had retained his commission when his regiment was disbanded in 1763. Instead of retiring men like MacDonald, the army had simply placed them on the inactive list, on half-pay, until such time as they might again be needed. In 1772 MacDonald was promoted to captain, and he remained alert to the possibility of returning to active service. In 1765 he had been settled in New York barely a year, but when the imposition of new taxes caused protests and riots in cities throughout the colonies, MacDonald promptly offered his services to the army. Evidently he remained keen for military service, and though on this occasion a political solution made that unnecessary, the old campaigner did not forget the idea.

In the vigorous political disputes of the 1770s, the Livingston faction gradually assumed leadership of the opposition to royal authority, partly because the rival DeLancey faction was in power and co-operating with the British governor and his administration, but also because the landed elite on its country estates had lost its sense that a strong tie to Britain was necessary. As the crisis deepened, Alexander MacDonald was invited to join his powerful relatives. A military command was offered to him, and the prospects for advancement were impressive: Richard Montgomery, another half-pay captain living in New York and married to a Livingston, would soon be a revolutionary general.

MacDonald rejected these approaches. His political sympathies lay more with the New York merchants who, whatever their opposition to arbitrary taxation, valued the empire and the trade it generated. In fact, MacDonald's loyalty was stronger even than that – Highland clan traditions had prepared few Scotsmen for notions of liberty and equality, and MacDonald had a visceral loyalty to the king and country he had served even when most of the Highlanders were Jacobite rebels. He found anything tainted with disloyalty odious, and, though willing to acknowledge some sympathy for colonial grievances expressed by his friends and neighbours, he expressed contempt and horror for actual rebellion. "I hope that all true Britons will spend their lives and fortunes sooner than suffer the offspring of these transports and gaolbirds to get the better of them" was his succinct verdict on the contest that loomed.

More prescient than most observers, or simply more inclined to put events into a military context, Alexander MacDonald was already convinced by mid 1774 that the issues at stake in America were profound and serious, and that the conflict would have to be settled by force of arms. It was already his conviction that "nothing can cure the madness that prevails all over America but the severest of measures," and he prepared to commit his own life and fortune to the struggle.

MacDonald's plan was bold and simple, and nicely advantageous to himself. On his own initiative, he began contacting other Highland veterans about the dangers facing America. He wrote to his cousin Allan in North Carolina, to John Small, a major on the army staff at Boston, and to veterans living in the Mohawk Valley, proposing to each the creation of a regiment of loyal Highland veterans to oppose the rebellion he believed to be imminent. In October 1774 he left Staten Island and headed up the river to begin recruiting among his old soldiers. When he had secured the agreement of more than a hundred, MacDonald went to Boston to place his new corps at the service of the army. If he succeeded, rebellion might be nipped in the bud – and there would surely be pay and promotion to reward MacDonald's vigour.

When Alexander MacDonald left his wife, family, and property on Staten Island in the fall of 1774, he must have had some sense of exile. Though he was confident of eventual victory – in fact he would return more than once to his rural farm – the commitment he renewed that fall to bear the king's arms inevitably dissolved many of his bonds to friends, neighbours, and kinsmen in colonial America. MacDonald had sensed very early the tremors of the approaching split, and he had made his choice without waiting or hoping for a compromise.

In 1774 James Allen was thirty-two and just coming into his own as a capable and successful Philadelphia lawyer. He had been slow to commit himself to a career. Only late in his twenties, a decade after he graduated from the College of Philadelphia, had he begun to apply himself seriously to the study of law. Now, as he mastered his fear of public speaking and discovered how to put his legal studies to practical use, he began to find the law both satisfying and profitable. Already married, with two daughters, he was just beginning to find himself "easy in his circumstances" and content with his lot. As his legal practice grew, James Allen remained less venturesome in other spheres than his surname might have permitted him to be. Allen was an important name in Philadelphia, for James's father and grandfather had been among the city's richest, most influential men during the years when it was rising to become the largest and busiest city in the Thirteen Colonies. Though it had been founded half a century later than the colonial settlements of New England, New York, and the Chesapeake, Philadelphia was already a substantial town when James's father, William Allen, was born there in 1703. Originally the capital of a refuge for Quakers, the town grew steadily through the eighteenth century. English, Irish, Scots, and Germans poured in to clear and plant the fertile lands to the west and north of Philadelphia, until by the 1770s Pennsylvania was home to 250,000 colonists. They had made Pennsylvania the breadbasket of the Thirteen Colonies, producing great stocks of flour and meat for export and colonial consumption.

William Allen had the ships and warehouses to store, sell, and transport the farmers' exports and imports. He owned great tracts of the land the settlers were making productive. His iron foundries in Pennsylvania and New Jersey produced many of the hardwares of the burgeoning colony, and his distilleries turned Caribbean sugar into the colonists' rum. As the gateway for Pennsylvania's commerce, Philadelphia had tripled in size in James Allen's lifetime, reaching 40,000 people in 1774, and its trades had grown even more rapidly. For the Allen family the result was security, wealth, and prestige. As a young man James Allen acquired a thriving rural estate at Northampton – eventually it would be Allentown – and the agricultural rents alone provided him with a steady income. He saw his sister marry Governor John Penn; he knew everyone of importance in Pennsylvania and the neighbouring colonies. His brother made the Grand Tour of Europe in the company of Benjamin West, for it was by William Allen's patronage that the young Pennsylvania-born artist was able to sail for Europe and the beginning of an international reputation.

In eighteenth-century British America, this kind of social prominence almost inevitably translated into political influence and political office. After a term as mayor of Philadelphia, William Allen had spent many years in Pennsylvania's colonial legislature, and simultaneously he served as the colony's Chief Justice. In the assembly he was conservative, leading the faction that supported the Penn family interests against attempts to curb the powers and privileges of Pennsylvania's founding family. Though the cause was conservative, Allen wrapped it in local pride, supporting the Penn family as a local institution threatened by the extension of royal power. As a local entrepreneur with all his wealth rooted in America, Allen frequently joined in colonial resistance to imperial measures. Allen's older sons followed his example as they grew up, and by the 1770s two generations of Allens were prominent Pennsylvania spokesmen for the colonial cause. Andrew Allen, who had become Attorney-General at the age of twenty-five, and two of his brothers received commissions in the colonial militia and appointments to the colonial congresses when they were formed, while William Allen donated ammunition to the militia companies.

James Allen was slower than his brothers to take up all these opportunities that were open to him. He had been elected as a Philadelphia alderman at twenty-five, but that seems to have been due more to his name than to his own ambitions, and he sought no higher office. He was the only one of the Allen sons who did not take a commission in the colonial forces. When the royal authorities asked him to prosecute colonists who evaded new colonial taxes, he took the job, even though he privately considered the new taxes unfair and despotic, writing angrily that "I am doing as a lawyer what I would not do as a politician, being fully persuaded of the oppressive nature of those laws."

James Allen's notion of legal practice seems to have shaped his response to the political crisis developing in the colonies. Initially troubled by his role serving causes he did not share, he gradually began to appreciate the uncommitted objectivity of the law. As he ceased to advocate his own views, his political stands began to mellow. When his brothers took commissions in a colonial militia that increasingly was aimed against royal institutions, James Allen merely did drill with the civic guard, telling himself his example was good for the unruly workingmen with whom he served. When he was persuaded to serve in the Pennsylvania assembly in 1776 – representing his Northampton tenants – he claimed his aim was to further the cause of peace and reconciliation. Born to colonial leadership, James Allen found himself less and less inclined to lead – or even to follow.

Even at the beginning of 1776, few would have predicted

that the Allens would become exiles and loyalists. Second- and third-generation Americans whose success was inextricably bound up with the progress of their community, they were used to shaping and articulating the political consensus of the colony. For decades William Allen had kept abreast of the shifting political currents of Pennsylvania, and now his sons were moving with the tide of colonial opposition to British rule. The strongest critics of royal authority were glad to have their support, and a rock-ribbed loyalist like Alexander MacDonald might easily have cited the Philadelphia Allens as examples of the kind of determined colonial resistance that would eventually have to be curbed by military power.

Yet in his developing preference for lawyerly objectivity, his wish to resist political commitment in the midst of turmoil, and his hope for peace and reconciliation, James Allen was already giving signs of discontent with the political trend. His brothers were still active in the opposition to British authority, but James Allen was already hedging. When he wrote, "I have an abhorrence of family quarrels and am convinced that good temper and civility will make friends and carry a man peaceably through the world," James Allen was referring to a domestic dispute, but the phrases captured the essence of his hopes for public life. In 1774 the revolution in the hearts and minds of Americans was just getting under way, but already James Allen feared things had gone too far. He was beginning to grow uneasy.

In the early summer of 1774, when Thomas Hutchinson was being driven from America and thousands of others were wondering about their future there, twenty-four-year-old Nicholas Cresswell was heading determinedly in the other direction. On May 15, 1774, aboard the merchant ship *Molly* five weeks out from Liverpool, Cresswell examined the Chesapeake Bay shores that lay level and pine-covered on either side and declared he had come into "one of the finest prospects I have ever seen".

Cresswell's own prospects were less certain. He came to America that summer with no fixed plans for his future there, and his immigration had been spurred mostly by his frustration with his life at home in Britain. A well-to-do landowner's son from the Derbyshire countryside not far from Manchester, Cresswell was educated but trained to no particular skill, and though of a prosperous family, he had few assets of his own. Unwilling simply to await inheriting the family estates and frustrated by his father's overbearing dominance, Cresswell decided abruptly, and against the advice of all his friends, to go to Virginia. Just before his departure the local parson preached a Sunday sermon on the parable of the prodigal son. "It is very strange that these sons of the clergy cannot forbear meddling in other people's affairs," wrote Cresswell in the diary he had just started, and off he went to America.

Virginia pleased him from the start. "The finest country I ever was in," he called it, "rich beyond conception, the face of the country beautiful and the air and situation healthy." Virginia and Maryland, the Chesapeake colonies that pleased Cresswell so much, were the tobacco colonies of America. The initial settlements begun around Jamestown in 1607 had barely survived until the region's potential for tobacco was recognized and exploited. With tobacco established, the colonies had never ceased to grow, and tobacco had shaped every feature of their growth. By the 1770s half a million people, a third of all the people in the thirteen American colonies, lived around the Chesapeake. As their numbers and the total acreage of their plantations increased, their Chesapeake tobacco became far and away the most important crop in America, alone providing forty per cent of all the colonies' exports to the rest of the world.

Though for most of its history the Chesapeake had only one crop, this monoculture had left Virginians and Marylanders neither poor nor dependent. The markets for Chesapeake tobacco in Britain and (through re-export) on the continent of Europe were substantial and reliable, and the demand for Chesapeake tobacco made these colonies among the richest in America.

Tobacco had also made Chesapeake society overwhelmingly rural. Though the planters might gather at Williamsburg, Annapolis, and other towns around the Chesapeake, these were mere villages by comparison with Philadelphia, Boston, or New York. It was agricultural land that mattered in Virginia. Elsewhere a diversity of products for many markets supported urban traders, shippers, and artisans in substantial towns, but in Virginia and Maryland, plantations lay scattered along the James, the York, the Rappahannock, the Potomac, and all the other river estuaries that cut into the flat tidewater coasts of Chesapeake Bay. The planters loaded their massive tobacco hogsheads not at the quays of great port cities but at scores of little riverside wharves along the long river frontages. Tobacco society could flourish without cities.

The tobacco colonies were large, and for a long time land had been easy to acquire for any credit-worthy white man. Those unable to acquire land drifted away to other colonies, and in Virginia a high proportion of the white settlers owned property. There was little need to keep poor white labourers in the colony, for since 1700 the tobacco plantations had turned to involuntary black labour. By 1770, forty per cent of Virginians were slaves. The settled Virginia plantation owners put their capital into land, slaves, and buildings, and they aspired to the life of rural gentry – independent, leisured, and self-sufficient – with their slaves producing enough tobacco to pay for everything the planters were inclined to purchase. Most of the intricacies of the international tobacco trade were left to the merchant houses of Britain. Convinced that rural life was better than town life, agriculture better than trade, and their new world better than Europe, tobacco society was closely knit, harmonious, and contented.

Soon after he arrived in the Chesapeake, Nicholas Cresswell found opportunities to observe plantation life. He visited George Washington's Mount Vernon plantation several times during his first months in Virginia, and in July 1774 he attended the public elections that returned Colonel Washington to the Virginia legislature. Cresswell enjoyed plantation opulence – Washington's entertainments "were always conducted with the most regularity and in the genteelest manner of any I ever was at on the continent" – but he was not awed by its pretensions. Though Washington owned hundreds of slaves, mills for linen and wool, and, all in all, "a very fine plantation and farm", Cresswell thought him only "roughly equal to the better sort of yeomanry in England", and he was not greatly impressed with the simple agricultural methods standard in the tobacco fields.

Had he emigrated twenty-five years earlier, Nicholas Cresswell would probably have stifled these criticisms and set about acquiring his own plantation, but Virginia was changing by 1774. Tobacco had actually passed its peak, for the best tidewater locations were long since claimed, and in many areas tobacco quality declined as constant cropping exhausted the soil. An ambitious immigrant was likely to look elsewhere.

Cresswell did. Both his shipboard friend Alexander Knox and his sole acquaintance in the Chesapeake, James Kirk of Alexandria, were more interested in trade than in plantations. These merchants were part of a new group in Virginia, Scottish traders mostly from Glasgow who had recently found a niche where they could prosper without either plantations or great shipping fleets. They had discovered that the French government, which controlled all tobacco sales in France, would buy even low-grade Chesapeake tobacco and would pay cash promptly for it. The merchants became middlemen, supplying Virginia's tobacco through Britain to Britain's traditional rival, but they quickly looked around for other opportunities in the colony. Where other crops had replaced tobacco, they shipped wheat or even timber to the West Indies, and they looked to the enticing frontierlands on Virginia's western borders.

Virginia welcomed the traders' business. By finding markets for even the poorest tobacco, they kept old plantations going. By handling the trading and shipping aspects of tobacco, they enabled the Virginian growers on their rural plantations to remain aloof from non-agricultural pursuits, secure in the conviction that someone would always buy their tobacco. But the traders made odd Virginians. Commercially minded and often transient, they kept one foot in the wide world of British and European trade. Virginia plantation society was becoming a closed community, and despite his origins in the gentry and his agricultural interests, Cresswell soon found common cause with the other newcomers.

Politics also kept Cresswell apart from the planters and bound to his new Scots friends. Resisting his father's influence had not made Cresswell into a rebel against authority. He remained a conventional Englishman in politics and religion, so he was shocked to find "the king openly cursed, . . . his authority set at defiance, . . . everything ripe for rebellion" in America. At first Cresswell blamed the New Englanders, who by "canting, whining, insinuating tricks have persuaded the rest of the colonies that the government is going to make absolute slaves of them," but by the fall of 1774 he began to understand that the wealthy, leisured, and self-sufficient Virginia planters themselves acknowledged no real or theoretical subservience to Britain – and particularly not to a British Parliament that proposed to set taxes on colonial wealth. Virginia might seem contented and conservative by comparison with New England's turbulent politics and mob violence, but the vast mass of Virginia society had grown hostile to the British government and ready to punish supporters of the Crown.

Throughout Virginia the transient merchants, outsiders in Virginia society and still closely bound to Britain, provided the only substantial loyal community, and as a result they were increasingly threatened and isolated. By 1774 Robert Jardine of Fredericksburg had decided to close down his business and return to Britain with the proceeds. Mary Douglass, who had come from Edinburgh to Maryland as a merchant's bride in 1771, found within a few years that life was made intolerable by "the people's jealousy against her husband as a Scotsman . . . and openly a friend to government." Identified both as foreigners and as loyalists, people like the Douglasses made easy targets.

Nicholas Cresswell was also finding his position intolerable. "It is as much as a person's life is worth to speak disrespectfully of the Congress," he discovered in the winter of 1774-75. "I am obliged to act the hypocrite and extol these proceedings as the wisest productions of any assembly on Earth, but in my heart I despise them." He was not very adept at hiding his convictions, and he realized his plans to establish himself in Virginia were being destroyed by the political turmoil and the general suspicion towards those loyal to the Crown. "Did I not think this affair would be over by the spring," he wrote in October 1774, "I would immediately return home."

Nicholas Cresswell was trapped. Having struck out for the New World on his own against the advice of family and friends, he regarded a return to Britain as a humiliation he would never live down, and he was convinced "that I can with a very small sum make a pretty fortune here" – if the political confusion would blow over. In the meantime, however, he was unable to establish himself unless he took an oath of allegiance and worked actively against British rule. With his money nearly exhausted, he was already running up debts with his friends.

Cresswell spent an uncomfortable winter, idle, indebted, frequently drunk, and increasingly fearful for his safety: "The Committees act as justices," he discovered. "If any person is found to be inimical* to the liberties of America, they give them over to the mobility to punish as they see fit, and it is seldom they come off without tarring and feathering." Finally, in the spring of 1775, with the crisis about to break, Cresswell found both employment and escape from prosecution. One of his Virginian acquaintances had acquired a tract of land far off in the western frontier and Cresswell agreed that, in exchange for a share of the property, he would go into the wilderness to inspect it. In March, Nicholas Cresswell set out on a dangerous expedition through Indian country to the Ohio and Kentucky rivers, one that would keep him out of settled Virginia until October.

Ironically, by venturing into the west in pursuit of a lucrative land-settlement scheme, Cresswell was taking the kind of action that might eventually have reconciled him to the Virginia rebels. Since 1763, frontier expansion had been restricted by the British government's treaties with the native nations of the interior. Once Cresswell's hopes for personal gain in the west had come into conflict with this imperial policy, the young immigrant might have begun to share the American resentment of British control over colonial matters.

When he set out for the frontier, however, the intolerance and hostility he had received in Virginia as a defender of British rule had actually reinforced his loyalty, and he would never be given a chance to change his ways. Just before leaving for the west, Cresswell wrote a series of letters to friends in Britain describing the difficulties he had been caused by the rebellious spirit that prevailed in Virginia. Cresswell then went into the wilderness, but because his loyalty was already suspected, his letters were seized and opened before they left for Britain. To colonial spokesmen whose concern for Virginia's autonomy

---

* Inimical, a vogue word of the revolutionary period, simply means unfriendly.

overrode their scruples about the right to privacy or freedom of opinion, the letters proved Cresswell "inimical to the rights and liberties of America". Virginia would no longer be safe for Nicholas Cresswell.

Before leaving Virginia, Cresswell had one day encountered four chiefs of the Shawnee nation; "tall, manly, well-shaped men", who were in the colony as hostages. During 1774, Virginia's royal governor, a Scots soldier named Lord Dunmore, had personally led the colonial militia westward over the mountains to attack the Shawnee. Dunmore shared Virginia's eagerness to annex native lands for settlement and profit. When the Shawnee were forced to seek terms, the colony laid claim to most of the territory that would later be West Virginia, and Dunmore brought the four hostages back with him as security for the good behaviour of their nation.

Less than a year after that conquest, Dunmore would be forced to flee, as the revolution swept away royal authority in Virginia. Soon the revolution would make Dunmore's recent Shawnee enemies into royal allies. Shawnee leader Weyapeirsenwah, called Blue Jacket, had been among the chiefs who fought and were forced to yield to Dunmore in 1774. But shared emnities can forge alliances, and many native leaders would find the Crown their friend against the rebellious – and still land-hungry – colonies.

Vigilant, still-powerful native nations like the Shawnees stood just west of all the Thirteen Colonies: Creeks, Cherokees, Miamis, Delawares, Iroquois. All these nations saw in the settlers' land hunger their greatest danger. To protect themselves, they had made many treaties with the British king, often yielding territory in exchange for promises of peace and protection. Now that the king was at war with his own colonial subjects, nearly all the native nations were ready to fight with him against the settlers. They would be allies, never subjects, of the Crown, and the price of their support was royal protection of their lands against settlement. In the war that was looming, scores of native leaders like Blue Jacket would fight alongside loyalists and British redcoats. In defeat, they would share routes of exile that sometimes matched the loyalists' paths.

Thomas Peters, of Wilmington, on the North Carolina coast, cared as little about colonial liberty and royal authority as did Blue Jacket of the Shawnee. For Peters, freedom was a far more tangible aspiration. Either African-born or the son of Africans carried unwillingly to the New World, he laboured as a slave on the plantation of a colonist named William Campbell. Peters was thirty-seven in 1775, and Lord Dunmore was no more a friend to him than to Blue Jacket. After fleeing the Governor's Palace in Virginia, Dunmore would seek compensation for the loss of the sixty-seven slaves he had abandoned there. But soon after, Dunmore and the royal cause would seek the help of slaves like Thomas Peters, much as they sought native alliances with Mohawks and Shawnees.

In the fall of 1775, Lord Dunmore held on to a small, swampy enclave of Virginia near Norfolk, besieged by rebels in overwhelming force. In November he issued a desperate proclamation: the slave-owning governor promised freedom to any rebel-owned slave who was able to bear arms and join His Majesty's forces.

Word of mouth carried Dunmore's proclamation across the slave plantations of the southern colonies, even after Dunmore himself retreated from Norfolk. His offer provoked no instant slave uprising, for lifetimes of servitude had made the slaves careful judges of the risks and possibilities of escape. Many loyalists were slave-holders, and no slave wished to make a risky escape simply for a change of masters. But the British would continue to offer freedom to the slaves of rebels, and wherever the British forces were strong and near, hundreds and even thousands of slaves would trade their rags for freedom and a British uniform.

Among the first was Thomas Peters. Early in 1776 he vanished from William Campbell's plantation and escaped to a British ship. Soon he was a sergeant in the Black Pioneers. Thomas Peters, like Blue Jacket, was hardly a loyalist when the revolution began, for he had been denied any chance to share in colonial politics. But the beginning of the American struggle gave these people new choices. Blacks and natives made tactical alliances with a power that offered them what they needed, even if that power was often in two minds about accepting its obligations to them. Yet Thomas Peters' flight to freedom had started him on an odyssey that would take him through all the way-stations of the loyalist cause – and finally back to Africa itself. He would never be a slave again.

For Moses Kirkland, of the town and district simply called "Ninety-Six" in the interior of South Carolina, "being possessed of a considerable fortune and held in great esteem" meant that he acceded almost automatically to a position of leadership in his community. Late in 1774 his neighbours made him their delegate to a political meeting being organized at Charleston on the coast. In January 1775, as he set out for Charleston, Kirkland probably expected to find himself arguing against the delegates from the coastal districts of South Carolina, for a seaboard-versus-upcountry rivalry was as traditional as anything could be in these comparatively new communities. This time, however, the issue would be greater than county boundaries or the salary of local magistrates.

In South and North Carolina – founded as one colony in 1669 and split in 1701 – and in adjacent Georgia, the youngest of the Thirteen Colonies, founded only in 1732, the seaboard communities were naturally the oldest areas, and they were also the most prosperous. Since 1700 the seaboard settlements had been growing rice and also indigo, a dye used in British textiles, and cultivation of these crops had made the Carolina seaboard rich. A plantation society, supported by slaves who soon far outnumbered the whites, sprang up along the coast, and South Carolina soon had a plantation gentry that may have been the wealthiest in America. The number of their slaves and the value of their crop grew ceaselessly from 1720, and the planters became secure, independent, and leisured, often living in comfort in their port city of Charleston.

The backcountry settlements of the Carolinas were distinctly different: even newer than the seaboard plantations and without either rice or indigo to bring them wealth and leisure. The inland communities that grew up after 1740 lived by lumbering, by stock- and wheat-raising, and by trade with the friendlier Indian nations, those that had been obliged to accept the new white presence. The upcountry settlers had little leisure for political discussion, but by 1774 they already had a tradition of resisting – sometimes violently – the domination of the colony's affairs by the wealthier and more populated seaboard community.

This resistance extended to the most fundamental issues. Living in a new and still fragile community, the upcountry settlers needed the support of strong authority that could protect and assist them, and the people who had elected Moses Kirkland to represent them were more sympathetic to royal power than the planters ever needed to be. The seaboard communities, like their counterparts in the Chesapeake, had grown increasingly resistant to British authority over colonial decisions, and they had instigated the political meeting to which Moses Kirkland travelled early in 1775 as an instrument of this opposition.

The meeting of elected delegates from every part of South Carolina was called a Provincial Congress, and, as in all the other colonies where similar meetings were being organized, the men who organized South Carolina's Congress intended it to be a vehicle for opposition to royal authority. Moses Kirkland, however, had other ideas. He and many other rural and inland leaders in the Carolinas and Georgia were not prepared to be stampeded either into submission to their seaboard rivals or into any expression of hostility to Britain and the empire.

Supported by a scattering of loyal planters and townspeople, backcountry delegates vocally supported the royal authorities and the colonies' ties to Britain. Wealthy plantation-owner Thomas McKnight attended the Congress organized in North Carolina early in 1775 solely "to oppose all disloyal resolutions", and a Savannah, Georgia, physician named Lewis Johnston complained that the effect of the Congresses "seems to be to exasperate and inflame". Dr. Johnston accepted the Congresses as legitimate only to the extent that they could articulate "a reasonable plan of accommodation between Britain and its colonies". He was willing to have them meet, but not to see them take independent and disloyal stances.

These were also Moses Kirkland's sentiments, and when the South Carolina Congress met, he moved that it condemn the disloyal proceedings of opponents of the Crown throughout the Thirteen Colonies. Kirkland's motion was defeated, for most of the delegates saw opposition to the Crown as the reason for the Congress's existence, and they would tolerate no other views. After being defeated in a similar motion of loyalty, North Carolina's Thomas McKnight was quickly declared an enemy to America, deprived of his seat, threatened with violence, and finally forced to flee for his life. In South Carolina, Kirkland prudently concealed the extent of his disaffection. When his motion was defeated, he left the Congress and avoided its proceedings.

The South Carolina Congress was not done with Moses Kirkland. In June 1775, with supporters of the Massachusetts Congress actually fighting British troops, the South Carolina body began making its own military preparations, and it tested Moses Kirkland's allegiance by offering him command of a militia company. If he refused, he could be arrested and held in Charleston. Kirkland accepted – but for his own purposes. Once he and his new militia company reached the upcountry, where Kirkland's personal influence outweighed Congress's, Kirkland was able to arrest his fellow officers and lead the men in a declaration of loyalty. With Thomas Brown and Thomas Fletchall, two like-minded neighbours of comparable influence, Kirkland began to gather thousands of loyalists at his home in Ninety-Six district.

Moses Kirkland's retreat to Ninety-Six was a fighting one. As armed resistance to British rule flared all over the colonies, the rallying of loyalists there offered one more proof that rebellion would not go unchallenged among the colonists. Yet it was none the less a retreat, a kind of exile from the centres of power and influence where America's future was being made.

Like Hutchinson and Stavers fleeing to Britain, Alexander MacDonald leaving Staten Island, or Nicholas Cresswell heading for refuge in the countryside, Kirkland's actions on the eve of revolution suggest not only exile, but a kind of isolation from the trends and developments that had set the Thirteen Colonies toward revolution. The people of Kirkland's Ninety-Six district were loyal to their king and his established authority because they needed the support of the empire, but also because loyalty was the natural condition. Ninety-Six had not changed its ways; it was the rest of America that had changed enough to drive men as diverse as Stavers, Cresswell, and Kirkland into exile from it. To see why, we need to consider what John Adams called the real revolution – the one that had turned the hearts and minds of America against loyalty and against the loyalists.

2
1763   1776

The Language of Liberty

BY 1775 THE THIRTEEN COLONIES WERE LOOKING LESS and less like thirteen colonies.

In the political theory of the day, colonies existed to benefit the nations that had established them. Since every empire-builder had to defend the enormous costs and efforts that colonial expansion demanded, writers and thinkers about the empire had constructed a theory that encouraged a hard financial assessment of colonization. This imperial theory drew attention to all the new products a colony provided to the founding nation and the new market it became for the home country's own production. The theory emphasized how distant colonies could be springboards for further profitable expansions and how they could absorb the surplus populations and restive minorities of the nation. The theory took it for granted that to maximize the benefits that justified the colonizing effort, the imperial power had to control as much as it could of the colony's activity, directing its economy, arranging its borders and its external relations, manipulating its finances, and even shaping its religious, cultural, and educational affairs. Not to do so was to neglect an investment.

In British eyes, the Thirteen Colonies stood up well enough to economic assessment. Englishmen of the late eighteenth century, increasingly aware of how closely the power and prosperity of Britain were linked to its success in overseas trade, understood that the American colonies, along with the West Indies and the Far East, were vital components of the trading system that was making Great Britain into a world power. If the loss of the colonies meant the loss of their trade – as the theory presumed – Britain's loss would be very great.

But the simple economic tally seemed to leave out a great deal that was fundamental about the Thirteen Colonies. The theory presumed that the goods of colonies would go to benefit the founding nation, but, from the start, merchants from ports like Boston, New York, and Philadelphia had been shipping their colonial fish and flour and lumber wherever markets offered, and the benefits seemed to flow back to the colonies rather than to London. Theory dictated that the raw materials of the colony should be exchanged for the manufactured goods of the founding nation; yet American shipyards had long been exporting completed vessels rather than lumber to Britain and Europe, and the cities of the Thirteen Colonies supported iron foundries, leatherworks, and many other skilled manufacturing trades that lessened American dependence on British output. Contrary to all theory about colonial boundaries and colonial troops, the Thirteen Colonies were increasingly taking the lead in determining their own western expansion, while their militia regiments and privateering fleets served colonial as much as imperial policies.

The gap between theory and practice was acute in the area of religion and culture. In theory the imperial power should have controlled and shaped these matters to ensure that the colony did not develop in ways that challenged or inhibited imperial interests. Yet nowhere in the Thirteen Colonies did the Church of England, the official, state-supported church headed by the king, have the power or prestige it enjoyed in Britain. Even in those colonies where Anglicans were in the majority and the Church of England was the established, state-supported church, there had never been a single Anglican bishop or any well-developed religious hierarchy. In New England, Pilgrim founders had officially established their Congregational church; elsewhere groups of Quakers, Presbyterians, Catholics, Baptists, and Methodists either rejected the established church or sought to preserve or impose their own authority. Along with religious diversity came cultural innovation; by 1775 the large and affluent cities of the Thirteen Colonies supported colleges, newspapers, painters, writers, and scientific societies that, while hardly independent of British influence, were surely not controlled by it. Britain might benefit from the existence of the colonies it had created in America, but in many ways it no longer could claim to control or direct them.

By the 1770s the American colonies covered a huge territory encompassing many peoples, cultures, and economies. The colonies had never been able to unite on any scheme for intercolonial government, they fought over their boundaries, and they competed for prestige and leadership. It was easy for Britain to see the thirteen as small and separate and needing the guiding hand of Parliament, yet in the colonies' very diversity lay the beginning of "America" and the idea of the limitless possibilities of being an American. Some colonists were beginning to think of America as the glory of the future, when Englishmen still thought of it as Britain's child. "America was designed by Providence," exulted John Adams, "for the theatre on which man was to make his true figure, on which science, virtue, liberty, happiness and glory were to exist in peace," and the statement was not a piece of campaign oratory, but an entry

in a private journal a decade before the revolution. Many rational and prudent colonists might have doubted Adams's utopian
faith, but to most Englishmen the claim would simply have
been absurd. The Indian in feathers and warpaint was still
Britain's favourite image of America. Britain continued to
think of the colonials as simple and rustic, while Americans
began to see Britain as aged and corrupt. The gap between colonial theory and American images was growing.

The most important gap between colonial theory and the
nature of the American colonies was political. When the colonies had to be justified by a stern economic accounting of their
costs and benefits to the founding nation, the separate interests
of a colony could obviously be given no weight: clearly the
colony had to be wholly subservient to the interests of the
founding nation that had invested in it. So went the eminently
practical theory of colonization. Yet the settlers of the Thirteen
Colonies were Englishmen who had never acknowledged giving up the rights of Englishmen merely because they had moved
from Britain to America.

From their earliest days, each of the thirteen American colonies had had an elected assembly that participated in governing and administering the colony. Distant and isolated from
Britain, the new colonies needed some form of governing institutions, and these assemblies arose, not from some high notion
of democracy somehow acquired in the ocean crossing, but naturally, out of standard British practice. In the colonies, as in
Britain, it was natural that the duty and responsibility of
administering the state should fall on those who had a stake in
society and paid taxes to support government: namely, the
property-owners. There was no sense that every citizen had a
natural right to a share in government, only the perception that
since property was the foundation of society, the property-owners naturally had a special interest in the sound running of society – particularly since it was taxes on land that paid most of the

cost of government. To have an elected assembly was the fundamental right of Englishmen, but those who voted and sat in the legislature were the white, male, adult, Protestant heads of property-owning families. To give voting power to anyone with a lesser stake in society was clearly irresponsible and dangerous to liberty and the English constitution.

The colonial assemblies of the Thirteen Colonies followed the British practice – there was no thought of giving the vote to wives, children, tenants, servants, slaves, and other dependants, or to Catholics or Jews, who, however wealthy, were outside the Protestant society. But the way the colonies were growing meant that the proportion of men who owned property was larger in America than in Britain. In Britain property-owners were few and perhaps getting fewer, as the expansion of great estates eroded the position of small proprietors. In the colonies land abounded, and property grants would freely be made to new settlers without threatening the position of other landowners. In most parts of the colonies it was relatively easy for a successful tenant or servant to acquire property on previously undeveloped ground.

As a result, more men voted and exercised the rights of Englishmen in the colonies than in Britain itself. Probably the majority of white adult males in the colonies had enough property to vote, while only a small proportion of men in Britain could vote or sit in Parliament. In America, as in Britain, it was property, not citizenship, that conferred the right to vote, but the large number of people in the Thirteen Colonies who owned sufficient property to vote meant that political activity, or at least the sense that one had a share in running one's community, tended to involve more people more directly in America than in Britain. It was a circumstance that depended on the newness of the colonies and their abundant land – by the 1770s there were already overcrowded areas in rural New England and in several colonial cities where the proportion of men who owned property and voted was actually in decline – but there remained a large number of colonials who, each time they went to the polls and voted, were reminded that they had a share in the rights of Englishmen.

The existence of elected legislatures in the colonies was normal and in conformance with British practice. Yet at the same time every colonial who voted had the opportunity to contemplate the paradox of Englishmen in the colonies: how could their constitutional rights as Englishmen be reconciled with the clear fact that the colonies they lived in were, and had to be, subservient to the nation that had invested in their foundation?

The paradox – on one hand the imperial insistence that colonies be useful to and controlled by the founding nation, on the other hand the conviction that Englishmen had certain constitutional rights wherever they lived – did not have to be confronted as long as it caused few practical problems. When the colonies were distant and peripheral to the central concerns of the British government, it was sensible to delegate to the colonial people – or at least to the colonial property-owners – the responsibility for ordering their own affairs. And the colonies were unlikely to take steps contrary to the imperial interest when they were small and new and acutely dependent on the founding nation for money and men and military support and most of the goods they ate and wore and used. Rights or no rights, the colonials' subservience was real, practical, and dictated by their circumstances.

For a century and more the contradiction remained muted and invisible. The colonials exercised their rights in their colonial legislatures. Imperial interests in the colonies were served by the governor and his appointed officers. Few fundamental disagreements arose. The governor ensured that the colony continued to benefit its founders and at the same time secured for the colony the assistance it required. Beyond these limits

Britain could administer its colonies with a loose hand, expecting only that trade should increase and royal sovereignty be acknowledged.

Since it was obvious that colonial trade was growing and profitable – in other words that the colonies were justifying themselves in strictly economic terms – it was not really necessary to observe or supervise colonial government more closely. Throughout most of the existence of the Thirteen Colonies, Britain's Parliament rarely received specific statistics or regular reports on colonial population, trade, or economic development. Many colonists in the Thirteen Colonies rarely even saw a royal official: local councils governed most of their daily activities. Even the governor of a colony was not necessarily a royal appointee, for several of the Thirteen Colonies had been privately founded and remained privately run. Pennsylvania, for instance, was the creation of the Penn family, who had received a grant of land from the king in 1680 and had developed the colony privately, giving or selling land as they saw fit but retaining proprietorship of the colony as a whole. William Penn had himself drafted the colonial constitution by which Pennsylvania property-owners voted and sat in an assembly, and throughout the colony's existence succeeding members of the Penn family were Pennsylvania's governors and proprietors. Whether royal or proprietary, a governor was rarely an agent of unwanted authority in the early years of any of the Thirteen Colonies, and colonial Englishmen exercised their rights largely unlimited by the political subservience a colony owed to its founders.

By the mid-eighteenth century, however, Britain could hardly afford to continue ruling its empire with so loose a rein, for running the empire was becoming as important as running Britain itself. The Seven Years War of 1756-63 had demonstrated vividly that world power and world commerce depended on victory in the colonial struggles: the empire was no longer peripheral. In that war an enormous, globe-spanning effort had had to be made and paid for, and the effort intensified a search for means by which central plans could be implemented and monitored around the world. In the last half of the century, as the British Empire struggled toward greater efficiency and greater organization, Ireland and the Scottish Highlands were integrated more closely into the British nation, and the nearly autonomous East India Company was obliged to recognize British sovereignty and parliamentary supervision over its activities in the Far East. As part of the same process, the Thirteen Colonies began to become increasingly aware that they were part of an empire run from London.

The evidence came in a series of acts following the close of the Seven Years War, acts aimed both at improving British supervision of colonial affairs and at having the colonials begin to contribute at least a small part of the growing cost of running and defending the colonies. At the end of the war, when it became clear that some of the British regiments that had protected the colonies and taken Canada from France would have to stay to garrison them, new regulations for quartering troops in the Thirteen Colonies were laid down. Relations with native nations were more closely regulated after the Royal Proclamation of 1763 recognized native territorial rights and forbade the acquisition of native land by private citizens. In 1763 and again in 1767, customs officials gained new powers to investigate and supervise trade. The 1764 Sugar Act revised duties on sugar and molasses, with the explicit intention of securing more revenue in North America to pay part of the cost of North American administration. The 1765 Stamp Act sought to raise further revenue in the colonies by placing a tax on the circulation of legal documents and papers. In 1767 new duties taxed tea, glass, and other trade goods. In each case, the imperial intention to supervise more closely and to collect additional revenue made imperial power increasingly visible to the people of the Thirteen Colonies.

Whether it was a matter of customs officials examining their commerce, of subsidized British tea cornering the colonial market, or of a garrison of troops demanding to be housed, the Thirteen Colonies were unused to interference of this kind. Unwilling to begin paying new taxes, particularly in the economic lull that had followed the wartime boom, colonists also suspected that the new acts infringed the rights of Englishmen as they had traditionally been practised. Used to exercising substantial authority in their own affairs, and assuming their authority would grow rather than shrink, colonists now confronted in a new way the British meaning of empire: the presumption that the colonies and their assemblies were subservient to Britain and Parliament, not merely in theory, not merely by supporting British commerce, but in specific and practical matters of obeying parliamentary regulations and contributing to the rising costs of empire. The paradox that had always existed – colonial subservience versus the rights of colonial Englishmen – had at last to be confronted.

The question that arose, in the most natural way, was acutely and fundamentally political. All details of taxation, tea, and stamps aside, the issue was the source of legitimate authority: given that colonial matters were vital to British power, would the basic decisions by which colonial society was run be made by the colonies or by the colonizing power? In an English-speaking society of the eighteenth century, there was only one language in which to discuss a fundamental issue of this sort: the language of liberty.

Eighteenth-century politics was uncomfortable with the idea of party or partisan interest. There remained in British – and American – society a strong sense of the natural authority of those intended to lead, and a sense that government was not a forum in which to fight for partisan advantage, but a place to render public service in running the nation wisely. Public service was not a wholly noble and disinterested service, of course – there were important rewards of personal patronage and preferment – but the role of the leaders was to discover the public interest and carry it out. Eighteenth-century Englishmen participated in politics to see that the state was well run, and they expected to find a consensus about what constituted a well-run state. Disputes might arise, and cliques and coalitions were inevitable, but the existence of permanently opposed parties or of chronic discord would be taken as an indication of failure, of a fundamental division that was likely to be fatal to good order and English liberties. To avoid tyranny the nation was supposed to be united. The concept of a loyal opposition, systematically opposing government policy and offering an alternative government with different policies, had yet to mature.

Quarrels over honours and preferment were to be expected, but really only one opening existed for the systematic expression of dissent, and that came from the historical sense that Englishmen were newly and uniquely favoured with the benefits of a fragile liberty, the liberty of sharing in the government of their country. In the 1760s, British history did not seem a long, peaceful record of parliamentary democracy: there were particularly vivid memories of 1688, when one king (the Catholic James II) had been deposed and another (the Protestant William of Orange) enthroned, specifically because of a perceived threat of royal tyranny. On the continent Englishmen saw absolute monarchs not merely preserving but extending their power. Liberty looked fragile, and so, besides helping to see the state well run, Englishmen acted in politics to preserve liberty.

The bulwark of liberty was the supremacy of Parliament, where the monarch, the nobility, and the people were all represented. Parliamentary supremacy was also new and fragile.

Englishmen were protective of its rights and powers, and cautious about surrendering those powers, whether to cabinet ministers or to colonial assemblies. The supremacy of Parliament was acknowledged as the main defence of liberty. If liberty were endangered, parliamentarians could legitimately oppose the government that threatened it.

Opposition for the sake of liberty was thus made respectable, at a time when other motives for opposition were denounced as faction and discord. Anyone who opposed the government in power had to take up the cause of liberty and call himself a patriot, claiming to oppose the government because, by negligence or corruption, it had become a threat to the rights of Englishmen. When Samuel Johnson coined the phrase "Patriotism is the last refuge of a scoundrel," he was not simply tossing off an epigram. In mid-eighteenth-century politics, a "patriot" had become synonymous with a "member of the opposition". Johnson, a government supporter, was accusing the opposition of trying to justify a partisan stance by taking refuge in a patriotic invocation of liberty and the rights of Englishmen.

Samuel Johnson might have been speaking of colonial Americans. When colonial spokesmen resisted British projects for the empire, they inevitably called themselves patriots or sons of liberty, and they phrased their political dissent in the patriotic language of liberty, the only acceptable language of dissent. To many observers in Britain, already accustomed to patriotism's being used as a mask for unprincipled political opposition, this raising of the cry of liberty from America was absurd. Nowhere in the world was there more freedom than in the Thirteen Colonies.

The Thirteen Colonies offered opportunity, property, land, and social ascendance to a degree unmatched in the rest of the world. It was the prosperity and wealth of the colonies that had permitted their people to increase their population by an explosive rate through early marriages and large families – in

1775 three-fifths of Americans were under twenty-one. Yet this rapid growth was not impoverishing the country. Despite the newness of the colonies, the white colonial population was challenging Britain for world leadership in per capita wealth, and wealth was certainly more evenly distributed in America than in the Old World. There were good lands for the asking, and reliable markets for commercial agriculture and a range of trades.

With work and luck, almost any white American male could aspire to become a property-owner of modest wealth and secure social standing, in an era when such an aspiration was much less realistic in Britain and nearly inconceivable in most of the rest of the world. And with property, the colonist became a voter, exercising the fundamental right of English liberty. It was true he elected only his colonial representatives, but, by compensation for his exclusion, the colonial voter was largely exempted from the taxes that British voters paid to defend and run the empire that underpinned both British and colonial prosperity. As a result, sympathy did not come quickly when Americans bemoaned the threats to their liberty. A slave-owning Virginia gentleman who used the language of liberty to protest that a tiny tax on tea would make him a slave to the British government was likely to get a sceptical audience among Englishmen who themselves paid heavy taxes to defend the empire and who were already used to hearing "liberty" dragged in to justify all kinds of dubious factional claims. "Why is it we hear the loudest yelps for liberty among the drivers of negroes?" asked Samuel Johnson.

The Americans who argued that their rights were being trampled had two justifications for the rhetoric of liberty they quickly mastered. First, the claim contained a germ of truth: despite their material prosperity and unmatched freedoms, American colonists did confront the paradox that set their cherished rights as Englishmen against the hard-won and not easily relinquished right of Britain's Parliament to be supreme over monarchs, armies, private fiefdoms – and colonial assemblies. But the other justification for crying liberty, the fact that liberty was the only language in which dissent short of rebellion could be expressed, may actually have weakened their chance to make their case and win changes by persuasion.

The problem with constant appeals to liberty lay in the speed with which they poisoned the atmosphere of reasonable discussion. Beneath all protestations of loyalty, the language of liberty was a language of extremism. Grounding every political protest in the fundamental rights of Englishmen meant that every protest became a matter of inflexible principle, where no compromise short of victory could be justified by either side. Preaching liberty encouraged stiff-necked righteousness as fast as it bred polarities. If one claimed to be defending the rights of Englishmen, then the Englishman who disagreed with you – probably by citing the rights of Parliament – was a traitor. If one cried out for liberty, then one's opponents became tyrants, whatever their outward appearance. And if Parliament itself, the bulwark of liberty, rejected one's claims, then a conspiracy had to be at work, preaching liberty and practising slavery, professing rights and scheming for power.

A fear of conspiracy was the dark side of the defence of endangered liberty. Once liberty became the issue in America, a conspiracy against liberty became the omnipresent danger. Parliament was supposed to be the forum where reasonable men, the natural leaders of the nation, reached consensus. When discord appeared, when factionalism persisted, when events occurred for which no one seemed willing to accept responsibility, men were quick to find the cause in conspiracy rather than in honest political disagreement. If liberty was natural and good, then the only threat to it was the conspiracy of corrupt men seeking unfettered power, and such traitors and tyrants would naturally conceal these plans and disguise their actions. Much of the heat of eighteenth-century politics came from the ease with which conspiracy was suspected: one's opponent was not simply disagreeing, he was probably a traitor and either a would-be tyrant or a hired servant of tyranny.

In this atmosphere of appeals to liberty and suspicions of conspiracy, the weakening bonds between the colonies and Parliament were eroded every time political issues were raised. There was a serious political problem to face – how to reconcile the right of colonists to participate in their government with the right of Parliament to be supreme throughout the British realm – but it could only have been solved if Americans and Britons had retained a reservoir of trust in each other. Instead, as the two societies grew apart, the assumption of shared interest became more difficult to maintain. When all political dissent was wrapped in a claim that one's rights were being endangered by a conspiracy against liberty, confidence in government and its institutions inevitably declined.

It is difficult to find much evidence that either side strove for reconciliation in the decade before the American Revolution. Americans, increasingly proud of their own society, grew convinced that Britain, becoming old and corrupt, was conspiring against the wealth and freedom of America. Englishmen, committed to the rule of Parliament and struggling to administer an ever-expanding empire, were easily persuaded that colonial demagogues were conspiring to steal the richest jewel of the empire by pretending that minor taxes were major attacks on their liberty.

The language of liberty had been part of political debate in Britain since early in the century. In the colonies, its domination of discussion – and its increasing radicalism – was seen as early as the Stamp Act crisis of 1765, provoked by one of the first British efforts to secure some revenue from colonial taxation. The act broke new ground in asserting Parliament's right to tax the colonies, and the nearly unanimous protests from the colonies were firmly grounded in constitutional rights, not in material objections, even though a post-war economic slow-down made new taxes particularly burdensome at that time. Even colonists of conservative temper and unquestioned loy-alty to the Crown objected to the Stamp Act, and since Parlia-ment itself had reservations about the policy, the act was eventually withdrawn. But the protests over the Stamp Act helped enshrine liberty as the vehicle of colonial opposition to British authority. The radical organizations formed that year called themselves "Sons of Liberty", colonial newspapers ener-getically discussed whether tyranny was returning under the guise of taxation, and lawyer William Smith earned the nick-name "Patriotic Billy" for leading protest campaigns in New York – "patriotic" naturally referring to his status as a mem-ber of the opposition. Smith, indeed, would later find him-self trapped by other people's definition of the word. Was he expected to be a patriotic American, or a patriotic colonial Englishman?

Liberty remained the focus of debate in the colonies after the withdrawal of the Stamp Act, even in issues when no great constitutional principle seemed obvious. When James Allen's father, the wealthy, well-connected businessman William Allen, resisted Benjamin Franklin's legislative campaign to end the proprietary power of the Penn family, he justified his own conservative stand to the voters as a fight for liberty, arguing that if royal governors replaced the Penns – one of whom was his future son-in-law – the Crown would have a new instru-ment by which to impose imperial policies on the colony and its legislature. In New York's factious politics, whichever coali-tion of legislators found itself temporarily out of power tended to rally support by accusing the group in power of being too close to the royal governor and therefore too neglectful of American rights.

This effective use of appeals to liberty for partisan advantage was often cynical, but it had the effect of politicizing and educating the American electorate. Traditional politicians, confident of their duty to lead, had rarely appealed to a mass electorate at all, and traditional voters had tended rather passively to elect their betters without much sense that they might have divergent rights or interests to pursue. In the wider suffrage of the Thirteen Colonies, politicians – particularly opposition politicians – had good reason to court the mass electorate, and to teach it about the rights and liberties they could preserve by participating in politics. Under this encouragement, the crowd became an active political force in the colonies, participating in rallies, marches, and festivals, and sometimes in mass violence in pursuit of political objectives. As the crowd was roused to a sense of its own liberties, the idea began to spread that voting need not be linked to property but might be a "universal" right, available to everyone who was adult, white, and male.

As the cause of liberty politicized an increasing slice of the population, it also came to turn an increasing range of grievances against the royal authorities. It became increasingly easy to denounce arbitrary authority as the root of all evil, and to perceive in every action of the royal authority another step in a conspiracy against colonial liberties. When the British government limited westward expansion to conciliate the powerful native nations west of the Thirteen Colonies, sound management of the empire may have been the motive, but colonial spokesmen perceived a threat, and not merely to their acquisition of new land. The conspirators of tyranny, they argued, were attempting to surround the colonists with savage enemies. The same interpretation was put forward in response to Britain's attempt to govern the French Canadians effectively after their conquest. Efforts to regulate the garrisoning of troops in America were denounced as the plans of a tyrannical standing army. Once the language of liberty dominated politics, the conspiratorial mindset ensured that whatever decisions Britain took would be interpreted as further evidence of conspiracy, until all trust in royal authority had been replaced with fear, suspicion, and hostility.

Eventually almost any action taken against royal authority could be justified in the name of liberty. In 1770 a small detachment of British troops on sentry duty, surrounded, challenged, and harassed by hostile Bostonians, fired into the crowd, killing several citizens. The confrontation had been provoked as much by the crowd's militancy as by the usual small hostilities between civilians and troops housed among them, but colonial spokesmen quickly turned the unfortunate incident into the Boston Massacre, a savage attack on colonial citizens by a murderous standing army. To partisans of liberty, all British authority in America was illegitimate, and British troops were automatically to blame whatever the circumstances, since they had no right to be present uninvited in the colonies.

Two years later, when a gang of Rhode Island smugglers seized and burned the British naval schooner *Gaspee* in retaliation for its unusual vigilance in pursuing customs violators, the lawbreakers were able to win wide support by casting doubt on the Royal Navy's right to operate against colonial shippers. Though the commander of *Gaspee* had been seriously wounded when his ship was pirated, Rhode Island's governor took no action and felt forced to criticize the navy's activity. The smugglers not only escaped prosecution but successfully laid charges against a slave who had identified them to the authorities. When incidents such as these could sincerely be seen as colonial defence of liberty against arbitrary authority, it was clear that the bonds between British authority and American patriots were almost totally dissolved.

The most famous and most consequential challenge to

British authority was Boston's "tea party" of December 1773. Tea had become controversial in America because of a clever move by the British government. The government wanted to tax tea imports to America, partly for the revenue, mostly as a symbol of Britain's authority to levy such taxes, many of which had already been abandoned. To soften resistance to the tax, the government dropped various duties that were charged on East Indian tea as it passed through Britain on its way to America. This reduction made British tea the cheapest tea in America, even though the colonials were charged a special import tax on it. It was hoped Americans would put their desire for a bargain ahead of their unhappiness about imperial taxation powers and tacitly accept royal taxation each time they bought British tea.

To prevent such a trend, the colonial leadership organized a comprehensive boycott of British tea in all the cities of the colonies. They threatened or persuaded the importers of British tea into compliance and proclaimed that the purchase of British tea threatened American liberties. Boston was actually slow to join this crusade, and a lot of tea was imported, but in December 1773, when a new shipment of tea arrived in Boston harbour, a well-organized Boston crowd seized the ships and dumped ninety thousand pounds of tea in the harbour. Boston's defiance was actually no greater than that of any other city, but because the "tea party" was a dramatic action under the noses of the authorities, it drove home the message clearly: a growing number of Americans held in contempt all regulations for the colonies enacted in London. The administration of government was collapsing.

Particular protests, mob actions, and midnight raids, however, were insufficient grounds for a revolution. Imperial authority might have lost its standing in the colonies, but before it could be thrown off, some new institutions had to be created to depose and replace the royal ones. Uncertainly, and largely to defend liberty against the conspiracy they feared, the colonial leadership began to lay the groundwork for independent institutions. They began with committees and moved on to congresses.

Colonial government had always required an alliance between the elected representatives who formed the colonial assemblies and the royal governors who administered the colonial government. As trust between the colonial spokesmen and the royal officials disappeared, each group used its power to thwart the other's program. Royal governors called and dismissed sessions of their legislatures each year, and they could use this power to neutralize legislative criticism or opposition: a hostile assembly could be sent home, or simply dissolved to face new elections. To free themselves of this obstacle, colonial legislatures began to appoint standing "committees of correspondence", to remain in session when the legislature was not meeting. The committees' original purpose was merely to maintain communications between the various colonial legislatures, but as resistance to royal authority grew more open, the committees quickly became independent centres of discussion and decision-making that still enjoyed quasi-legal status as committees of the royal legislature but could not be restrained or removed by royal authority. By the early months of 1774 every colony had such a committee.

In the end it was Boston's tea party that set in motion the events that would transform legislative committees of correspondence into an independent American government. Parliament had decided that this flagrant violation of order and respect for law required an assertion of its control over the colonies, and Boston was chosen as the place where the lesson would be taught. Early in 1774 a series of punitive acts removed the Massachusetts assembly's right to appoint its executive council, abolished town meetings, closed the port of Boston indefinitely, and moved the customs house that Boston's trade required. The British military commander in America, General Thomas Gage, became Massachusetts' new governor, and he arrived in Boston with four additional regiments and renewed authority to use force against civil disturbances. "They must obey and we must prescribe" had been British statesman William Pitt's succinct definition of the essential relation between the colonies and Parliament in 1770, though Pitt was widely thought sympathetic to the colonials' cause. Now Parliament prepared to see itself obeyed.

In America the "Coercive Acts" aimed at Boston confirmed every patriot's fear of a tyrannical conspiracy launched against America by a corrupted Parliament. With Massachusetts' legislature decapitated, and the colony run by a military governor and his appointed council, the leading members of what had been the legislature transformed themselves into a provincial congress, still carrying an aura of legitimacy as the colony's properly elected representatives, but now entirely independent of royal sanction.

The British government had seen Massachusetts as the centre of rebellion, because the "patriots" were firmly in control and widely supported there. But it quickly became apparent that generally similar views of colonial rights and British oppression held sway in most of the colonial legislatures of America. Throughout the colonies, the colonial leadership recognized that the power being levied against Massachusetts could be aimed against any or all of them, and there was a rapid and widespread movement to vest colonial power in provincial congresses free from royal interference. In some colonies, the new congress was simply the old legislature redefined, but in those where a majority of legislators were hesitant, indecisive, or leaning toward a more moderate course, the radical leaders or the committees of correspondence simply acted on their own to establish provincial congresses that competed with and soon undercut the royal legislatures.

In the summer and fall of 1774, the newly established provincial congresses, supported by town and county councils, and often by mass meetings and demonstrations, became the government of America. Reorganizing the colonial militias as their arm of resistance, voting a boycott of all trade with Britain, and establishing committees of safety to protect against conspiracy and subversion, they simply defined out of existence the agencies of government that represented British authority in America. In the fall of 1774, these provincial congresses took the first steps to unify themselves: in September the first Continental Congress, of delegates from every colony except Georgia, came together in Philadelphia.

The Continental Congress furthered the plans to boycott British trade. In essence, it attempted to coerce Britain just as Britain had attempted to coerce the colonies by its punitive laws against Massachusetts. The Congress also took steps to secure its authority in America: every American was invited to sign the articles of association that defined the boycott of British goods, and every American who refused was judged inimical to the liberties of America.

Congress still sought accommodation with Britain, sending petitions to the British people and to George III explaining its actions and asking for royal and popular support against the corrupt Parliament. Yet it might have been at this time that John Adams, a Massachusetts delegate to the Continental Congress, formed his belief that the revolution in America had been accomplished. It would take more than a year to see the Declaration of Independence ratified, but by the start of 1775, a government free of British influence, with wide support reaching down to the smallest communities, and armed to protect itself, now governed virtually the whole of the Thirteen Colonies. The provincial and continental congresses still claimed to be loyal and patriotic assemblies upholding the traditional English liberties, but the almost unlimited powers they had claimed for themselves – and their savage repression of their opponents – made a collision with the remnants of British authority in America inevitable. After a lull in which both sides awaited the response to their demands, the first spark of conflict came. Again Massachusetts, where the only large body of British troops was garrisoned, gave the lead.

In April 1775 General Gage sent a few hundred troops out of their base at Boston to seize an illegal stock of arms at Concord, a few miles away. Shots were fired at Lexington, and the war had begun. Almost immediately Gage found himself besieged at Boston, first by a cordon of angry militia, then by a steadily growing army with artillery and siege tools. In June a pitched battle was fought at nearby Bunker Hill. The debate over liberty was suddenly a war.

Elsewhere in the colonies, battle came more slowly, feeding the illusion that rebellion was essentially a New England matter. There was little actual conflict away from the garrison town of Boston, but only because there was almost no British force to be confronted anywhere else. In colony after colony, the British governor, rendered powerless by the establishment of a defiant provincial congress and a provincial militia, either fled to a naval ship or a coastal fort, or else yielded to the American cause. Governor Trumbull of Connecticut changed sides and became the revolutionary governor. Governor Wanton of Rhode Island permitted himself to be eclipsed and remained quietly where he was. Governor Franklin of New Jersey, the illegitimate son of Benjamin Franklin, who had risen higher than his father, remained in office in search of conciliation until a revolutionary congress arrested him and sent him off to detention in Connecticut. The southern governors took to ships and forts.

Between 1774 and 1776 America underwent a rapid and astonishing transformation. For more than a decade colonial spokesmen had been objecting to the powers they were sub-jected to, powers they considered strong and arbitrary enough to be called parliamentary tyranny. The open and massive use of this power – both political and military – against Boston and Massachusetts had been the spark that turned their protests toward revolution. Yet when armed resistance did begin, America suddenly discovered how remarkably limited the power of the tyrant really was. The revolution conceived and justified as a backs-to-the-wall defence of liberty seemed to expand effortlessly outward, and the feared authority of Parlia-ment melted away wherever it was challenged.

Everywhere governments and congresses sprang into being, defined their powers, and organized local hierarchies and lines of authority. The Continental Congress began to print its own money, and soon a willingness to accept Congress money at face value became one of the tests of support for the colonial cause. Armies and supply systems were created, each province raised its own regiments and militias, and the Continental Congress established a national force, the Continental Army, under George Washington's command. Sources of ammuni-tion, artillery, clothing, and food were identified and reorgan-ized to serve the needs of the new army. From the shipping ports arose a naval power in the time-honoured tradition: as war reduced peaceful sea trade, the ships and sailors turned to war. The new state, or collection of states, soon initiated foreign relations. A congressional representative opened negotiations with Britain's traditional adversary, France. Invitations to join the revolution went to the Canadian colonies to the north and to the native nations to the north, west, and south.

And suddenly the nation-in-the-making was even under-taking foreign adventures. In the fall of 1775 the Continental Congress sent not ambassadors but an army up to Lake Cham-plain and down the Richelieu River into Canada, to seize Montreal and attempt the siege of Quebec City. A smaller force ventured out of Maine into the St. John River valley and the Nova Scotia isthmus, seeking to rouse the small population there into joining the rebellion. From Rhode Island an enterprising sailor named Ezek Hopkins led a privateering assault on New Providence, the capital of the Bahama Islands. Another privateer landed on Prince Edward Island to attack Charlottetown and take the lieutenant-governor prisoner. Successful enough as looting ventures, none of these expeditions found the local people much inclined to welcome them as liberators or join in the crusade against tyranny, but these optimistic and outward-looking expeditions at least helped to define the boundaries of the revolution.

The intellectual transformation of the revolution's first years was perhaps as startling as its easy victory and broad geographical sweep. For many years, every protest against British policy and every assertion of American rights had been kept within the boundaries of traditional theories of Englishmen's liberties. No matter how radical, American actions had been defended as the legitimate exercise of colonial rights. Colonial spokesmen had simultaneously defied British authority and claimed to be loyal subjects of the Crown. Even in the early battles with British troops around Boston, the Americans had claimed to be fighting only the "Ministerial Army" of a corrupted government, not against Britain or the king. That style of argument was now making room for other voices, as Thomas Paine showed in his pamphlet *Common Sense*, published in Philadelphia in January 1776.

Common Sense broke decisively with the "patriot" tradition that claimed to seek for American colonists the traditional liberties guaranteed to all Englishmen. Instead of demanding for Americans the rights of all loyal subjects, *Common Sense* offered a vitriolic attack on King George, "the hardened sullentempered Pharaoh of England, the royal brute of Britain".

Paine denounced Parliament and parliamentary government, declaring that the vaunted sharing of powers between king and Parliament was "a mere absurdity", and Parliament far too ignorant to deal with American matters. He denied Britain's claim to be the source of liberty, stating, "Europe, not England, is the parent country of America. This New World has been the asylum for the persecuted lovers of civil and religious liberty from every part of Europe." Himself a dissident Englishman who had been in America for only a year, Paine cried out not for an Englishman's rights but for an American Utopia, "an asylum for mankind" under "the noblest, purest constitution on the face of the earth", and his declaration struck a responsive chord.

Common Sense was a publishing sensation. In the first three months of 1776 one copy of *Common Sense* was sold for every four white men in the Thirteen Colonies, though it was only the most successful of hundreds of widely circulated political pamphlets. The long-developing and widespread American habit of participating in government and debating fundamental political matters now bore revolutionary fruit, and the language of dissent was transformed: just as "patriot" had shed its meaning of "member of the loyal opposition" and begun to signify a friend to the revolution, so "liberty" ceased to refer to the rights of Englishmen and began to mean American freedom from the English tyrant.

The great concluding symbol of this intellectual break was the Declaration of Independence. Drawn up by Thomas Jefferson at the request of the Continental Congress, the Declaration was formally adopted on July 4, 1776. The last large body of royal troops in the Thirteen Colonies had evacuated Boston early in 1776, retreating to Halifax to regroup. Revolutionary authority had been established the length and breadth of the Thirteen Colonies, and only a few isolated pockets of organized resistance remained to be attacked or coerced. The revolution had succeeded, not only in hearts and minds, but all across the territory of the Thirteen Colonies, and the Declaration of Independence seemed to state the basis of a *fait accompli*.

From its opening phrases, "We the people of these United States . . .", the Declaration of Independence took it for granted that Britain was foreign, the king a tyrant, and Parliament corrupt. The Declaration made plain the triumph of the radical notion that sovereignty and power resided in the people and were conferred on government by them and not by any higher agency, human or divine. America would be a republic. Less explicit in the Declaration, but developing elsewhere, were other characteristic American values, such as the notion of universal suffrage giving voting rights to every adult white male. Perhaps even the notions of equality and democracy were buried therein – though deeply buried for the moment. The slaveholders of America had obliged Jefferson to erase from the Declaration an attack on King George as a supporter of the slave trade.

In the summer of 1776, the revolution seemed to have triumphed. Hundreds of thousands of Americans who had not shared the roller-coaster ride from loyalty through patriotic dissent to rebellion now faced a confident, jubilant, and unforgiving new nation.

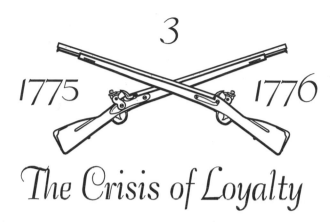

The Crisis of Loyalty

BY THE SPRING OF 1775 SAMUEL CURWEN WANTED OUT of Salem, Massachusetts. The Harvard-educated son of a clergyman, Curwen had spent most of his life as a Salem merchant, and over the years he had acquired most of the attributes of the settled and successful businessman. He had been a justice of the peace for many years, a deputy in the vice-admiralty court of Massachusetts – a post he acquired after marrying the senior judge's sister – and an officer of the local militia. Though hardly important in Massachusetts' affairs, he was acquainted with most of those who were. But now the affairs of the colony were so turbulent that Curwen thought it prudent simply to leave for a while.

Curwen's political ideas were limited and conventional. Though he had exercised leadership as a captain of colonial troops at the siege of Louisbourg in 1745, he never sought political office or offered his opinions about the rights of Englishmen. As a man with a stake in society, he preferred peace and order to any disturbance, and so it was his natural inclination to support the established government that could maintain order. In 1765, when most American merchants had vigorously opposed British plans to tax colonial trade, Curwen's greatest concern was the demonstrations and disorders that occurred in Salem. "We who have property to lose and are lovers of peace, security and good government have, we hope, reasonable grounds to expect this town to continue as it has done hitherto in a laudable state of peace," was his longest opinion on the crisis. As colonial agitation continued in the following decade, Curwen seems to have seen its threat to orderly government rather than its attempt to create a new government, and his support for government was instinctive and almost automatic. It was natural that he – and many of his fellow merchants of similar temperament – would sign Salem's address of welcome to General Thomas Gage when the strong new voice of royal authority arrived to be Massachusetts' governor in 1774, though by doing so he marked himself for retaliation from those who called Gage a tyrant.

Curwen, who was fifty-nine in 1775, had simply never learned the language of liberty. A well-informed man who had visited Europe and read widely, he appreciated the almost unmatched degree of freedom and prosperity that the Thirteen Colonies enjoyed, and he did not see a threat to liberty arising from the colonies' place in the British Empire. He had not even complained about paying the new taxes Britain had begun to impose on its colonies, and so there was little chance he would see the abstract principle of Parliament's right to tax as a threat to freedom or the first step of impending tyranny. Content with the society in which he lived, Curwen was satisfied to leave debates about the rights of Englishmen to others. The vigorous political debates of colonial Massachusetts seem never to have engaged his interest very deeply.

Since contentment with his lot kept him passive in politics, Curwen rapidly fell out of step with the march of opinion in his

community, for colonial spokesmen and their crowds took politics very seriously. With every British action scrutinized for evidence that the enslavement of America was under way, a
neighbour who did not share their concerns and who doubted
that liberty was threatened quickly became suspect. For his
part, Curwen began to find a real threat in his townspeople's
political obsessions, for the boycotts, marches, and confronta-
tions of the Patriots undermined the peace and prosperity that
Curwen valued. Never convinced of an external danger to his
liberty and prosperity, Curwen saw a greater danger in the
increasing madness of the "furious partisans who now compose
almost the whole body of the people".

The fighting at Lexington and Concord destroyed Samuel
Curwen's life in Salem. He thought the clash between British
troops and his own colony's militiamen was "an unhappy
affair", but since he considered the Salem crowds and the colonial militias the primary threat to peace and order, he would
not condemn the troops that had attempted to impose lawful
authority on them. Such views were intolerable to Patriots,
who had seen all their warnings of tyranny and armed oppression vindicated by the British military action, and angry crowds
attacked Curwen and others like him. "For four days after the
19th of April 1775," Curwen wrote later, "I had the mortification to hear myself and much better men than myself reviled,
excoriated, and menaced with immediate destruction." On the
fifth day Curwen boarded a merchant ship and left Salem.

This he hardly saw as a political choice. Political debate had
ceased to be possible, and Curwen was simply protecting himself from "the looks, words and actions of the mad rabble – and
indeed in that time of confusion almost all were mad and all
were rabble." Curwen used the word "mad" quite seriously.
Never having made sense of the language of liberty, he now
believed the neighbours who had created so much strife were
"licentious and enthusiastically mad and broke free from all

restraints of law and religion." His lifelong home now filled him with "dreadful apprehension" and he was glad to be able to sail for a "safe asylum" in Philadelphia. He arrived there early in May 1775 and he arrived alone, for there was a personal dimension to his flight from conflict. Curwen and his wife had been on bad terms for years, and she had declined to accompany him, saying she preferred the risks of civil disorder to those of a sea voyage.

In Salem and in Philadelphia, Curwen was distressed to find himself labelled a "tory". The epithet "tory" was one of the words he had fled from Salem to escape, and so he was agitated when a Philadelphia friend greeted him at the dock with the words "We will protect you though a tory." "Tory" had once meant a diehard supporter of the king, one who stood for absolute royal power unfettered by Parliament. That tradition was long discredited and nearly extinct, so Curwen, who was no great admirer of George III and a supporter of parliamentary rule, saw no reason to accept the label. But by defining all British authority in America as arbitrary and unjustified, the Patriots had adapted the word "tory" to cover any supporter of British rule. Once men like Curwen could be identified with the imaginary tyrants scheming to enslave America, no one who was less than fluent in the language of liberty was safe. Being teasingly called a tory on his arrival in Philadelphia was a hint to Curwen that he had not yet found his safe asylum, and though he was politely received there – and even enjoyed an apolitical encounter with George Washington – he boarded another ship after ten days and sailed away to Britain.

Samuel Curwen was not rare. Many active, well-informed Americans simply never perceived the original threat to liberty that inflamed the Patriots and grew increasingly out of touch as their communities progressed from opposition to particular taxes, to fear of tyranny, to alienation from all things British. It was possible to become a tory inimical to the liberties of

America simply by continuing to express the views that had been the basis of all political discussion a decade or two earlier. Samuel Curwen, who had found those views perfectly adequate, had been driven out of Salem virtually for being too satisfied with his lot there.

Yet many Americans who were labelled and exiled as tories, and who came to call themselves loyalists, had participated actively in the political debates of the colonies and had shared in the demands for the rights of Englishmen. Lawyer Samuel Hale of Portsmouth, New Hampshire, who was probably one of the men of standing who had saved Bart Stavers from the mob in 1774, was a more political man than Samuel Curwen. He retained no small sympathy for the Americans' opposition to arbitrary authority, and even after the revolution he went out of his way to explain that "the people of these provinces, seeing and feeling their connection with their own provincial legislatures, must from their habits and prejudices be attached to them."

Hale's political sense had allowed him to define a crucial issue in the debate over colonial liberties: the way the colonists' growing sense of being Americans predisposed them to give their first allegiance to their colonial leaders rather than to a distant Parliament in Britain. He thought he knew why many of his neighbours had come to prefer their colonial institutions, for, as he explained, "The laws of Parliament, acted partially, were feebly executed and were not all perceived and felt by the great body of the people." Yet Hale's awareness of the growing distance between his people and the government in Britain did not convert him to the American cause. Instead, ranking himself among "the more cool and consistent" who ought to lead the misguided people, Hale attempted "to show them the inferiority of their own Legislatures and to point out to them the connection they all had with the supreme Legislature and their necessary dependence."

Hale would soon find that teaching New Englanders to accept their necessary dependence had become an impossible task, but as a sympathizer with the colonies who still insisted on their submission, Hale seems to have shared the viewpoint of many New England loyalists, including Massachusetts' exiled governor, Thomas Hutchinson. Believing with Hale that the colonies ought to accept dependence rather than "break off our connection" with Britain, Hutchinson argued that the colonies could not survive alone and needed, for the sake of their prosperity, to be part of Britain's empire. This seemed a hesitant, pocketbook kind of patriotism – loyalty for the rewards of empire – and Americans found it easy to abuse Hutchinson as a traitor sold out for royal pay and preferment. But in men like Hutchinson and Hale, the claim that America could not survive alone masked a deeper emotional tie. Vividly aware of the greatness of the empire and confident of the part the Thirteen Colonies could play within it, they rooted their own patriotism in the effort to increase America's role in the empire. These men could accept and justify "the inferiority of their own Legislatures" because they had a deep conviction that the British constitution, enshrining the supremacy of the British Parliament, was the underpinning of liberty and prosperity for Englishmen both in Britain and in the colonies.

Defending the empire and Parliament as the colonies' best government was particularly important to colonials who had honestly and diligently made their careers as servants of the Crown. From Hutchinson and his attorney-general, Jonathan Sewell, down to minor officials like customs collector Isaac Hubbard of Stamford, Connecticut, or even the humble postman Bart Stavers, defending the empire and all it represented meant defending their personal honour; none of them believed that he had chosen to serve the cause of tyranny.

But one did not have to be in the royal pay to believe that

Americans and Britons should remain one people under one government. Samuel Hale accepted it as his duty to defend the empire in Portsmouth. Daniel Leonard, a lawyer from Taunton, Massachusetts, who had been an advocate of the liberty cause for years, broke with his friends and allies soon after the Boston Tea Party made plain that a total break with parliamentary authority was impending. Leonard denied his views had changed. He still wanted to expand the colonists' share in the exercise of Englishmen's liberties, he said, whereas his former colleagues had moved on to treason.

In an atmosphere less poisoned by fear of conspiracy, these advocates of colonial liberties within the empire might have been able to propose some peaceful settlement, but at a time when any defence of the empire could successfully be denounced as toryism by what Hale called "the factious and designing men", the advocates of reformed parliamentary government found it necessary to take a firm stand against the colonial cause. Daniel Leonard published a series of pamphlets defending his views, and he publicly accepted a royal appointment to the council named in 1774 to replace the dismissed Massachusetts legislature. At once an armed mob surrounded his home in rural Taunton, fired shots at the house, smashed the doors and windows, and committed "various other outrages" that forced Leonard to seek military protection in Boston. Samuel Hale also found "his natural influence destroyed by all possible calumny" after he advocated the necessity of submission, and he accepted that British rule would have to be reimposed by force of arms rather than persuasion. Along with John Wentworth, the colonial-born governor of New Hampshire, and other Portsmouth loyalists, Hale fled to Boston in 1775 to join General Gage and was soon appointed a military commissary.

Many colonists whose loyalty was to American liberty

within the British Empire followed Hale's example, however through 1775 and into 1776 others resisted a decisive commitment to war and continued to hope for a reconciliation. In New York, where Patriot radicals and advocates of moderation vied for influence, politician William Smith, the "Patriotic Billy" of ten years before, proposed plan after plan that would confirm American liberty, preserve the empire, and spare the colonies from war. Smith withdrew from the increasing dangers of New York City to a rural retreat early in 1776. Drawing on old friendships to protect him from Patriot wrath, he continued to offer compromise plans to both sides. Not until 1778 would Smith abandon the hope of reconciliation and choose a side, the loyal one.

James Allen, the reticent Philadelphian who hoped that good temper and civility would carry a man peaceably through the world, had espoused political beliefs even more sympathetic to the Patriot cause than those of Samuel Hale or William Smith. The Allen family, in fact, had taken the language of liberty to its limits, for they were even willing to fight British troops for the rights of Englishmen: Allen's brothers had marched north to attack British garrisons in Canada in 1775. James Allen had discovered doubts, however, and just as he was pushed into the political role that most men of his family accepted as natural, he began to retreat from the momentum of the colonial cause.

Allen's neighbours from rural Northampton elected him to Pennsylvania's Patriot-dominated provincial assembly early in 1776, but already he was alarmed to see the colony's leading spokesmen abandoning their demands for Englishmen's liberties. In October 1775 he had despaired over "the madness of the multitude" and the powers of the mob. "I love the cause of liberty," he wrote, "but cannot heartily join in the prosecution of measures totally foreign to the original plan of resistance." By the spring of 1776, when the popularity of Tom Paine's

Common Sense was demonstrating the depth of animosity toward the British political tradition, Allen's continued adherence to the cause of Englishmen's liberties and his total rejection of independence was making him part of an increasingly abused minority in his city. Customs official John Smith "was severely persecuted by the rebels who imprisoned him in the common jail and plundered his house, etc., under pretense that he held a secret correspondence with the king's friends in England." Hugh Stewart, a retired naval officer and merchant seaman who was urged to command a Patriot frigate of war, tried to be excused by pleading age and infirmity, but when he finally refused outright, "he was obliged to secret himself from that time."

Soon James Allen also retreated. "I have been very active in opposing independence and change of government, but the tide is too strong," he wrote, and as the Declaration of Independence was ratified he returned to his estate at Northampton and abandoned both politics and Philadelphia, "which from the current of politics began to grow disagreeable."

"I cannot conceive what will become of all those who have no estates," wrote Allen at Northampton, where income from his tenants maintained him as his Philadelphia law practice collapsed. For men like Allen, rural estates seemed to offer an escape from the political frenzy of the city, and also a welcome reservoir of apparent loyalty to the Crown. The rural interior had seen less political debate than the coastal cities, and so the language of liberty had never so totally dominated political discussion. In areas of recent settlement, new immigrants were still grateful to the empire that had enabled them to cross the ocean to new homes, while the preoccupations with becoming established kept them remote from political debates.

James Allen's rural Pennsylvania was particularly attractive to a loyalist seeking a retreat from politics. Many of Pennsylvania's farmers were Quakers or Mennonites, who avoided political involvement beyond offering a due submission to lawful authority. Their pacifism alienated them from the increasingly demanding Patriots, but their example might have comforted Allen as he attempted to become "a calm spectator of the civil war".

Many more Pennsylvania farmers were German immigrants. Retaining a sense of the dynastic links between America, the British Crown, and the German states that had enabled them to immigrate, the Germans because of their rural location and separate traditions had been largely immune to the debate over the rights of Englishmen. Those who were politically active often supported the established authority, as did the two Christopher Sowers, father and son. The Sowers, whose family had come from Germany to Germantown, Pennsylvania, early in the eighteenth century, "carried on the business of printing and circulating a very extensive public paper in the German language through the provinces, by which . . . they gained the general esteem and confidence of the Germans and other inhabitants." Many of their readers would have avoided strong political commitments, but as publishers the Sowers had to take a stand on the issues, and they "opposed to the utmost of their power the rising sedition, as well by frequent publications in their paper as otherwise." Among such opinions, and bolstered by the traditional deference his tenants showed to the powerful Allen family, James Allen, devoted both to Pennsylvania and to the British Empire, still hoped to find a quiet escape from the political turmoil he had come to detest.

Alexander MacDonald knew none of James Allen's hesitations. The veteran soldier and determined foe of revolution had travelled north from his home on Staten Island to New York's Mohawk Valley frontier late in 1774, not to avoid commitment, but to recruit the settlers there for loyalism and the regiment he intended to raise.

The most influential men in the Mohawk Valley were great landowners who doubled as royal Indian agents in a region that was still bounded by Indian territory. Pre-eminent among these landlords at the end of 1774 was Sir John Johnson, son and recent heir of William Johnson, the Irish immigrant who had helped persuade the Iroquois to accept white settlement in their vicinity. William Johnson had mediated the conflicts that arose between white and native, and then had prospered by acquiring land and bringing in tenants. Men like the Johnsons remained close to the royal authority they served, and their loyalty was never in doubt.

Tenant settlers on the Mohawk Valley estates were equally responsive to MacDonald's approach. One, Luke Bowen, would describe himself as a settler who "resided previous to the rebellion four years on Abraham Windle's estate and rented a hundred and twenty-five acres. . . . At the commencement of the rebellion I opposed the measures of the rebels under Captain Alexander MacDonald." Even tenants whose landlords did not share their loyalty could be rallied to the Crown. "At the Mohawk Valley I deserted my master to manifest my loyalty," proclaimed Donald Cameron, a future recruit to MacDonald's regiment, "and lost my hire for a year." Veterans of British regiments who had settled in the Mohawk Valley after the conquest of New France tended to have the attitude of one aged ex-soldier, Derby Lindsey, who, "being unable to join the British corps by reason of age and infirmity" when the revolution broke out, "sent two sons to join His Majesty's Forces."

The lands of the valley were still attracting many new settlers whose loyalty matched that of Johnson or Lindsey. In 1773 a large Highland family, the MacDonells of Glengarry, had emigrated from Scotland with their followers and tenants to take up some of Sir William Johnson's lands. Their loyalty, too, was fixed and certain. Though there were Patriot committees and spokesmen for the liberty cause in the Mohawk Valley, the revolutionary message of Boston merchants and Virginia planters meant little to most of the settlers there, and Mac-Donald had received a warm response. Archibald MacDonnell, a newcomer engaged in trade in the Mohawk Valley, accepted an officer's commission, and scores of young Scots immigrants enlisted with him. As recent migrants, often Gaelic-speaking, and mostly tenant farmers, they were still bound to the traditional loyalties of the old clan system.

Not only Scots favoured the royal cause. It was nearly as popular among the German communities of the New York frontier. Early in the 1700s, a wave of refugees from war-torn Germany had come to the Mohawk Valley. In the 1770s they remained a tight-knit cluster, still German-speaking and mostly still devoted to Britain's Hanoverian kings, whose German connections had helped make their migration possible. Some German colonists did choose the revolutionary side, but many Cryslers, Casselmans, Loucks, and Hoffs soon enlisted in John Johnson's newly formed King's Royal Regiment of New York and in other loyal corps. Even those inclined to pacifism or simply to keeping their heads down were gradually driven to the loyal cause by the violent intransigence of the rebel forces.

With support for his regiment confirmed, MacDonald had travelled in the spring of 1775 to Boston, then the centre of royal power in America. Most of the British troops in the Thirteen Colonies had been gathered there to enforce the punitive laws enacted after the Boston Tea Party, and men whose loyalty jeopardized their safety in the rest of New England retreated there to join the forces. Samuel Hale, Daniel Leonard, and Jonathan Sewell had already taken shelter in Boston, or were about to do so. Zaccheus Cutter of Amherst in New Hampshire had aided British officers in the pursuit of deserters in March 1775, "by which means he rendered himself so obnoxious to his countrymen that it was utterly unsafe for him to return home." Merchant Samuel Bliss, "largely concerned in trade" in

Greenfield, Massachusetts, was forced by the town's hostility to head for Boston, and young Thomas Gilbert of Berkeley arrived there by a more dangerous route. Gilbert was an officer of his father's Bristol County militia regiment, one of the few loyal militia units in Massachusetts. During the spring of 1775 Gilbert and his three hundred men had "mustered and marched into various parts of the country to still the people and prevent riots." Finally, on the eve of the fighting at Lexington, Patriot militias preparing for war moved to silence this dissident element within their own ranks. Gilbert and many of his men were seized, briefly jailed, and forced to sign an oath of allegiance to the revolutionary cause. Like a great many other Americans who would take such oaths under duress in the coming years, Gilbert repudiated it the moment he was free. Escaping to a naval vessel off Rhode Island, he reached shelter in Boston.

This influx of loyalists was outweighed by an exodus of Bostonians who supported the revolution. Boston's civil population fell from 16,000 to 3,500 during 1775, and the British garrison found itself with its back to the sea facing a hostile population all around the city. In June the costly assault on Bunker Hill across the harbour from Boston had confirmed the strength and determination of the New England militias, which were soon reinforced by the new Continental Army units led by George Washington. The British and their loyal allies found themselves besieged in Boston.

The loyalists in Boston were quickly drawn into the defence forces. Bookbinder William Cross became a sentry in the town guard, and merchant Archibald Cunningham "joined the North British Association and did duty in that corps during the blockade." Those who did not bear arms gave other services. John Joy, a Boston carpenter who had led a crew of New England artisans to assist General Wolfe's siege of Quebec in 1759, was again recruited as a military carpenter, this time to construct defence works around his own town. Dr. John Jeffries became physician to the troops and treated many of the wounded after Bunker Hill. Boston tax-collector Abraham Savage found himself appointed a supply officer and was dispatched to Cape Breton Island in search of coal for the garrison, "which coal he actually brought in to their great relief."

In the midst of his civil and military duties, General Gage also turned his attention to Alexander MacDonald's proposal for a regiment of loyal American Highlanders. MacDonald had a well-placed ally in John Small, a major on Gage's staff, but they soon discovered that an influential rival had arrived from Britain. Allan Maclean, an army lieutenant-colonel, had conceived a plan strikingly similar to MacDonald's: a new regiment of American Highlanders to prevent or defeat rebellion in the colonies. Maclean, a former Jacobite who had been pardoned and had commanded Highland troops in America during the Seven Years War, was senior to both MacDonald and Small, and he had already acquired a royal warrant for the regiment he planned.

Just a week before the battle of Bunker Hill, General Gage resolved the rivalry by creating the Royal Highland Emigrants as a two-battalion regiment. Maclean would have overall command, but each five-hundred-man battalion would be run independently, one by Maclean, one by Small. Alexander MacDonald's personal plans – to become a major and second-in-command of a regiment – were dashed. Outmanoeuvred by Maclean, he found himself only a company captain in Small's battalion, and it was Maclean who set off, travelling in disguise to avoid capture, to enlist the men of the Mohawk Valley whom MacDonald had persuaded to serve. Maclean reached the Mohawk, gave commissions to several of the leading men there, and almost at once led his new recruits north to defend Montreal and Quebec against the American invasion. Major Small remained at headquarters in Boston, fought at Bunker Hill, and supervised the dispatch of commissions to

Highlanders in North Carolina. Alexander MacDonald, who had already travelled from Staten Island to the Mohawk Valley, back to New York, and east to Boston, was dispatched to Halifax, Nova Scotia, along with Samuel Bliss, the Greenfield merchant who had accepted a lieutenant's commission in the new regiment.

The siege of Boston continued through 1775, as General Gage was replaced by Sir William Howe. Forced to bring in supplies by a long and vulnerable sea route, the embattled garrison of Boston was barely able to sustain itself, and what Boston loyalist Richard Lechmere called "the fatigues of a tedious, dangerous and disagreeable siege" were doing little for the loyal cause. As the troops began a harsh and unproductive winter in the heart of rebellious New England, royal authority was demolished in the rest of the Thirteen Colonies. With all the royal forces committed to Boston, New York City fell to revolutionary authority despite a large body of moderate opinion there, and in Pennsylvania the radicals were able to neutralize those who still sought reconciliation.

In Virginia the governor, Lord Dunmore, attempted an armed resistance to the revolution, but though he boldly offered freedom to any slave who joined him, the small loyal force he mustered was soon driven from the mainland and left holding only some small islands in Chesapeake Bay.

The Highlanders of North Carolina also attempted armed resistance. Letters and then commissions in the Royal Highland Emigrants reached Alexander MacDonald's kinsmen Donald and Allan MacDonald, and they soon raised nearly fifteen hundred newly settled Highlanders from the North Carolina backcountry. Attempting to march to the coast, this small army was cut off and defeated by rebel militias. Many were killed. John McRae, who had abandoned a plantation to enlist, "lost his right arm by a gunshot, after which he suffered captivity," and Torquil MacLeod "was forced to secret himself from the face of the enemy in the back parts of North Carolina." Allan MacDonald was captured and "sent from gaol to gaol til at last closely confined in Philadelphia," while his wife, Flora, the Jacobite heroine, was left behind in rebel territory. North Carolina loyalism had been driven underground.

In South Carolina, Moses Kirkland of Ninety-Six district was more cautious about offering armed resistance. Though Kirkland claimed the support of five thousand men, the loyal settlers of the South Carolina backcountry were isolated, poorly armed, and outnumbered. Rather than suffer the fate of the North Carolina Highlanders, the loyal militia decided to disband and make temporary submission to the revolutionary powers on the sea-coast, while Kirkland and his twelve-year-old son set out to alert the royal army to the situation in the southern colonies.

Kirkland's mission soon took him the full length of the Thirteen Colonies. Managing to reach the sea-coast and to board a naval vessel that South Carolina's exiled governor had made his headquarters, Kirkland was sent south to the British fort at St. Augustine in Florida, and then, in October 1775, north to Lord Dunmore's tiny loyal enclave in Virginia. In November, Kirkland decided to carry his information directly to General Howe, who had replaced Thomas Gage in command at Boston, but his ship was taken by a rebel privateer within sight of that port, and Kirkland was sent as a prisoner to Philadelphia. Far from securing aid for his neighbours, he had only learned that all the loyalists of America were as beleaguered as those of Ninety-Six.

A few months later, in March 1776, General Howe gathered enough ships to evacuate Boston, and just as Washington pushed his siege lines close enough to make the town untenable, Howe retreated to Halifax with nine thousand soldiers and a thousand loyalists. Richard Lechmere, though he claimed to have foreseen that his loyalty "would expose him to many great difficulties and dangers", found the voyage from Boston hard to bear. "He embarked for Halifax," he wrote of himself later, "with his family consisting of a wife, six children and four servants, having only three days' notice to prepare himself and his family for a voyage in a small ship crowded with near one hundred persons (exclusive of the ship's crew). . . . In this very confused and distressing situation they remained from the beginning of March 1776 til their arrival the end of the same month, experiencing every species of indelicacy and inconvenience." Lechmere, however, was spared the inconvenience of capture, unlike Robert Campbell, a New Jersey loyalist who had fled first to New York and then to Boston. At the evacuation of Boston, Campbell boarded a sloop for Halifax, "but she was unfortunately taken on her passage by an American privateer" and Campbell spent a year in a Boston jail.

With the retreat from Boston, just months before the Declaration of Independence, the crisis of loyalty ended in the loss of royal government everywhere in the Thirteen Colonies. Thousands of individuals had stood by their principles against both the coercive power and the persuasive rhetoric of the revolutionaries. Entire communities, from the Mohawk Valley to South Carolina, had instinctively responded when invited to affirm their loyalty. Nowhere, however, had loyalism been dominant. The faith that Americans and Britons were one people who could work out their differences had fallen victim to the Patriots' corrosive distinction between the interests of America and the distant authority of Britain, and many colonists who might have been passively loyal under continued British rule either accepted the fact of American independence or chose not to resist it.

Those still committed to the empire now looked to Britain and the force of its arms to restore the imperial bonds. A military contest would determine the future of the loyalists.

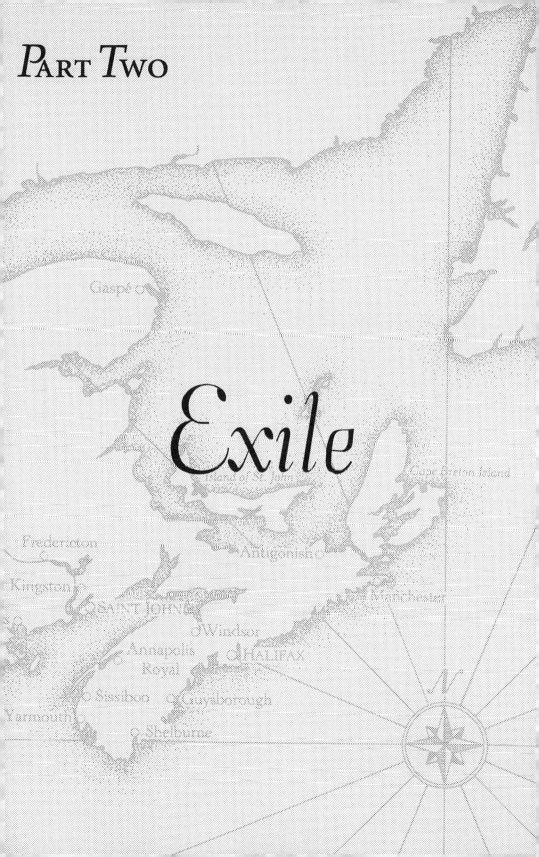

PART TWO

Exile

The King's War

AT HALIFAX, NOVA SCOTIA, IN THE SPRING OF 1776 Alexander MacDonald was beginning to recover his habitual optimism after a very bad winter. During his months as a recruiter in Halifax, his Staten Island farm and the family he had left there had fallen into the hands of the rebels, and the little news that reached him was alarming. His cousin Allan MacDonald had been defeated and captured in North Carolina, and his regimental commander, Allan Maclean, was besieged at Quebec. In March, MacDonald saw the British garrison of Boston arrive at Halifax after escaping from Massachusetts and leaving the revolution triumphant throughout the Thirteen Colonies. Yet, as early as February 1776, MacDonald was predicting the approach of victory: "This wretched, miserable, unnatural contest must be decided in the course of this ensuing year," he wrote as he considered the way the war was developing. The instrument of decision was not to be the loyal citizenry of the Thirteen Colonies. Now that the

Continental Congress and the Patriot committees had established their authority and raised an army, declarations of loyalty could not be enough. MacDonald, always inclined to put the American crisis in military perspective, understood that the armed forces of Great Britain would be required to restore parliamentary authority in America. For a solution to the crisis, MacDonald looked to Britain, and what he saw made him hopeful of quick victory.

The American cause had always had friends in Britain, for Britain had its own patriot opposition. Much of the language of liberty that had been the prevailing ideology of American resistance had initially been worked out by English radicals, and American grievances had often received a sympathetic hearing across the Atlantic. The outbreak of war, however, rallied the British behind Parliament and the Crown. Few in Britain believed that American grievances justified armed rebellion against a Parliament that Britons still considered as the bulwark of liberty, and righteous anger demanded a strong response to the conspiracy that had somehow led the colonists into rebellion.

The American Revolution challenged two of Britain's proudest attributes, its world-wide empire and its parliamentary government, and many Englishmen feared one might be lost and the other discredited by American independence. "A small state may certainly subsist," said George III, "but a great one mouldering cannot get into an inferior situation but must be annihilated."

Britain had become a great state, the leading power of Europe, as early as 1763, when it consolidated a global empire at France's expense. Now that Britain's wealth lay less in land and agriculture than in overseas trade and commerce, the sense was strong that losing the large and valuable colonies in America would trigger a global slide that would send Britain into decline, much as Spain and Holland had declined from imperial glory to secondary importance. Britons also considered their parliamentary government as a special and fragile accomplishment, and the American claim that Parliament was corrupt and tyrannical directly challenged British pride in the slowly developed political system that guaranteed the Englishman's rights and liberties. The national consensus to defend British greatness and the good name of parliamentary government translated into large parliamentary majorities in favour of war measures and war taxes.

The war, however, would not be an all-out one. Britain itself was not directly threatened. Europe and the rest of the empire were at peace, and the usual preoccupations of peace continued unabated. There may have been willingness to fight for America, but no one was yet ready to accept the kind of effort that a major European war would have demanded. No one wanted the raising of massive armies, the conscription of merchant sailors for a great naval expansion, the crippling of peacetime trade and commerce. Above all, the men who controlled Parliament did not want the enormous taxes of an all-out war to be levied on them just a decade after the end of the most recent struggle with France. Britain was nearly unanimous in favour of a war, but not yet for a total war.

The European situation reinforced the desire for a quick, decisive military commitment. Britain's rivals France and Spain and its estranged ally Prussia, all monarchies, could hardly be keenly supportive of the radical ideology of the American revolutionaries – Alexander MacDonald in Halifax believed that every Crown in Europe would help to stamp out the republican heresy – but they would be eager to profit from Britain's misfortune if the war lasted and grew. This danger of a challenge in Europe meant Britain could not send all of its standing army or all of its navy to stamp out the American resistance. Twenty thousand men with all their supplies and equipment, with a fleet of up to sixty warships, was the government's minimum estimate for the force needed to smash the rebellion. Yet in the winter of 1775-76 there were fewer than ten thousand soldiers on active service in Britain. The British high command faced a dilemma: how to crush the rebellion by an overwhelming show of force while at the same time protecting Britain and keeping within the spending and recruiting boundaries of a limited war.

The problem was resolved in Germany. In January 1776 Britain signed treaties with the principalities of Hesse, Brunswick, and Waldeck, by which eighteen thousand disciplined, experienced officers and men were recruited to serve Britain during the American war. Sending foreign mercenaries against colonial Englishmen probably helped to alienate wavering colonials from the British cause, but without the German troops, Britain could never have fielded a professional army of adequate size in 1776, and the decision to use mercenary regiments was not seen as anything unusual in a century when most wars were not ideological conflicts but limited and pragmatic contests for power and prestige. By early spring of 1776 the German regiments were arriving in Britain to join English, Irish, and Scots regiments, until there were twenty-six thousand men preparing to cross the Atlantic, ten thousand to relieve Canada and prepare the way for an invasion of the Thirteen Colonies from the north, the rest to go directly to the attack.

By an extraordinary effort, all these men, and a ton of supplies for every three of them, actually did cross the Atlantic that spring. Though the peacetime merchant navy and the trading fleet of the East India Company were left largely untouched by the limited war, enough transport ships and escort frigates were gathered together to move all the men, horses, weapons, food, and equipment out to the theatre of conflict. Military officials were pleased by this unprecedented success; in the coming years they would discover that similar logistical feats would have to become an annual event of the far-off American war. As the army of reconquest sailed from Britain, British commanders – and observers such as Alexander MacDonald – could find cause for optimism in a survey of Britain's remaining strengths.

Sea power was the first element of Britain's remaining hold over the colonies. The large merchant fleets of New England and the middle colonies were turning into a privateering navy, capable of harassing British shipping and bringing in supplies and ammunition for the Continental Army, but these small vessels could never face and defeat the Royal Navy, which was still maintaining a close surveillance on American ports and preparing to impose the tightest of blockades on the rebel coast. Sea power also gave Britain its surviving foothold on the southern edge of the continent, the outpost colonies called East and West Florida. The Florida peninsula and all the Gulf coast west to New Orleans and the Mississippi, acquired from Spain in 1763, controlled a major sea route out of the Gulf of Mexico and kept watch over Spanish activities on the Mississippi. Neither part of Florida had been extensively settled, and small military garrisons at St. Augustine and Pensacola kept the Floridas loyal to the Crown and useful as potential springboards for action against rebellious Georgia and the Carolinas.

While the navy carried British power up to the shores of the rebellious colonies, the preservation of Canada from American attack had secured a strong British presence on the northern and western boundaries of the revolution. Canada in 1776 remained a French society with a British veneer. A few English and American merchants, a few retired military men settled on seigneurial estates, and the officials of the colonial government comprised the British population that had come since the fall of New France in 1763 to live among 140,000 French-speaking *Canadiens* in the towns and farms along the lower St. Lawrence. In 1774 Canada's governor, Guy Carleton, had secured passage of the Quebec Act, intended to win *Canadien* support for British rule by giving official recognition to many rights and practices preserved from the French regime. Carleton trusted that the act would unify the *Canadiens* behind his government, for in the same year he had had to send most of his troops south to assist General Gage in Boston.

Without these troops, Carleton had been unable to defend Canada's borders when the Americans attacked in 1775, and despite the Quebec Act, the *Canadiens* saw little reason to rally to the support of a British regime that was collapsing in Canada and throughout the continent. The Americans captured the border forts and occupied Montreal. By December 1775 Carleton had seemed as vulnerable in Quebec City as General Howe did in Boston. Yet Carleton managed to hold Quebec and recover Canada that winter, and much of the credit went to Alexander MacDonald's recruiting rival and commanding officer, Allan Maclean.

Maclean had managed to gather only a couple of hundred recruits in the Highland communities of the Mohawk Valley before he was forced to flee to Canada, where he soon found himself the colony's senior military officer after Carleton. As the American invasion rolled up to the walls of Quebec City in December 1775, Maclean's professional experience was invaluable in making the most effective possible defence of the town. "I really believe the gates would have been opened . . . by the disaffected and faint-hearted among us if it had not been for the colonel," wrote an observer. Maclean established a command post in the famed Quebec City tavern called The Golden Dog – giving an ensign's commission to the tavern-keeper's son, Samuel Prenties – and his small force of soldiers and a larger collection of new recruits, sailors, and townspeople proved just adequate to hold Quebec City. The momentum of the American attack was stopped, and winter, disease, and supply shortages eroded the strength of the invading army. When they launched a desperate assault on the town on New Year's Eve, the loyal defenders repulsed them. One of Maclean's officers was credited with giving the first warning of an attack. Alexander MacDonald's kinsman and ex-colleague Richard Montgomery died at the head of the American troops, and the power of the invasion was broken. "I will say that my regiment did keep Quebec and save Canada," exulted Allan Maclean.

By spring, with British reinforcements coming up the St. Lawrence, the Americans were in full retreat. They had found themselves even less successful than the British in winning co-operation or support from the cautious *Canadiens*. Carleton soon re-established Canada's borders, strengthening the border forts close to New York and regaining contact with the western military posts along the Great Lakes. By the spring of 1776 a long defence line from Quebec and Montreal, south to Lake Champlain and west to Niagara, Detroit, and distant Michilimackinac once more challenged revolutionary power on the northwestern frontier.

The British posts on the western frontier of Canada provided bases from which to carry the war back into the Thirteen Colonies, and they helped protect the still-valuable fur trade, but their most vital role was as embassies to the native nations. Native territory bounded all the long western frontier of the revolutionary colonies, and the native nations could be crucial to the future of the war. During 1775 and 1776 the leaders of each tribal confederacy had been working out their policies on this complex and puzzling war, and the route west from Montreal remained Britain's lifeline to these hesitating potential allies.

One nation for whom the revolution posed particular challenges was the Iroquois, or Six Nations, Confederacy, the most powerful native nation of eastern North America. The Iroquois had once been allied with the Dutch and the English of New York, and they had fought fierce wars against the French in

Canada and France's native allies, the Hurons. But by 1700, with the Hurons destroyed, the Iroquois had seen the advantage of remaining neutral when the white men fought each other. They had managed to limit their involvement in most of the eighteenth century's French-English wars and in the native uprising that followed Britain's victory in 1763. In the meantime the Iroquois had prospered. They had always been an agricultural and trading people, and on their lands south of Lake Ontario and west of the Mohawk Valley, their farms and settlements flourished. The political issues of the revolution meant little to them, but they had the strongest incentives for remaining friendly both with the New York neighbours whose settlements were coming increasingly close and with the royal soldiers and officials whose treaties guaranteed the natives' title to their lands and homes. Nor did the Iroquois relish having either side as their enemy. On one hand, the growing numbers of land-hungry New Yorkers would welcome the excuse to dispossess the Iroquois. But on the other, the Iroquois had long and intimate knowledge of the royal army's power to punish native nations that resisted it.

At the start of the conflict, the councils of the Iroquois voted for the traditional policy of neutrality, but the issues at stake were too big and the people of the Confederacy too enmeshed in the Europeans' politics to remain above the fray. For most of a century the Iroquois had been abiding by royal treaties and dealing intimately with royal officials, and this link with the Crown seemed stronger than the promises of the revolutionary committees. The case for the British alliance was put with particular force by Thayendanegea, or Joseph Brant, a well-educated and ambitious young Mohawk whose sister Konwatsi-tsiaienni, or Mary Brant, was both an influential member of the Iroquois matriarchy and the widow of Sir William Johnson, the royal agent and Mohawk Valley landowner. In native society, war, with its opportunities to display courage and leadership, had always been a forum for young men seeking to advance themselves within the tribe, and now Brant made his claim. Against the tradition of neutrality, he could cite the traditional alliance with the British king; and the ever-present land issue gave weight to his cause. In rapidly expanding New York, settlers who had renounced the king's native treaties would make dangerous friends, while a grateful British government might be a useful ally.

Brant's case did not convert all the Iroquois. Despite his arguments and his sister's influence, many of the elders on the Six Nations council still wanted neutrality, and the Oneida tribe, nearest neighbours of the Americans, leaned toward the revolutionaries. The Six Nations Confederacy was to be tragically divided, but gradually the largest part of the Iroquois nation began to lean toward an alliance with Britain. As the American invasion of Canada collapsed, the Iroquois became a powerful and much-feared British ally close to the northern edges of the rebellious colonies. The adherence of the Iroquois to the royal cause shored up the support of tribes all down the western frontier of the Thirteen Colonies and added significantly to Britain's power to fight the revolutionary colonies.

Back in Halifax, where news of the successful defence of Canada had brought surprise and relief, Alexander MacDonald would have been only vaguely aware of the distant politics of the Iroquois alliance, though he knew the power of the native nations from having fought them in 1763. MacDonald, however, was making his own contribution, both to securing royal authority in the Maritimes and to building the regiment he served into a force capable of participating in the recovery of the Thirteen Colonies.

The expanding war was restoring Halifax to its intended function as a military headquarters. Founded as a garrison town in 1749, Halifax had done well enough in peacetime as the capital and trading centre of the growing colony of Nova Scotia, but now the collapse of British authority to the south had again underlined its strategic importance. It remained a town of fewer than two thousand people, tiny by comparison to the older cities of the Thirteen Colonies, but it had long both had an army garrison and been the headquarters of the Royal Navy in North America. From Halifax, naval patrols along the long coasts of the Bay of Fundy, the Atlantic, and the Gulf of St. Lawrence struggled to turn back waves of rebel privateers sailing north from New England, while small garrisons detached from Halifax secured the sometimes doubtful loyalties of the twenty thousand colonists of Nova Scotia – almost half of whom were originally New Englanders.

In May and June of 1776, Alexander MacDonald had the privilege of being in Halifax to watch as General William Howe made his rendezvous with the thousands of troops, mountains of supplies, and scores of vessels arriving from Britain. Howe then sailed away to begin the reconquest of the Thirteen Colonies by an invasion of New York. Contemplating the strength of Howe's army, the network of ships, forts, garrisons, and allies surrounding the rebels, and the great reserves of strength held by the empire, Alexander MacDonald had reason to hope that his prediction of a quick resolution to America's civil war would soon be proven correct.

In the same week that the Declaration of Independence was signed at Philadelphia early in July 1776, William Howe's army and a naval fleet commanded by his brother Richard arrived off New York harbour to begin the reconquest of America. The Howe brothers' forces were imposing, as one officer cheerfully recorded in a survey of the opposed armies: "General Howe now had the satisfaction of finding himself at the head of full twenty-four thousand fine troops, most comfortably furnished and appointed, commanded by the ablest and best officers in the world. Mr. Washington, a gentleman of property in Virginia . . . had the chief command of the rebel army and called himself General. The utmost of his collected forces did not amount to sixteen thousand men, all of whom were undisciplined, unused to war, deficient in clothing and even necessities, and very ill-provided with artillery and ammunition. His officers were tradesmen of different professions, totally unacquainted with discipline and consequently utterly unskilled in the art of war."

Apart from a clearly superior army and the arrogant confidence it inspired, General Howe had brought with him the conviction that two decisive steps could seal the fate of the revolution during 1776. Howe intended to seek and fight a battle in which his well-trained regular troops could destroy George Washington's fledgling Continental Army, and he intended to couple this demonstration of power with an offer of pardon and reconciliation that would enable the revolutionary leaders to accept the inevitable and submit to royal authority. The conviction that a few hard blows and an offer of pardon would destroy the revolution governed British strategy in 1776 – and, when a second campaigning season proved necessary, this strategy continued in 1777.

The first stage of Howe's invasion, the battle for New York City, seemed to justify the confidence of British and loyalist observers. Howe successfully managed the difficult transfer of his troops from ship to shore, taking first Staten Island and then Long Island, and then crossing to Manhattan to capture New York City and send Washington retreating rapidly north and west. By the end of the summer, New York City and a broad stretch of territory all around it had passed into British hands, and the British conviction that Howe's regulars were virtually invincible on the battlefield had been reinforced by a series of British victories.

Loyalists rushed in to greet and join the British, and Howe added many of them to his forces. Francis Blackburn, a tailor from Oyster Bay, Long Island, had been "harassed and disarmed

by the rebels on account of his loyalty to the king and attachment to the British government" and he had fled into the
woods for refuge from the Patriots. Blackburn emerged to meet
the British army on Long Island, and soon he was serving in a
loyalist militia troop. Jesse Hoyt, a sailor from Norwalk, Connecticut, had not even waited for the success of the landings,
but had joined the fleet at sea and helped to pilot it into New
York harbour. Young Ichabod Oliver of Elizabethtown, New
Jersey, "on the arrival of the Royal Army at New York in 1776
was fifteen years old and, actuated by the same principles of loyalty that inspired his father, left his home and joined the pro-
vincials that were then raising." Knowledge of the local terrain
made loyalists like these useful to the British, and many of them
soon saw action in the battles around New York.

Despite several successful battles, the taking of New York
City did not give Howe the decisive victory he had hoped for,
for the Continental Army had shown it preferred retreat over
the prospect of a last-stand battle it was sure to lose. In search of
his battle, Howe pursued Washington deep into New Jersey in
the last months of 1776, and both the speed of his advance and
the number of loyalists rallying to support him sustained the
British commander's confidence that the revolution might simply collapse from its own weakness.

Howe was not alone in this optimism. When a New Jersey
doctor, Abraham Van Buskirk, "obtained a commission of Colonel and began to raise a regiment out of the loyalists who were
then flocking in and taking refuge under the British standard,"
he offered a major's commission to Gabriel Van Norden of
Newbridge, a close friend of his who had been active in opposition to the revolutionary cause. Van Norden, however, was so
confident "that there would soon be an end to the war and that
British Government would soon take place" that he declined
the commission and remained at home.

Van Norden's confidence – and Howe's – was misplaced, for

Washington's army remained intact and dangerous despite all its retreats. On Christmas Eve, 1776, the Continental Army made a counter-attack on a British outpost at Trenton, and General Howe felt obliged to withdraw his overextended troops back toward New York for the winter. Van Norden, who was left behind, was captured by the rebels and jailed for two years. Arrested at the same time was a Hackensack cooper named Dan Jessup, who had guided British troops in New Jersey that fall, but Jessup managed to escape from custody to reach New York, where he enlisted in Van Buskirk's new regiment. Less fortunate were Margaret Thomson and her husband Thomas, a loyal schoolteacher. Washington's troops used their Trenton home as a temporary headquarters, then plundered and burned it as they departed.

In 1777 Howe renewed his search for a decisive battle and a quick victory. Taking his army by sea to Pennsylvania, Howe advanced on Philadelphia, the revolutionary capital, where the governing Continental Congress met. Again Howe's better-trained and better-equipped regiments won a series of victories. The British soon occupied Philadelphia, and again loyalists who had been lying low under Patriot authority flocked to the British standard.

Yet once again Howe found himself denied the great victory on which he had counted. George Washington had recognized that a decisive encounter – and his near-certain defeat in it, given the weakness of his troops – would destroy the Continental Army, the vital military arm that kept the revolution alive. Washington had quickly learned the advantages of retreat, and the huge American countryside always offered space into which he could withdraw, emerging only to spring raids like the one at Trenton, which had reassured his troops and mocked the power of the British army. In 1776 Washington had abandoned New York to the British and made no attempt to protect New England. In 1777 he allowed Philadelphia to fall, though its loss forced the Continental Congress to flee and obliged Washington and his army to endure a cold winter at Valley Forge. General Howe's army wintered comfortably in Philadelphia, but Howe had begun to learn that there was no vital centre Washington had to defend – and hence no decisive battle that Howe could coerce his enemy into fighting and losing.

The survival of the Continental Army and its ability to retaliate had also negated Howe's offers of pardon and negotiations, for while the British insisted that submission to royal authority would have to precede a reconciliation, the revolutionaries still felt able to insist on a recognition of American independence as the first step toward any settlement. Against this impasse, no headway could be made by those rare conciliators who still believed the differences between Britain and America could be resolved peacefully.

By 1777 the Patriots had also given proof that their revolution was hardly so weak as the British had hoped. Though their military units were not yet able to achieve battlefield victories against the professional army Howe had brought from Europe, their political organization was growing strong, supple, and resilient. If Howe spread his army out to police large areas and assist the loyalists against Patriot harassment, the enemy attacked his small detachments, but if he gathered the army together, rebel organizations reasserted themselves in the countryside. Howe had sought to smash the revolution by a decisive battle and a show of force because he understood the impossibility of imposing military occupation on the whole continent. Now the resilience of the revolutionary forces was challenging the assumption that Britain could ever win without achieving such an occupation.

The British army's attempt to bring the revolution to a quick collapse finally died at Saratoga in northern New York. While Howe was capturing Philadelphia in the fall of 1777, General John Burgoyne had left Montreal with an army of seven thousand to invade the Thirteen Colonies by the Richelieu–Lake Champlain route the Americans had used to invade Canada in 1775. Burgoyne's plan was based on the unspoken assumption that the rebellion could be toppled simply by a determined show of force, for once he reached the Hudson River, his army would confront a heartland of the revolution without any prospect of reinforcement or even retreat. Only if the revolution had been a weak conspiracy without popular support could Burgoyne have succeeded.

Like Howe, General Burgoyne received enthusiastic support from American loyalists all along his route. George Boyle of Skenesborough piloted part of the army down Lake Champlain, as did George Brenner, a lakeside settler who "was in all the engagements with General Burgoyne". Samuel Anderson raised sixty-four loyalists in Pownal, Vermont, and joined a detachment of Burgoyne's army at nearby Bennington. The wife of James Clarke, a farmer with five hundred acres of Mohawk Valley land, reported that "nothing would serve her husband, an Englishman, when General Burgoyne came down from Quebec than to join the army as a volunteer."

Despite the courage and loyalty of men like Anderson and Clarke, their support never gave Burgoyne's army the strength to compel the mass of northern New York's population into obedience. Instead, the small Continental Army that faced the British advance recruited thousands to resist the British invasion. By fall Burgoyne was cut off in the midst of the American forest at Saratoga, his route back to Canada severed and an ever-increasing force of armed civilians surrounding and harassing his troops. When Samuel Anderson's sixty-four loyalists joined the conflict at Bennington, "all but eight were killed or taken prisoner by the rebels." James Clarke was killed at Saratoga, where Burgoyne suddenly found himself vastly outnumbered by an enemy he had expected to subdue almost without a struggle. Burgoyne surrendered in October 1777.

Anderson, Brenner, Boyle, and hundreds of other loyalists either were captured or fled north through the woods to Canada.

Saratoga transformed the war. After two seasons of the British campaign to smash a colonial revolt, America's revolutionaries had actually won a major victory over one British army while avoiding fatal defeat at the hands of the other. The growing evidence that the revolution was real, serious, and deeply rooted turned the colonial revolt into a European war, as Britain's traditional rivals seized their opportunity to reverse the defeats of previous wars. France entered the war against Britain early in 1778, and by summer the Royal Navy was fighting to retain control of the English Channel. In 1779, when Spain joined France, their combined fleets outnumbered the British navy and threatened an invasion of England, and by the end of the year Britain was also fighting Holland, which had wished to remain neutral but insisted on its right to trade with the American rebels. By 1780 Britain was fighting to preserve its bases and colonies in India, the Mediterranean, and the West Indies, and was finding its naval and military resources stretched too thin in every direction, though the army had grown to 150,000 men. All hope of a quick, economical war had vanished, along with the hope that a mere show of force could bring victory in the American colonies.

The Patriot cause in America gained much-needed supplies, naval support, and eventually troops from France, but the first consequence of the international war was a lull in the fighting. Britain's powerful army could still largely control the pace of the colonial conflict, and in 1778 the British were retrenching in America, transferring ships and men south to defend the West Indies and withholding the annual reinforcements needed for offensives against General Washington's increasingly experienced army. That summer General Howe abandoned Philadelphia and moved his army back to New York

City. At the end of 1778 the British controlled little more of the Thirteen Colonies than they had in 1776. General Howe was replaced by General Henry Clinton, who began seeking a new strategy by which to recover the Thirteen Colonies.

In these years, the world-wide obligations of the British army put new burdens of responsibility for the colonial war on the loyal Americans, and British commanders began to seek ways to reinforce loyal Americans rather than confront the revolutionary heartlands. In 1778 the British ceased to pursue the decisive battle in Pennsylvania, New Jersey, or New York, and turned to areas where they hoped the loyalists were stronger. After 1778 British strategy aimed to surround and isolate the revolution instead of confronting it, and so the royal cause looked south. Troops from Florida recovered most of Georgia early in 1778, and in the following year the British captured most of a Continental army at Charleston, South Carolina, and launched a major offensive in the southern colonies.

Once again British and loyalist regiments won a series of victories. By the end of 1780 most of Georgia, South Carolina, and North Carolina were in British hands, but in the south the British aimed not just at military victories but at political success. The aim was now the creation of loyal provinces, from which reorganized loyal governments could be spread northward. Military victory in the southern colonies would sever a large part of America from the revolutionary cause, but only political success would show war-weary Patriots that loyal government under the British Crown could be made to work for the benefit of the American colonies.

Loyalists were active in every part of the campaign for the south. Torquil MacLeod, one of the loyal North Carolina Highlanders whose rising had been smashed at Moore's Creek Bridge early in 1776, had hidden in the North Carolina backcountry until news of General Howe's advance into Pennsylvania encouraged him to traverse Virginia and Maryland in secret to join the royal forces at Philadelphia. Quickly enlisted in the 71st Highland Regiment, MacLeod became part of the force that entered Georgia in 1778 to begin the reconquest of the south. When South Carolina was invaded in 1780, much of the army consisted of loyalist troops, including even five companies of the Royal Highland Emigrants, trained by Alexander Mac-Donald in Halifax and now beginning their active service after a spell in garrison at New York.

Also among the invaders was Moses Kirkland, whose career since his flight from Ninety-Six district in backcountry South Carolina in 1775 had typified the restless, dangerous wanderings many southern loyalists had endured. Kirkland's attempt to reach Boston in 1776 had led him to Florida and Virginia and then to capture by a rebel privateer and imprisonment in Philadelphia. He had escaped from captivity, seen Howe's reconquest of New York, and eventually earned an assignment in Florida. For a year Kirkland had worked as an native agent, travelling on the frontiers urging the Seminole natives of East and West Florida to ally themselves to the royal cause. Administrative oversights and the death of his superior denied him his pay for this service, but Kirkland joined the invasion of Georgia, helped to defend Savannah against a French-American siege late in 1779, and then joined the invasion of South Carolina. Finally, in May 1780, five years after his escape in disguise, Kirkland returned in triumph to his home in Ninety-Six and took up his original role as a loyal militia officer.

Men like Kirkland at Ninety-Six and James Cassells, a Georgetown, South Carolina, plantation-owner appointed to a militia colonelcy, became the backbone of the attempt to build a loyal government in the south. Loyalists who had been forced to flee or conceal themselves since 1775 came forward to rebuild a loyal economy based on rice exports to Britain. Taking on roles in the new loyal governments of their districts, they helped "reclaim the province to a due obedience of the just and lawful authority of His Majesty's Government." Former rebels or sympathizers were forced or persuaded to accept the new regime, and loyalist exiles began to return, hoping to rebuild their lives in a once more loyal and peaceable South Carolina.

Despite the strength of southern loyalism, however, the rebels had not conceded either Georgia or South Carolina to the Crown, and soon South Carolina was suffering under the worst cruelties of a civil war, as loyal and patriot militias skirmished and struggled all through the inland counties, burning towns, savaging plantations, and hanging prisoners, with each side attempting to terrorize the enemy into submission and to avenge the sufferings of friends. Continental armies from Virginia and North Carolina menaced the loyal territories, and rebel guerrilla leaders raided behind the British lines. Against them loyalist cavalry and infantry units like Tarleton's Raiders and Edmund Fanning's King's American Regiment swept through the countryside in a vicious war of raid and reprisal. "The Whigs and Tories pursue each other with the most relentless fury, killing and destroying each other wherever they meet," was one soldier's summation of the South Carolina campaigns.

To General Cornwallis, commanding the British forces in the south, it began to seem that the prospect of political victory there would be lost if the colonies just to the north were left free to raise armies against his loyalist government-in-embryo. Each time a Continental army advanced toward South Carolina, people who had "recently given their most solemn assurances of submission and support to His Majesty's Government" betrayed their allegiance and put in question the possibility of stable royal government. Cornwallis faced the problem Howe had discovered in New Jersey in 1776: should he spread his troops out to pacify a large area or concentrate them to attack rebel armies that carried the seeds of rebellion?

In 1781 Cornwallis resolved to move north, risking a rebel

resurgence in South Carolina in order to hammer the staging grounds of the Continental Army. In the course of that year he took four thousand men on a long march into and across the interior of North Carolina, down to the coast for reinforcements, then far into Virginia. It was a virtuoso display of the professional skills that the British and German regiments had demonstrated throughout the war, for though Cornwallis was crossing hostile and unfamiliar territory and constantly warding off militia raids on his army's flanks and rear, he managed to advance without interruption and to defeat a much larger Continental army in a major battle. But the victories did not quell opposition, and in the fall Cornwallis brought his army down to the Virginia coast at Yorktown on Chesapeake Bay, to await reinforcement or withdrawal by sea.

In his free-wheeling march through the enemy interior, Cornwallis had remained confident that the skill and discipline of his regular troops would overcome all obstacles, but he also counted on being able, when necessary, to turn to the sea and rely on the Royal Navy to resupply him or remove him from danger. This command of the sea-coast had been fundamental to British strength throughout the war. No other British general had ranged as far inland as Cornwallis. However, in the fall of 1781 sea power failed, briefly but critically. When Cornwallis reached Yorktown and looked out into Chesapeake Bay, he found not a friendly British fleet but a hostile French one. George Washington, seizing his opportunity to go on the offensive, massed sixteen thousand French and American troops against Cornwallis at Yorktown. The army that had marched through hundreds of miles of enemy territory undeterred found itself trapped. Cornwallis surrendered in mid-October 1781.

As Cornwallis marched into the trap at Yorktown, the loyal provinces of South Carolina and Georgia crumbled under renewed rebel attack. Militia colonel James Cassells of Georgetown saw his plantation wrecked when "a party of Americans under General Marion made an eruption into that district, burning and destroying his crop" and carrying away "thirty-eight slaves together with the horses, oxen, cattle and other articles." Michael Egan of Camden, who had become a captain of loyal militia, had to abandon his home and property when the royal authorities evacuated that area, and Moses Kirkland soon found himself obliged to withdraw from the violence around Ninety-Six and settle on a rice plantation he had acquired near Savannah in Georgia, one of the few coastal enclaves the British and loyalists retained in the south.

Cornwallis's surrender and the shrinking of the loyal south to a few coastal bases did not mark a conclusive American victory, however. Britain still maintained a thirty-thousand-man army in America, still controlled a circle of territory all around the Thirteen Colonies, and was about to recover naval supremacy from the French. If Britain chose to fight on, it could continue to deny the American Patriots the fruits of their revolution. After years of war and hardship, this sense of endless inconclusive struggle overcame one American, Silas Deane, a Congressional representative in France. Writing advice for the Congress just before Yorktown, Deane wrote, "Let them weigh fairly the probable chance for their succeeding to establish independent sovereignty, and if they find the probability against it, let them honestly confess it, and put an end to the calamities of our country by a peace on honourable terms." In his despair, Deane himself would actually switch to the British cause, and the suspicions he had voiced were shared by many more committed Patriots, for whom American victories, even after Yorktown, were still too rare, too costly, and too inconclusive.

But if the Americans were war-weary, the British were more so. Since 1778 Britain had been fighting a global war instead of a colonial rebellion. With its armies and fleets tied up in America, Britain risked losing control of the sea, thus endangering all its other colonies from the Caribbean to India. In 1775 it had seemed that to accept American independence would mean conceding the end of Britain's imperial greatness, but by 1781 Parliament began to fear that continuing the war in America might be even more directly dangerous to the preservation of the empire. Cornwallis's surrender provoked the conviction that the American war was unwinnable and a drain on more vital interests, and so the decision to give up America was made. In 1782 Parliament threw the war government out of office, resolved to cease fighting in America, and instructed its commanders to begin withdrawing British troops and officials from every part of the Thirteen Colonies, pending a treaty of peace between Britain and the independent United States of America.

2
1775   1781

The Loyalists' War

FOR A BRITISH GENERAL, OR EVEN FOR A SOLDIER IN A provincial regiment, the revolutionary struggle from Lexington to Yorktown was a war of a conventional kind, made up of offensives and withdrawals, of battles, marches, spy missions, and all the problems of arming and supplying troops in the field. For Captain Alexander MacDonald and even for politician / Indian agent / militia leader Moses Kirkland, the war mostly meant soldiering, and though the places of service were fast-changing and unpredictable, the objective remained the same: military victory leading to the surrender of the enemy.

Most of the loyal citizens of the Thirteen Colonies fought a different war, a local and domestic struggle that went on in every county and town of the embattled colonies. Many loyalists fought desperate campaigns far from the battlefield, seeking only to save their farms or to avoid a beating and a stay in jail, and the bitterness of persecution helped to shape unswerving loyalty in many colonial Americans who might otherwise have

tried to avoid choosing between their king and their neighbours. Two years before the war began, Bostonian Mather Byles
had defended his loyalty in the face of mass protests against
British rule with the ironical question, "Which is better – to be
ruled by one tyrant three thousand miles away, or by three
thousand tyrants not a mile away?" Facing the vengeful anger of
a population in arms, many loyalists became all the more
convinced that tyranny in the name of liberty was more
threatening to their lives and freedoms than the rather abstract
injustices said to flow from parliamentary taxation.

Thomas Barker, justice of the peace in a loyal community in
New York's Dutchess County, discovered the reliance on force
that underlay apparently democratic processes early in the war,
when independent committees and militias were forming in
many communities throughout the colonies. A neighbour
named Leonard Reid described the process in Barker's community. "In June 1775, the rebellious people appointed a town meeting to choose committeemen, to which Esquire Barker went on
purpose to oppose and if possible to frustrate their design. At
this meeting Esquire Humphreys, one of the rebellious party,
nominated such people as he thought proper for committee
members and requested the people to signify their approbation
by holding up their hands. I suppose there was about ten or
fourteen hands held up. To this Esquire Humphreys said, 'It's a
clear vote.'

"Esquire Barker objected and requested Humphreys to re-
new the signal and let such people as did not wish a committee
signify to the same token.

"To this Esquire Humphreys objected and said, 'The vote
was clear.'

"Esquire Barker spoke to the people, saying, 'All you that
wish no committee signify it by following me,' and stepped out.
The number of people that followed, I suppose, was near two

hundred. Some time after this, Esquire Barker was made a prisoner by the rebellious people."

Confined under surveillance in neighbouring New Hampshire, Barker was unable to reach loyal territory in New York City until 1778. Long before that, the committee whose formation he had sought to prevent had established firm control of Dutchess County, and many of Barker's hundreds of supporters had been forced into prison or exile. When the revolution became a war and the colonies declared themselves independent, each new state officially authorized exile, property seizure, and other penalties for anyone unwilling to give allegiance to the revolutionary authority, though – as Barker could have testified – the punitive laws tended to follow, rather than to direct, popular resentment of loyalists.

The strength of resentment against loyalists varied greatly. In areas where patriot appeal was strongest, loyalists were occasionally ignored as harmless. In a few areas, as in part of the Mohawk Valley, so many citizens were loyal or sympathetic to the loyalists that their enemies had to restrain their hostility until military force settled the issue. Anti-loyalist measures tended to be harshest where the contest was roughly even, or where the approach of military units, either British or Continental, provoked communities into action. Physician Azor Betts of New York, "a very zealous and active loyalist . . . being thought to have influence among the people, became immediately very obnoxious to the malcontents," but his enemies did not dare to attack him until November 1775, when, with "the fury reviving upon the expectation of General Lee's arrival at New York", the Patriots felt strong enough to seize Betts, who was jailed until the following summer.

Potential leaders and influential spokesmen for the loyal cause were always targets. "He gave such opposition to the measures of the usurping power in the province where he resided that he was obliged for the safety of his person to quit his home and property and seek protection" was New Jersey loyalist Robert Campbell's account of his own experiences, but harassment was directed almost as vigorously at the least powerful of loyalists, the wives and children of men who had already left home on account of their loyalty.

In the pre-revolutionary disturbances in colonial America, nearly all the troubles, from Stamp Act riots to Patriot marches to the Boston Tea Party, had been urban phenomena, and peace-loving men had adopted the habit of retreating to their country houses when conflict loomed. Some similar habit seems to have governed the conduct of many loyalist husbands and fathers who chose or were forced to leave home and join the British or loyalist forces. Men whose wives and children were living in small towns or on country farms seem to have felt they would remain safe there, and urban loyalists sometimes sent their families to country retreats. "To secure his family from the impending danger he removed them to Monmouth in New Jersey" was the explanation of New Yorker Benjamin Garrison. Once the war began, however, the situation was reversed. Most of the major colonial cities were occupied by British troops at some time during the war, and even when they were not, the cities provided opportunities for loyalists to gather together or to escape by boat. The rural interior was more often controlled by rebel committees and Patriot militia, and isolated loyalists there were easy to identify and punish: Benjamin Garrison was arrested when he went to visit his family in Monmouth. After he had joined the army and gone to Halifax, Alexander MacDonald learned from his wife, Suzanna, that "soon after my coming away from Staten Island, a parcel of fellows went to my house with more than savage rudeness, rummaged the house (as they pretended) for arms, swore they would have me dead or alive, and frightened her out of her senses." Scores of wives and children left in supposed safety were exposed to this sort of violence from their Patriot neighbours, while their husbands were safe and helpless in distant British garrisons.

Sometimes wives and families of loyalist soldiers or refugees were merely ejected from their homes and obliged to join their men in exile. When Poughkeepsie lawyer Bartholomew Crannell fled from his estates to New York City, his "wife and unmarried children were afterwards banished and sent off to him, without permission to take any other of her property than a Negro slave, their clothes and necessary bedding." After Alexander Grant joined the British forces and was killed storming a rebel fort north of New York City late in 1776, his wife, Sarah, "with her five children was stripped of everything, not even a change of linen being left them, and sent into New York." When New Jersey Quaker Samuel Moore, "disliking the measures carrying on by the Americans and being in personal danger," retreated to New York City, "a party acting under orders of the American government came and violently forced his wife and children out of his house, put them on a wagon, and sent them under a flag of truce to the British line at Amboy."

Other families were used as hostages. After Daniel Begal of the Albany district in northern New York fled first to Burgoyne's army and then to Montreal in 1777, he joined Jessup's Rangers, a corps which sometimes made raids into the Albany area. As a result, "his wife and three children were detained with a view of taking him, until the year 1778," when they were dismissed and sent away to Canada. More often the hostility directed against families of serving loyalists was direct and personal, as Lemuel Goddard noted when he lamented the ill-treatment of his wife and five small children – behaviour that he found "but too common at this period to the persevering loyalist and his adherents". Mary Hoyt of Norwalk in Connecticut, whose sailor husband had joined the Royal Navy as a coastal pilot in 1776, had a spectacular tale of her misfortunes. "Living in their dwelling house in Norwalk with her family, she was frequently on account of her husband's being in the King's service insulted and abused, both by the leading and common people in the rebellion, the soldiers when marching by firing balls into the house. On the night of the 17th February 1777 a number of armed men, supposed to be about fifty, came to the house, broke open the doors, instantly rushed in upon her and closely confined her, and immediately plundered and destroyed all the household furniture and clothing they could lay their hands on, leaving her and her family consisting of five children naked and destitute of clothing at that inclement season." One of the children died soon after, and the rest of the family were "harried through town" and finally sent off to New York City.

As the Patriots' congresses and local committees became more organized, attacks against loyalists became matters of official policy as much as of popular wrath. Throughout the Thirteen Colonies, local Committees of Safety undertook active searches for disaffection, frequently investigating rumours and denunciations and threatening arrest or exile to anyone who refused the oath of allegiance to the American cause.

John Cummings, a Catskill merchant visiting the Hudson River town of Kingston, discovered the power of these committees in March 1777, after he dropped into the house of Joannis Freer and joined a discussion between Freer and another neighbour, George Lawson. Talk soon came around to the military situation, for Kingston seemed likely to become a battlefield that year, whether the British struck north from New York City, or south from Canada, or both. A successful British occupation of the Hudson Valley would split the rebels of New England from their allies further south, and early in 1777 it seemed that that might spell the end of the rebellion and of the pretensions of the Continental Congress.

Such at least was Cummings's analysis. According to George

Lawson, who appeared before the Committee for Detecting Conspiracies that same afternoon, Cummings had offered his opinion "that the regular army would conquer the American army and that Congress money was nothing but stuff."

Cummings made no explicit statement of his allegiance at this time. He may have been a devoted loyalist, arguing "all Europe is joined against us" because that seemed the best way to win over suspicious neighbours. Nevertheless, the "us" he spoke of was the people of the Thirteen Colonies, and it may simply have been despair that led him to assert, "It is better for us to give over now than to hold out any longer." Or he may have been coldly rational that morning, just making a business-man's assessment of the future worth of "Congress Money", the revolutionary government's paper money in which everyone was obliged to deal. But Cummings was known to be ac-quainted with British army officers who had served at New York City, and he admitted having gone into the city on business not long before. Testimony like Lawson's confirmed the commit-tee's suspicions about Cummings, who soon realized what his prospects were. Long before the British army put Kingston to the torch in the fall of that year, John Cummings had fled to the safety of the British lines around New York City.

A suspected loyalist who did not flee could be summoned before the committee and asked "to show cause, if any, why he should be considered a friend to the American cause." Fre-quently such an interrogation became a cat-and-mouse game, in which a witness unwilling to commit himself by oath or ser-vice to the revolution struggled to avoid incriminating himself by a straightforward expression of his views. Asked to prove his friendship to the American cause, New Yorker Samuel Martin could only say he had never done anything against the country and should be sorry to be considered its enemy. Pressed to state his opinions in a series of detailed questions about Parliament's right to tax the colonies, Martin prevaricated, offering the excuse "that he is not a politician and has confined his studies to his profession." Another witness that day, Whitehead Hicks, had an honest but evasive answer to the same questions, heartily responding "that he would be very unwilling to be taxed," but refusing to reject all parliamentary authority. The committee resolved that both Martin and Hicks were not friends to the American cause. When John Willett, asked two days later which side he supported, replied "that he wished those might succeed who had justice on their side," the committee found him "not a friend" and forced him to post a £2,000 bond for his obedience to the revolutionary government.

For loyalists who incurred the suspicion or the wrath of their local committees, an invitation to join the Continental Army was sometimes both a test of loyalty and a punishment. William Free of Westchester, New York, invited to prove his allegiance to Congress by appearing "complete in arms to stop the progress of the British", promptly "made the best of his way into the British lines and joined the Westchester Refugees." Samuel Dickenson "ever opposed all Committees and Congress, for which reason he was in May 1776 drafted by the rebels to go into their service as a private soldier." More often, known loyalists were seized and detained, either in remote regions or in Congressional jails. When Alexander Fairchild was convicted and sentenced to two years in jail for high treason, "as it was termed by the usurped power of the rebels of the province of Connecticut for his attachment to the British government," he was sent to a jail that became infamous among loyalists. Simsbury Mines was "a cavern seventy feet underground" where prisoners were housed in the abandoned shafts of a former mine, and in the course of the war it held hundreds of loyalists, including William Franklin, deposed royal governor of New Jersey and the son of Benjamin Franklin. Other jails were almost as harsh: physician Azor Betts thought his seven months in Cooperstown jail were "cruel to the last degree and enough to kill a more robust constitution". Some loyalists saw several jails. When Vermont loyalist Paul Gardiner was captured at the battle of Bennington, he was jailed first in Bennington, then in Albany, then in irons aboard ship in the Hudson River, and finally at Hartford, Connecticut. When British troops approached White Plains late in 1776, Samuel Jarvis and his brothers were removed from prison there, "chained up each with a Negro on their right and marched to Fishkill," where another prison awaited them. William Bustis of Westchester, captured during a spying mission, "was stripped and flogged thirty-nine lashes, carried in irons to West Point Fort, and, tried for a spy, was condemned to be executed." With the death sentence commuted, Bustis was eventually paroled, only to be caught and jailed twice more on subsequent scouting expeditions.

Despite their harshness, Congressional jails were not very secure. Jails for long-term prisoners had been rare in the Thirteen Colonies, and the revolutionary committees lacked the manpower to keep their prisoners in permanent detention. Though one unfortunate prisoner named John Anderson "was detained four years and part of the time in jail at Newbury with his family, which ruined his health and apparently was the cause of his death and his wife's," many loyalists seem to have been able to escape within a few months of their imprisonment. Alexander Fairchild even escaped from Simsbury Mines. "After lying in that dreadful situation four months," Fairchild somehow escaped "with the greatest risk of his life, attended with hunger and fatigue" and fled to New York City. Samuel Jarvis and his brother escaped from Fishkill Prison after friends disguised them in women's clothing, and "after laying many nights in the woods and fields" they both reached safety in New York.

Exile and imprisonment were usually a cover for or prelude to property confiscation, whether the victim was a wealthy landowner like Thomas Barclay, whose goods and property filled a twenty-six-page inventory when they were sold at public auction in 1777, or a tenant farmer on the frontier like Luke Bowen, who "rented 125 acres of land for which I got a deed right and title forever for £6 a year New York currency." Barclay had fled to New York and been commissioned a major in the Loyal American Regiment, while Bowen was one of Alexander MacDonald's early Mohawk Valley recruits and eventually a refugee soldier in Montreal.

When an area was firmly under rebel control, this kind of property confiscation could be done by the more formal process of revolutionary law. "John Bates now or formerly of White Plains in the County Westchester, yeoman, did with force and arms, etc., adhere to the enemies of this state against the peace of the People of the said State of New York and their Dignity, wherefore his land is forfeit" read one expropriation notice of 1782.

When territorial control remained in dispute, destruction of property was as common as seizure. Each side waged economic war against the other, partly to supply their own troops, partly to punish their enemies. Over the course of the war, the revolutionary control over the countryside, maintained by the network of committees and militias, generally proved more flexible and resilient than the British and loyalist command systems, and so the rebels were generally able to bid higher in the contest of terror. Even in far-off West Florida on the banks of the Mississippi, loyalist James Bruce lost his plantation to a rebel raiding party that "burned his and all the loyal plantations after coming down the Ohio and Mississippi rivers."

One man who observed almost the whole range of sanctions the revolutionary government applied against loyalists and neutrals was James Allen, the Philadelphia lawyer, who had begun as "ever so warm a friend to constitutional liberty and the old cause". Disenchanted with the revolution before it had even begun, Allen had retreated from Philadelphia to his estates in rural Northampton shortly before the Declaration of Independence. During the fall of 1776 he remained "a calm spectator of the civil war but occasionally gave violent offense to the violent whigs in Northhampton." In December, when the Pennsylvania Congress included the Allens in a list of citizens considered inimical to the liberties of America, his brothers, who had once held commissions in the Continental Army but who opposed independence absolutely, all fled to the protection of General Howe's army in New York, decisively cutting all their ties with revolutionary Pennsylvania.

James Allen soon regretted not following them. Still convinced that "a vast majority of the people wish a reconciliation" and unwilling to make such a total break with the colonial cause in which he had been raised, Allen tried to remain quietly in Northampton, but he was not to be left in the peace he sought. Soon after his brothers' flight, a troop of soldiers surrounded Allen's house, arrested him, and took him to the Committee of Safety in Philadelphia. By pledging "not to say or do anything injurious to the present cause in America", and probably also by drawing on old friendships and the surviving respect for the Allen name, Allen won his release and permission to return to Northampton. But as he observed Pennsylvania "divided into two classes of men, those that plunder and those that are plundered", and learned of old friends being sent off to jail in Virginia lest they join General Howe, he concluded that the revolutionary proceedings "bear the mark of the most wanton tyranny ever exercised in any country." Expecting further harassment despite his pledge, "as I am extremely obnoxious," he began to think his brothers "happily out of the way".

Allen remained in his country home through 1777, hostile to and threatened by the revolutionary government, yet never quite able to hope wholeheartedly for a British conquest of his home. Frequently abused and threatened by the local militias, he also discovered that for all his wealth he was no longer protected from the economic upheaval the revolution and the war had brought. "My tenants whose rents are due in sterling often pay off arrears of six or seven years in continental money at the old exchange," he wrote in October 1777, when the paper money's value had fallen to a sixth of its official worth, "yet I dare not object, though I am as much robbed of my property as if it were taken out of my drawer." The cost of purchases had risen greatly – "in some, as butter, meat, cheese, etc., ninefold" – and for Allen's once-sheltered family, as for the poorest rural citizens, loyalist or patriot, "misery begins to wear here her ghastliest face. It is impossible to endure it. Ruin can't be far distant."

Early in 1778 James Allen decided to give up the struggle to remain safe and quiet in the Pennsylvania countryside. "I will endeavour to get to Europe, where I will live for a while with great economy," he wrote, estimating that his income for the year would not cover the taxes levied on him. During a lull in the fighting around Philadelphia, he and his brothers managed to meet briefly at the boundary of the British and Continental lines. In February he and his wife celebrated the birth of a son, James junior, and planned how they could escape to Europe.

James Allen never did get out of Pennsylvania. His last diary entries mentioned his ill health and constant chest illnesses, and in the summer of 1778, thoroughly alienated from America and laying plans to leave as soon as possible despite the certain confiscation of all his lands, he grew sick, took to his bed, and died.

James Allen's divided loyalties and his deep attachment to his Pennsylvania home and the security of the wealth it provided made him unusually – and at last fatally – slow in deciding to abandon everything in a flight from revolutionary tyranny. More often, the success of the revolutionary committees and militias in detecting and oppressing loyalists meant that Americans who resisted the revolution found themselves obliged at an early point in the struggle to abandon their belongings, and often their families, to flee for safety. Brothers Isaac and David Bennett of New Rochelle in Westchester County "were both in the early part of the late horrid and unhappy war much persecuted by the leaders of it in the county where they resided, from whence they were driven and finally obliged to abandon and sacrifice a large estate both real and personal and seek by flight protection among His Majesty's troops." Thomas Haycock of Orange County "for his loyalty was obliged to flee to New York for protection," and well-to-do lawyer Bartholomew Crannell of Dutchess County "in consequence of his loyalty was obliged precipitately to abandon his home and family in December 1776 . . . and take refuge within the King's lines."

For fleeing loyalists like these, the most frequent consequence of a successful escape was enlistment in a royal regiment. Ever since Alexander MacDonald had left Staten Island late in 1774 to enlist the veterans of the Mohawk Valley, ambitious and influential loyalists had been organizing military regiments to fight the revolutionary threat. Military service provided thousands of loyal Americans with the chance to fight for their beliefs, and there were many veteran soldiers, many victims keen for revenge, and many uncomplicated loyal servants of the Crown who never considered any alternative to military service. For men driven from their homes, with their property seized, their incomes cut off, and their businesses ruined, military service was also the likeliest available means to earn a living. Loyalist refugees like Joannis Ackermann of New Jersey, "who, having brought nothing with him save the daily wearing apparel of himself and family, had to begin the world anew to provide for his family," were usually ready to listen to the recruiters seeking men in New York City, Montreal, or wherever the royal armies penetrated.

Ordinary farmers and workingmen who "rallied to the Royal Standard" simply joined the regiment whose commanders were known to them, or, failing that, any regiment needing men. For potential officers, however, the enlisting process was more complicated, for social concerns were intimately involved in the creation of regiments. Military command always carried social status with it. At a time when their estates were being destroyed or seized, when their professional practices were collapsing and their private incomes were being cut off, prominent and influential loyalists naturally saw military rank in a new regiment as a useful way to preserve and even improve their social standing. The ability to recruit large numbers of men was often rewarded by high military rank, and recruiting ability was often a sign of social prominence. Sir John Johnson, the Mohawk Valley's largest landowner after the death of his father, Sir William, in 1774, found it relatively easy to enlist a thousand of his tenants and neighbours, and he quickly became a lieutenant-colonel commanding his own regiment, the King's Royal Regiment of New York, also called the Royal Yorkers. The prosperous New Jersey doctor Abraham Van Buskirk had much the same success with his regiment of New Jersey Volunteers, and James DeLancey of the influential DeLancey family of New York soon built a full regiment of Westchester Refugees from tenants and neighbours in Westchester County. DeLancey's uncle, Oliver DeLancey, was an even more successful recruiter, and his New York Volunteers, raised mainly in the loyal communities of Long Island, became the largest of all the New York loyalist corps.

Loyalists whose social standing was less certain, or whose neighbours did not share their belief in the royal cause, faced greater difficulties and risks to their dignity. Timothy Hierlihy, an Irishman settled in Middletown, Connecticut, had won both military rank and social standing in the Seven Years War, gaining his first militia commission after marrying the colonel's daughter and then rising to major by long and dangerous service on battlefields as diverse as Ticonderoga and Havana. In 1776, when he fled to New York, Hierlihy felt his military rank and experience entitled him to command a new corps called the Prince of Wales American Regiment, but a rival who brought in more recruits displaced him and Hierlihy angrily resigned, to spend much of the rest of the war struggling to bring enough recruits into Hierlihy's Independent Companies to justify the rank and pay he claimed. John Eagles of Westchester County, New York, who brought fifty-two men with him when he fled to New York, was offered a lieutenant's commission in the New York Volunteers, but Eagles thought he could do better. "Knowing his extensive acquaintance with the loyalists in the said county of Westchester, he was determined to raise a full company and command them himself." So Eagles became a captain in the Queen's Rangers – until it was discovered that officers from Britain had been promised places in that regiment. Eagles was displaced, along with twenty-six other loyalist officers. In this kind of competition for rank and status, officers frequently quarrelled vigorously over their seniority or the status of their corps: Alexander MacDonald, already bitter at being a captain instead of a major, was furious when his commanding officer inquired about rumours that he was offering commissions to mere tradesmen, though Colonel Maclean himself had made a tavern-keeper's son one of his ensigns.

Few loyalist officers left a better description of the labours involved in building a regiment than Captain MacDonald, who spent most of the war administering and training a battalion of the Royal Highland Emigrants in Nova Scotia. From Halifax, and later from Windsor, Nova Scotia, MacDonald wrote of his struggle to recruit soldiers and to give them some training. ("Send some drummers and fifers as I have got a parcel of fine pretty boys to be taught.") He borrowed and begged to secure uniforms and equipment. ("Once more I beg for the clothing to be sent down, for this very day some of the men came to me with their toes through their shoes frostbit, and there is not a shoe nor a bit of shoe leather to be had in Halifax for either love or money.") He tried to respond adequately to the army's frequent demands that he detach companies of his men for garrison duty all over the Maritimes. ("I went up to Windsor . . . to review the barracks and found them unfit to shelter a dog a gentleman had a regard for.") In these tasks Mac-Donald, like many other loyalist recruiters, got more hindrance than help from local authorities, who had their own warrants to raise troops. MacDonald's rival was Nova Scotia's Governor Francis Legge, who disliked MacDonald's competition and hindered the Highlander's recruiting efforts. Though he was sure he could raise men more successfully than the unpopular governor ("If the Governor will raise 300 men in three years, I will give my head for a football"), the weight of these administrative problems made MacDonald's letters harried and complaining, but as the war dragged on far beyond his original optimistic prediction, his regiment gradually acquired the standard of training that permitted loyalist regiments, raised wherever their officers had a chance to recruit, to serve with distinction in virtually every campaign of the war.

Units of the New York Volunteers actually participated in the invasion of their home territory in July 1776, and other New York corps such as the Westchester Refugees went into action around the city within weeks of their founding. By the following summer some provincial regiments were playing an important part in the British war effort, for even as the Continental Army struggled to acquire the organization and discipline that might permit it to face the British army on the battlefield, the royal forces needed to learn the irregular tactics and skirmishing skills demanded by the North American terrain. Loyalist guides and scouts became part of every British force, and units like the Queen's Rangers, where experienced British officers led a colonial rank-and-file, were vital in bridging the gap between professional training and local knowledge.

All the experiences of the loyalists' war – persecution, flight, loss, and service in loyal military regiments – reinforced and made permanent the sense of exile that the pre-revolutionary agitations had been breeding in thousands of American loyalists. As the war continued and loyalist refugees found new commitments to replace old ties to home towns and colonies, thousands of loyalists, though they certainly had not become British, had ceased to see themselves as Americans. They now rooted their identity instead in their wartime regimental affiliation, their service to the loyal cause, or simply their place as part of the vast and dispersed community that the war had created, the community of loyalists.

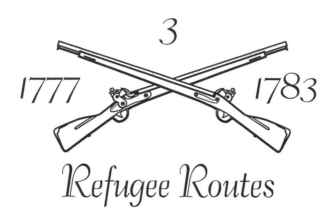

Refugee Routes

AMID THE CHAOS, LOSS, AND DANGER THAT THE REVO-lution brought to most loyalists, New York City had been a place of safety for Captain Peter Berton. Berton, like many of his fellow sea captains and merchants of New York, had been convinced by his pre-war career "in the London trade to and from New York" that the colonies' ties to Britain were vital to American prosperity and progress, and he had opposed the rev-olution from the start. Though he and his wife and eight chil-dren had retreated to a farm on Long Island early in 1776, when Patriot-loyalist disputes and the threat of a military attack drove nearly four-fifths of the city's population to seek shelter in the countryside, Berton returned to the city behind General Howe's British army later in the year. He spent the whole of the war there, close to the centre of British and loyalist strength in America.

Peter Berton's personal circumstances seemed not greatly changed by the war. Instead of taking up arms in one of New York's many loyal regiments, Berton stuck to his business.

Indeed, he was probably busier than ever in his trade, for New York had quickly become the supply centre that sustained all the British efforts in America, and a merchant experienced in the London-New York trade would have been more useful maintaining the flow of goods than carrying a militiaman's musket. Busy with his commerce and his large family, Captain Berton – he had earned the title as a sailor, not by a military commission – passed the war holding no office but the secretaryship of the New York Marine Society. By the end of the war he owned a store and a twenty-two-acre farm on Long Island and another store in the city, and he was also co-owner of a whaling company and several merchant ships.

New York City was spared from fighting after 1776, and the war made Peter Berton's city the capital of loyal America. As a major port with a fine harbour, it was the essential supply depot behind the British armies in the field, and it also became the naval base from which the Royal Navy could quickly reach any part of the American coast and to which its ships could retreat for shelter or repairs. As the headquarters of each of the British commanders-in-chief, New York had become the largest garrison town in the colonies. More than fifteen thousand soldiers and sailors were stationed there during most of the war, and the presence of the military headquarters made New York the centre of strategic planning, political decision, and administrative organization.

As the most secure loyal city in the Thirteen Colonies, New York drew thousands of loyalists, not just those who came on foot or by small boat from adjacent counties, but refugees from every colony, who arrived by every route. Southerners like Thomas Farrar of Norfolk, Virginia, fled north in their ships, though Farrar's brig *Peggy* was captured *en route* by an American privateer and he reached New York only after being rescued by the Royal Navy. Scores of New Englanders who had served in the defence of Boston arrived at New York by following the

army, as did Marylanders and Pennsylvanians like Christopher
Sower, the German-language printer who aided the British in a
battle near his home in Germantown and retreated with them
to New York in 1778. From the northern colonies men like
Robert Fowles, the former King's Printer of New Hampshire,
usually fled into Canada, but Fowles was one of many who went
on to New York City, where he helped organize "a corps of gentlemen called Governor Wentworth's Volunteers". Joining the
army or rebuilding civil careers in New York, thousands of loyalist refugees like these helped rebuild the commerce and society of the city. For a native New Yorker like Peter Berton, New
York was a safer and more prosperous community during the
war years than it had been in the stressful years preceding the
revolution.

Some of the refugees who reached the safety of the British
lines around New York preferred to settle on rural Long Island
and Staten Island, just across New York harbour from the city.
William Frost and William Bates were two of the many Connecticut loyalists who brought their families across Long Island
Sound to swell the population of Lloyd's Neck, "whose inhabitants," according to Bates, "were wealthy farmers, churchmen
and Quakers – all loyalists." The farms developed by refugees
like these helped to provision New York throughout the conflict, but the rural areas were not entirely quiet and peaceful.
Joseph Thorne, one of many New Jersey loyalists who settled
during the war on Staten Island, had to raise the alarm when
rebels attacked. Bates and Frost regularly participated in guerrilla raids into Connecticut, and their fellow refugee Filer Dibblee, a Stamford lawyer, was plundered twice during enemy
retaliations against Long Island.

As loyalists crowded into the city and surrounding countryside, the New York area began to resemble a self-sufficient city-
state around the mouth of the Hudson. The population grew
steadily, and the city soon became larger than it had ever been

before. Midway through the war, civil government was restored for the loyal territory around New York, and leading loyalists found administrative and judicial employment. In 1778 influential loyalists from several colonies established the Board of Associated Loyalists to co-ordinate loyalist military efforts in the New York area, thereby creating another lever of political and military influence in the city. Half of all the regiments raised by the loyalists had their start in New York, and most of the rest did part of their service there.

Wartime growth made New York's commerce busier than ever – in 1777 a visitor counted "six hundred square-rigged vessels, exclusive of the small craft and the four sail of the line," in New York harbour. Peter Berton and the other merchants of the town now worked not only to maintain the trade with Britain, but also to supply the swollen military establishment and to sustain the vital sea routes to British and loyalist outposts all along the American coast. Berton's own business routines were probably not much altered by the war, and he did not report the loss of a single vessel to enemy privateers, perhaps because large merchant ships sailing to Britain travelled in convoy. Other loyalists who turned to the supply trades were not always so fortunate. Thomas Gilbert, the young officer of loyalist militia from Massachusetts who had escaped captivity to join the British at Boston, spent three years as captain of a transport vessel based in New York – until his career was ended by his capture by a rebel privateer on the Connecticut coast. Despite the risk of privateers, James Van Emburgh of New Jersey preferred the coastal trade out of New York City to his previous service. Early in the war he had served as a spy behind enemy lines in his home territory, but, "finding that lying out of nights proved harmful to his constitution, he entered into the Quarter-Master General's Department and took charge of a sloop, half of which was his own property." Thomas Hazard of Rhode Island went into a supply trade of the simplest kind. He "obtained a small vessel and began plundering sheep, livestock, and supplies for the support of the garrison," and once brought in a hundred sheep and sixty head of cattle to feed the royal army.

As war activity and the population of New York grew, many of the amenities of life were preserved, at least for prosperous merchants and refugees well connected to the military establishment. The theatres flourished, and public holidays, particularly the king's birthday on June 4, were celebrated with salutes, fireworks, and the commander-in-chief's military ball. The influx of prominent loyalists and aristocratic military officers enlarged the city's social elite. "Money is here in plenty," said an observer, "and there is a set of people who, from the nature of their professions and their uncertainty of life, spend it as fast as they can." Charlotte Sergent, a Philadelphia doctor's widow obliged to leave her home town "for having received and entertained the loyal in her house", discovered that, despite the war, New York society could provide a social life of its own, and during the war years in New York her daughter met and married a German officer of the Anspach regiment, who eventually took her back to Germany. Taverns and coffee-houses prospered, hosting meetings of every kind, and they became centres of debate as loyalist opinion-makers strove to redefine their positions amid the shifting fortunes of war.

A regular flow of political pamphlets also contributed to this debate, and several loyalist newspapers were distributed. Though physician Samuel Stearns complained that his forced move from New England to New York "totally impeded the circulation" of the *Almanac of Astronomical Calculations* he had published annually, newspapers that could inform New York about the progress of the war and the state of America found an avid readership.

Of these the most notable was John Rivington's *Royal Gazette*, which enlivened its news and commercial notices with rumours and allegations designed to appeal to the hopes of its readers. Rivington had seen the presses of his newspaper smashed by a radical mob in 1775, and he had been forced to seek safety in England, but in 1777 he returned to New York determined to use the power of the press to match if not outdo the excesses of Patriot rhetoric. Rivington regularly published news of the death or capture of George Washington, and when these reports proved false, he announced that a New Jersey tavern-keeper's daughter had borne Washington a son. The *Royal Gazette* frequently reported mass desertions, regimental mutinies, and smallpox epidemics in the Continental Army. When France entered the war in support of the revolutionaries, Rivington announced that the Continental Congress had bound itself to cede New England to its new ally and to welcome the scores of Jesuit missionaries France was about to send. Fortunately, news, advertising, and commercial information balanced Rivington's enthusiastic distortions, for even New Yorkers who wanted to believe the worst about the enemy learned to read their newspapers cautiously. "I believe there is as many lies in the papers here as among the rebels" commented one disillusioned refugee who had had a chance to make the comparison.

The newspaper critic was Nicholas Cresswell, who spent several months in New York City in 1777. Cresswell's disillusionment went beyond wartime journalism to the city itself and to all of America. The young English immigrant who had arrived in Virginia in 1774 with high hopes and ambitions now looked at America from a perspective radically different from the one that could be maintained by secure and well-established citizens, such as Peter Berton, who could still hope a British victory would preserve and even extend New York's prosperity as the centre of a loyal America.

Cresswell had reached New York after eighteen months as a virtual prisoner in Virginia. In 1775 a land-speculation venture had taken him over the Appalachian mountains to make a long canoe voyage on the Ohio and Kentucky rivers, but though he had been impressed by the vastness of the North American frontier – and also by its risks of starvation and warfare – he had eventually been obliged to return to Virginia without much to show for his explorations. In Virginia the political opinions he had expressed in private letters, which had long since been seized and read by the revolutionary committees, ruined any hopes he still retained about establishing himself in the colonies. He was spared jail when a Virginia friend guaranteed his promise not to take arms against the revolution, but he was by now a confirmed outsider in revolutionary America, and none of his attempts to establish a profitable career bore fruit. Frequently drunk, heavily indebted, and alternately fearful and contemptuous of the revolutionary scene, Cresswell worked for his keep as a bookkeeper, attempted to manufacture saltpetre, and later travelled to Philadelphia. His standing as a gentleman, even a tory one, continued to serve him well, for his Virginia guarantor gave him an introduction to Thomas Jefferson, and Jefferson secured his permission to travel freely. But an attempt to escape to the British lines in 1776 roused suspicion again, and Cresswell returned to Virginia under closer surveillance than ever. Finally, with another persecuted loyalist, he managed to steal a boat and sail out to a lucky encounter with a British naval squadron, which brought him safely to New York in May 1777.

Realizing that his efforts to establish his personal independence in America had failed, Cresswell was preparing to return shamefaced to Britain and his family, and this personal bitterness darkened his attitude to loyalist New York. Though he was introduced to General Howe and was impressed both by the number of vessels crowding New York harbour and by the liveliness of New York society, Cresswell dwelt more on the disasters the revolution had brought to America than on the surface of prosperity. "When I see this once flourishing, opulent and happy city," he wrote, "one third part of it now destroyed, it brings a sadness and melancholy upon my mind, to think that a set of people who, three years ago, were doing everything they could for the mutual assistance of each other, and both parties equally gainers, should now be cutting the throats of each other and destroying their property whenever they have an opportunity."

The ruined third of the city that Cresswell mentioned had been razed by a fire during the Continental Army's retreat from New York, and such surviving evidence of war's destruction moved Cresswell more than the city's wartime prosperity. He noted how all the ditches and fortified places built by the rebels in their ineffectual attempt to hold the city were now "full of stagnant water, damaged sauerkraut, and filth of every kind", and he decided New York could provide abundant subject matter "if any author has an inclination to write a treatise upon stinks and ill smells." A trip outside the city provided more evidence of destruction and decay. "The country seems as if it had been prosperous, but this cursed rebellion has totally ruined this part of it. Almost every house seems to be deserted and the major part of them in ashes."

Forced by his poverty to take lodgings "at a little dirty pot-house", and distressed by the high cost of living, Cresswell expressed his strongest sympathy for victims of the fighting who had no part in the wartime prosperity. "Drank tea with some very agreeable young ladies," he wrote. "These people before these unhappy disputes lived in ease and affluence, but are now obliged to wash and sew for bread." He disliked the greed and immorality of the city, even as he yielded to it. His disgust was only heightened after he attended a dinner party and found himself seduced by the wife of an army major.

While many loyalists were anticipating that Howe's 1777

advance on Philadelphia would cause the collapse of Washington's army, Cresswell already foresaw difficulties. "General Washington is certainly a most surprising man," he wrote from New York, "one of Nature's geniuses, a Heaven-born general if there is any of that sort. That a negro-driver should, with a ragged banditti of undisciplined people, the scum and refuse of all nations on earth, so long keep a British general at bay, nay, even oblige him, with as fine an army of veteran soldiers as ever England had on the American continent, to retreat – it is astonishing. It is too much." Scoffing at yet another report of Washington being captured, Cresswell predicted that the American commander's great caution "will always prevent him from being made a prisoner to our inactive General."

In July 1777 such a statement was virtually a prediction of defeat for the British. Cresswell's ability to foresee the misfortunes of the British army grew out of his personal experience of the strength of the revolutionary cause, and his scepticism made him an early prophet of the end of loyal America. The sense that in leaving New York he was escaping a disaster – "my misfortunes have been unavoidable, and the common lot of thousands besides myself" – was his only consolation later that month when he boarded ship to sail back to Britain and the paternal authority he had been hoping to escape. By the time Yorktown signalled the collapse of loyal America, Cresswell had made a conventional marriage among the English gentry and had abandoned his dreams of the New World and independence.

In 1777 loyalists bound to America by years or generations of residence inevitably had more reason to continue hoping for the defeat of the revolution than did Cresswell the disillusioned newcomer, but in the following years the pessimism about the future of loyal America that had overcome Cresswell began to infect more members of the loyal population of New York. Many refugees there were gradually embittered by the reverses of the war, by their personal sufferings, and by the disappearance of the loyal America they had hoped to save. From the brutal treatment meted out to them in the name of liberty, many loyalists had learned to hate and despise not only the revolution but also their countrymen who supported or tolerated it. They looked for vengeance rather than reconciliation, and as a succession of British generals proved Cresswell's pessimistic predictions correct, they began to doubt Britain's commitment to the war.

These men – among them William Franklin, the formerly conciliatory royal governor embittered by his own maltreatment and the death of his wife – became estranged both from America and from Britain. Their disillusionment grew as complete as Cresswell's, but where Cresswell could abandon America, men like Franklin stayed in New York, complaining of Britain's failures of strategy and lack of resolve and proposing a ceaseless war against revolutionary America no matter what the cost. Under Franklin's leadership the Board of Associated Loyalists advocated and carried out a policy of harassment and guerrilla raids against rebel territory all around New York.

Some of the loyalists of New York opposed this resort to a war of vengeance. The case against it was put most clearly by William Smith, the New York politician whose commitment to peace and the possibility of reconciliation kept him wavering between the two sides until as late as 1778. Smith's perspective had always been that of the New York mercantile community of which Peter Berton was a part, practical trading men who retained a faith that America and Britain needed each other and could yet resolve their differences. The program he proposed expressed all the optimism the loyalists of New York City could continue to muster despite the setbacks of the war. Smith recognized despair in the plan of the embittered refugees for a war of vengeance, because the exchange of atrocities that guerrilla war encouraged could only stiffen resistance and poison relations between Americans. Smith argued instead for a more restrained military campaign, intended to encourage negotiations rather than continued war.

After Yorktown, when Britain resolved to cease hostilities and negotiate a treaty of peace with the Americans, a new commander-in-chief arrived in New York with policies and objectives surprisingly like William Smith's. Guy Carleton, the defender of Canada at the beginning of the war, did not see the cessation of hostilities as the end of the British presence in America. Like Smith he believed that there remained shared interests between loyal and rebellious Americans, and in 1782 he reassured the edgy loyal population of New York City that he would not be "a mere inspector of embarcations". Carleton and Smith, who became a key advisor to the new commander, still held out hope of a future in America. William Franklin and Nicholas Cresswell would have mocked the belief that any tolerance could be won from the revolutionaries by mere persuasion, but Peter Berton, protected from the fury of war, still prosperous, and still hoping to preserve a place in America, was probably eager to grasp that possibility.

No such hope remained for the other parts of the Thirteen Colonies where British and loyalist troops still held power. Within a few weeks of his arrival, Carleton made New York more than ever the heart of loyal America by ordering the prompt evacuation of all the British troops in the southern colonies.

Given the realities of Yorktown, Parliament's commitment to a ceasefire, and Carleton's need to make a strong stand at New York, the evacuation of the loyal enclaves of the south was strategically sound and politically inevitable, but the facts made the news no less of a shock to thousands of southerners who considered their colonies not only the most loyal in America but also the scene of the most successful British campaigns. The first city abandoned was Savannah, Georgia, and the shock there was great, for Georgia had been loyal territory since 1778, the only colony of the rebellious thirteen to return to the royal fold and be fully re-established under a royal government. Though the rebels had overrun much of the interior of Georgia since the fall of Yorktown, Savannah had seemed safe. Many loyalists there believed that a small detachment of troops would be able to preserve Georgia, but the orders from London and New York were unequivocal. Moses Kirkland, the loyalist from Ninety-Six district who had seen the war in every part of the colonies from the Mississippi to Boston and had finally settled on a plantation near Savannah as the safest and most promising site in which to establish himself, was among seventy-five hundred loyal troops and citizens obliged to pick up and abandon Savannah in July 1782.

The second loyal city to be abandoned was Charleston, South Carolina, where more than sixteen thousand loyalists and troops were gathered. Many of the civilians had retreated to the sea-coast town to rebuild lives and careers shattered in the see-saw fighting of the southern backcountry, and others had been attracted from other parts of the Thirteen Colonies. Thomas Farrar, a Virginia exile, had returned to the south from New York. He and another Virginian named John Hardey had been optimistic enough to return to Virginia when the British occupied Yorktown in 1781, thinking, as Hardey put it, "the war nearly concluded and that he might in security hold his estate." Farrar and Hardey held their estates there for only six weeks, but Farrar had gone on to Charleston and had spent nearly a year establishing himself when the news of its abandonment came.

Neither East nor West Florida had ever leaned toward rebellion, and neither had been successfully penetrated by the Continental Army during the war. St. Augustine, the fort that guarded the strategic waterway out of the Caribbean, seemed the most secure British possession south of Halifax, and the settlement around it grew from a few thousand to fifteen thousand in the space of a year, as the evacuees from Savannah and Charleston headed down the coast, sometimes in small open boats. But in 1783, the final negotiations of global peace transferred the Floridas from Britain to Spain, and virtually all these refugees were sent once more into exile.

The emigration of refugee loyalists from the southern colonies was made a much larger, and very much more complicated, affair by the presence among them of a large number of blacks. Black loyalists and blacks who were the property of white loyalists probably outnumbered all the white loyalists who were preparing to leave from Charleston, Savannah, and St. Augustine in 1782 and 1783, and the often contradictory interests of the black and the white refugees powerfully influenced the directions in which they travelled.

Even before the outbreak of war, slavery and the large black population in the Thirteen Colonies had complicated the political issues for both Patriots and loyalists. That many of the leaders of the Patriot cause, who so vigorously proclaimed liberty, the rights of man, and representative government, were themselves slave-owners and defenders of a society built upon slave-holding had not gone unnoticed in Britain, where slavery had been prohibited some years earlier. Defenders of the Crown pointed to the slave-owners' hypocrisy as further proof that all the Patriots' talk of liberty and resistance to tyranny was merely a cover for their malevolent conspiracy. Throughout the war, the British offered freedom, first to slaves who would bear arms, then to any slave who fled rebel owners and reached British-held territory. By the end of the war, escaped slaves were a vital minority in the loyalist forces.

Thomas Peters, the North Carolina slave who had fled his owner's plantation in 1776, had made his way to a British ship and been carried to New York City. There he enlisted in the Black Pioneers, a labour battalion of freed slaves, and served out the war in the New York City area. By 1779, when he had risen to the rank of sergeant, he married another escaped slave, named Sally, who had also joined the Black Pioneers.

Other black loyalists' wartime exploits had been more dangerous and eventful. Boston King of Charleston, South Carolina, was only fifteen when the revolution began, and he remained enslaved through the early years of the war. Soon after the British occupied Charleston in 1779, however, he fled his master and, as he later recalled, "began to feel the happiness of liberty".

He also felt the pains of smallpox, which swept through the crowded encampments of free blacks in war-ravaged Charleston. Once he had recovered, he worked as a servant and a dispatch carrier. Apparently, King never joined any of the black loyalist military corps, but his freedom was guaranteed by a new British promise. In 1779, General Clinton promised freedom, not only to the able-bodied men who joined the forces, but to all slaves who fled rebel masters. King did serve on a British naval vessel, and while aboard it he was captured by Patriot naval forces and returned once more to slavery. He managed to escape, but was almost enslaved a third time. This time it was by a loyalist who had lost his slaves to rebels. King managed to preserve his freedom and get safely away to New York City, where he married Violet, a slave who had escaped from North Carolina.

Thomas Peters and Sally, and Boston King and Violet were just four out of thousands of slaves who sought freedom by opposing the American Revolution – the first mass escape in the history of American slavery. A few blacks found freedom in the military service, but the British attracted the vast majority of refugees from slavery, including many of George Washington's slaves from Mount Vernon.

In the later years of the war, as loyalist and Patriot militias fought guerrilla campaigns back and forth across the southern plantations, as many as a hundred thousand blacks may have fled from their owners, and the aid given to escaping slaves became a major part of American complaints about the British army's behaviour in territories it invaded. Only a few of these hundred thousand runaway slaves maintained their freedom, and not all of them sought to join the British, but in each of the southern enclaves being evacuated by British troops and loyalists in 1782 and 1783, blacks were the largest group in the departing population.

Yet free blacks were outnumbered by slaves among the evacuees, for white loyalists in the south had never been abolitionists, and many of them had tenaciously held on to their slave property. Conservative, often propertied, and committed to the preservation of a status quo in which mass slavery and plantation agriculture had long been fundamental, southern white loyalists were either slave-holders themselves or at least members of a society that considered slave-holding as a natural and essential aspect of life. To keep the support of the loyal southerners, the same royal authorities who offered freedom to escaping slaves of Patriot plantation-owners had to guarantee that loyal plantation-owners would have their property, including their slave property, protected.

When white loyalists stood up for the preservation of British authority in the southern colonies and were dispossessed of their property by their Patriot rivals, the most valuable assets stripped from them were often their slaves. Thomas McKnight, an influential North Carolina plantation-owner who had been evicted from the provincial congress for his commitment to royal government, described how his rivals, after failing to assassinate him, seized his "lands, negroes and the usual stock of a Carolina plantation . . . and to hurt me still more, they took my house negroes and such as were born in my family and, carrying them some hundred miles into the back country, sold them there." Georgia loyalist William Knox lost "twenty slaves carried off" when rebels attacked his two-thousand-acre rice plantation, but he managed to preserve "102 Negroes, all of which he was fortunate enough to carry off with him" when he abandoned his lands.

A few slaves were often the only property left to refugee loyalists, men like customs collector James Kitching of Georgia, who "fled to sea in an open boat with one negro boy." Kitching and his companion underwent a series of escapes and misadventures and, when they reached loyal territory, Kitching was finally forced "to the disagreeable necessity of selling his negro to procure a little money". Holding on to a few of the slaves he had once kept busy on his plantation seemed no compensation to Thomas Fenwick. When he fled from South Carolina, he described himself as a loyalist "deprived of all he was worth, except a few negroes, and is now reduced to a state of poverty and distress."

For men such as these, slaves remained a potentially valuable asset, without whom plantations and plantation society could never be rebuilt. As a result, slaves owned by Patriots became a target for British and loyalist raiders in the later stages of the war in the south. Apart from being a vital part of the economic warfare waged against rebellious planters, the capture of slaves meant that compensation in kind could be given to loyalists who had lost their own slaves. As a result, a slave who had refused or been unable to flee from his Patriot master ran the risk of being seized by a British or loyalist patrol and awarded to a loyalist awaiting evacuation. By the end of the war there may have been ten thousand slaves in the loyalist enclaves of the south, and a smaller number of free blacks.

Because most of the southern loyalists had always lived in plantation societies, and because they still owned large numbers of slaves, the migration out of the American south was largely directed towards the Bahamas and the West Indies. Some of the troops and many of the free blacks headed north for New York City, but most of the fifteen thousand or more white loyalists and slaves eventually sailed for the West Indian islands, where slave-holding was standard practice and where plantation agriculture offered the exiled loyalists a chance to rebuild their prosperity by the labour of their thousands of slaves.

The largest group of southern loyalists went to Jamaica, which may have received ten thousand white loyalists and slaves. Jamaica had long been one of Britain's most productive sugar colonies, with a population of more than two hundred thousand before the Revolutionary War. Loyalists were only a part of the influx which spurred Jamaica toward continual population growth after the war, and so the American refugees and their slaves were quickly absorbed into the thriving sugar economy. William Knox of Georgia, who had managed to maintain possession of 102 of his slaves despite raids, sieges, and the confiscation of his estates, soon had them working on a Jamaican plantation.

Another southern loyalist who finally found a home in Jamaica was Moses Kirkland. Since fleeing from Ninety-Six district in 1775, Kirkland had been a courier, an Indian agent, a militia colonel, and a plantation manager, and in each place and career the hazards of war had made his efforts unsuccessful and his dispossession rapid. The move to Jamaica in 1782, with his old Ninety-Six colleague Thomas Edgehill and a small number of their slaves, seems to have marked a more lasting improvement in Kirkland's fortunes. Within a year both Kirkland and Edgehill had acquired plantation lands in Jamaica's Portland parish. Moses Kirkland was soon appointed as the local justice of the peace and could use his loyalist credentials and his new title to support his fellow refugees' claims for compensation and support. Within a few years, the Jamaica loyalists seem to have been absorbed into the larger population of the thriving island. A similar process of assimilation occurred to the smaller groups of American loyalists who migrated with their slaves to Dominica, St. Lucia, and the other sugar islands of the Caribbean.

The islands most influenced by loyalist immigration were the Bahamas, long a British colony but twice occupied during the Revolutionary War, once by an American privateering fleet and once by the Spanish. Britain had recovered the islands in the treaty that gave Florida to Spain, and to hurry matters along a small invasion force of loyalists led by South Carolinian Andrew Deveaux seized Nassau before the official exchange. With that incentive, groups of loyalists who had gathered at St. Augustine began making the short voyage across the strait to the Bahamas. Fewer loyalists went to the Bahamas than to Jamaica, but since the settled population there had been small, a few thousand loyalists doubled the white population of the islands and tripled its black population.

Granted land by the colonial authorities, the white loyalists began settling and developing many of the previously uninhabited Out Islands. The relatively large island called Abaco in particular became a loyalist community, as transplanted southerners and their slaves built up the many small sea-cotton plantations that became the mainstay of the Bahamian economy. Other loyalists preferred to settle in Nassau rather than in the Out Islands. The newcomers were close to a majority in the town, and they clashed with the established population, who feared that the loyalists were intent on having the whole colony turned over to them as compensation for their losses in America. For several years loyalists and old settlers fought for control of the colonial assembly and Bahamian society. Some loyalists gave up the struggle to find a niche in the islands. In 1786 New York loyalist John Shoemaker and his family left Abaco to seek their fortune in Quebec. William Moore, who had retreated from North Carolina to South Carolina to Florida and then to the Bahamas, found himself "unable after so many movements and losses to procure a living, and being not only reduced in circumstances but afflicted with sickness and the infirmities of old age", he moved from the Bahamas to London. The few thousand who remained gradually became an accepted, important, and influential part of Bahamian society, who retained the memory of their loyalist origins into the twentieth century.

The clearing of the loyal south made New York City more than ever the focus of loyalism, as regiments from the evacuated towns returned to New York, bringing with them many southerners, particularly black southerners, who preferred not to settle in the Bahamas and the Caribbean. But while loyal New York grew larger and stronger, Carleton's plan to make the city the site of a vigorous negotiation with the American Congress had long since collapsed. The British government that had committed itself to a cessation of hostilities was determined to have a peace treaty signed as soon as possible, and it intended to control the vital negotiations closely. Paris rather than New York became the site of peace talks, and Carleton had no opportunity to test his proposal for an amicable settlement that would protect the interests of the loyalists.

Carleton at first hoped that the Paris talks would fail and thereby reinforce his own claim to be given the opportunity to conduct direct negotiations with the American leaders. But the British government was determined on peace, even at great sacrifice. It would accept terms much less favourable than those Carleton proposed for the sake of reaching a settlement before the global war turned even more seriously against Britain. The Paris peace talks prospered, and as Carleton realized he had been bypassed, he attempted to resign his command in America.

Carleton's failure did not surprise those embittered and intransigent loyalists who always expected the rebels to demand total victory and who always feared that Britain's commitment might falter. Loyalists who followed this line of thought had never been prepared merely to await the outcome of decisions taken either at Carleton's headquarters or in London and Paris. By August 1782, when New York learned that Britain planned to recognize the independence of the United States unconditionally and in advance of a negotiated treaty, an independent spirit had grown among loyalists in the city. Feeling they had been failed by Britain's commanders and were now to be abandoned by its politicians – despite a promise that Britain would seek guarantees of protection for the loyalists and their property – groups of loyalists decided to have done with the Thirteen Colonies and head for new homes without awaiting the final consequences of the peace talks.

Where should they go if they left New York? The islands to the south remained open, and some New Yorkers did join the southerners' migration to Jamaica and the Bahamas, but the islands were chiefly attractive to those used to, and seeking the restoration of, plantation societies. Nor was Britain an adequate refuge.

Britain had been the safest and most comfortable refuge for loyalists throughout the war, not only for the well-placed and well-connected – Governor Thomas Hutchinson, James Allen's father, William Allen, and many of the attorneys-general, chief justices, and customs officers of the Thirteen Colonies – but also for a substantial number of lesser loyalists. During the war, Britain made room for as many as seven thousand Americans, including unrenowned and often impoverished loyal colonists like Bartholomew Stavers, the postman and shopkeeper driven from Portsmouth, New Hampshire, and Enoch Hawkesworth, a former merchant driven out of Alexandria, Virginia, for refusing militia service, who was reduced to working as a household servant in Bath, England, and who finally lost even that post through failing sight and the fact that he had become "very depressed and nervous".

Even men infinitely better placed than poor, half-blind Enoch Hawkesworth began to dislike their situation in Britain. Early in an exile they had expected to be brief, Samuel Curwen, Thomas Hutchinson, and other wealthy refugees had settled amid groups of loyalists in various parts of London. They patronized the New York or Philadelphia coffee-houses and founded clubs where they exchanged news and gossip. They lobbied parliamentarians and published long analyses of the war and the colonies. As symbols of American devotion to Britain's cause, they could even hope for presentation at court. Yet most grew disenchanted as the novelty of life in Britain wore off. Britain pursued its own policies, and the Americans often felt uninfluential and even patronized. In 1776 Samuel Curwen wrote angrily about a conversation with a British officer on leave from war service: "It piques my pride (I confess it) to hear us called *our colonies* and *our plantations*, as if our property and persons were absolutely theirs."

Many of these refugees grew poor in Britain. In 1778 Archibald McCall explained in a petition that he and his family had "left a fortune in Virginia in lands, negroes, houses, debts, etc., to the amount of £30,000 at least and, not doubting but the rebellion would have been quelled before now and they reinstated in their estates, did not mean to be troublesome to Your Lordships, but . . ." In short, the McCalls were ruined. Patriot control of Virginia had cut them off from their estates, and without that revenue they were reduced to soliciting charity, joining a line of loyal petitioners that grew longer every year.

Above all, loyalists in Britain felt superfluous. Guests for the duration of the war, they had no role to play unless they abandoned their American roots and became Britons. Many returned to the colonies when the war news was encouraging, as did apothecary Christopher Carter, who sailed for his home in Philadelphia in 1778 but "had the mortification to hear His Majesty's troops had evacuated that city" and had to land at New York instead. Their reports on loyalist life in Britain were unlikely to encourage migration in that direction, particularly when the loyalists most hostile to the revolutionary cause were now also embittered by Britain's weakening ardour for the cause. Britain might still attract the wealthiest and those most certain of influence, but few others.

Instead, the New Yorkers who would no longer depend on British intentions or revolutionary tolerance looked north and east, and the first sizeable migrations toward Nova Scotia began. Several hundred sailed for Annapolis Royal and Halifax in the fall of 1782.

Peter Berton and his family were not among the groups abandoning New York for Nova Scotia in the fall of 1782. A powerful army and fleet still defended New York City, and the demand for shipping to transport the southern loyalists made it impossible for more than a few hundred to sail out of New York that fall. In any case, the Bertons may not have wanted to go. As part of the New York mercantile community that had always sought a compromise between imperial and colonial interests, Berton may well have shared the moderate, optimistic loyalism aimed at reconciliation and backed by General Carleton. That fall of 1782, it was still possible to hope that astute negotiations and Patriot magnanimity might yet make it unnecessary for New York to be abandoned by its loyal population.

Yet the danger signs were obvious, and loyal New York could not neglect its preparations against disaster. The news from Europe was not yet conclusive, but every development so far suggested that Britain was acceding to virtually every Congressional demand. Fearing a collapse it still hoped to avert, New York made its plans. General Carleton rounded up every military transport and merchant vessel that the navy and the commercial fleets of Britain and loyal America could provide. He wrote to Nova Scotia and Britain urging that lands be prepared, that rations and supplies be stockpiled, and that funds be allocated in readiness against one of the largest mass migrations ever seen in the New World.

The loyalists made their own plans, giving a new role to the Loyalist Associations spawned by the war. During the war the Associations had been essentially military, a way to organize militia units and govern occupied territory, but now they were adapted in preparation for an exodus. Families and relations, rural or urban neighbours, church congregations, business associates, and militia companies began forming themselves into Associations, the better to arrange their departure and eventual resettlement, not as vulnerable individuals but as groups of mutually supportive neighbours and partners.

Each Association was headed by an elected captain, a senior man capable of organizing and directing a party of refugees and of negotiating for the services and assistance they would need. As the Associations took shape all over New York, Peter Berton, after tending his commerce as a private citizen through all the years of war, was at last drafted to leadership and was elected captain of one company of about a hundred and fifty Associated Loyalists.

As winter wore on and the news grew ominous, the destination of all these nascent Associations of civilian loyalists became more clear. Agents for the New Yorkers had accompanied the first flock of immigrants to Nova Scotia in the fall of 1782, and during the winter they had been discussing the prospects of migration with Halifax officials, exploring the ground themselves, and sending back reports to New York.

Two great destinations were emerging. Port Roseway, near the southern tip of the Nova Scotian peninsula, seemed only to need a population to rival Halifax or even Boston as a fishing port, trading town, or naval base. Pre-revolutionary efforts to develop a settlement at Port Roseway had spread notice of its attractions widely in the colonies, and it seemed the likeliest candidate for development in Nova Scotia.

Some loyalists looked to Halifax or Annapolis Royal, but in the winter of 1782 the other settlement candidate that surged to the fore was the long valley of the St. John River. Amos Botsford and two other agents of the New York loyalists sent back enthusiastic reports on the settlement potential of this region, and it quickly attracted many who preferred an agricultural frontier to a seaport like Port Roseway.

In the spring of 1783 the news came from Britain, and it confirmed the disaster against which the loyalists had been preparing.

The preliminary treaty of peace between Britain and the United States of America was signed on November 30, 1782. The final version, joined to peace treaties with France and Spain, would not be signed until September 1783, but the terms of the agreement were made known in New York City in March, and the formal cessation of hostilities took place on April 19, 1783, the eighth anniversary of the battles of Lexington and Concord. Britain had made a total and unconditional recognition of the independence and sovereignty of the United States of America. Nothing of the old Thirteen Colonies would be retained by Britain – indeed, enormous territorial concessions increased the boundaries of the new United States far beyond what the Continental Army had controlled or conquered during the war. Finally and surely it was confirmed that there would be nothing in the treaty for the loyal Americans.

The loyalists had been the subject of intense debate in the peace negotiations. American negotiators, convinced that anti-loyalist sentiment would permit no concessions to be made to them, wanted to omit all mention of them, but the British were unwilling to gloss over the damages inflicted on their unfortunate American supporters. Eventually an intricate compromise was worked out. The American delegates agreed that Congress would recommend to each of the thirteen states that they restore seized property, redress grievances, and permit loyalists to return home to live under the new jurisdiction. For British readers of the treaty terms, it was possible to imagine that a Congressional "recommendation" to the states would be binding in the same way that parliamentary "advice" bound the British king. But in America the clause was meaningless. Congress duly and without fanfare approved the recommendation but neglected to publish it, and none of the states paid the least attention. Most were busy passing new laws to supervise the eviction of loyalists and the transfer of their property to friends of the revolutionary government and veterans of the Continental Army.

Loyalists who attempted to make some private reconciliation with the victorious Patriots discovered that victory had actually increased the hostility toward Americans who had opposed the revolution. George Gillmore, once the Presbyterian minister of Voluntown, Connecticut, had been driven from his parish when he declared his loyalty at the start of the revolution, but he and his family of seven managed to pass the war years in another Patriot-dominated community, living "in low circumstances, preaching sometimes . . . and teaching school" for the few people willing to accept the teaching of a man "bearing the name of tory". The triumph of the revolution, however, made matters even worse, and in 1782 "poverty and popular odium" at last forced the Gillmores to flee north to Montreal.

With the peace treaty signed, a few loyalists in New York City did attempt to return home, if only to salvage a few possessions. Though he had spent most of the war plundering livestock, Thomas Hazard of Rhode Island "judged he had a right to go unmolested into any of the states to settle his affairs," but as soon as he reached his home he was arrested, jailed, ordered deported, and had his ship seized to cover the cost of getting rid of him. After the peace, merchant Richard Mackie "returned to Virginia in hopes of trading as a British subject, but was soon seized by their mobs, beaten and threatened to be tarred and feathered for his activity against them during the war, and ordered to leave the country within twelve hours or be hanged on the first convenient tree." At New York City, soldier John Siger of the Loyal American Regiment thought he could go to bid farewell to old friends, but he was seized just outside the city by four men who flogged him, shaved his head, threatened to decapitate him, and finally sent him back "to let his friends on Long Island know that every rascal of them that attempted to come back among them would meet with the like accident."

Events such as these finally resolved all differences of opinion in the crowded loyalist community of New York, Long Island, and Staten Island. It was now clear to those most hopeful of reconciliation, as to those most alienated from America, that there was no future in the revolutionary republic for anyone identified as a loyalist. In the spring of 1783, virtually the whole population of a city of fifty thousand people prepared to pack and go. As Governor Carleton announced that his troops would not surrender New York until all the civilians who wished to depart had settled their affairs and sailed, the dismantling of the city began. Soon Peter Berton, at last caught in the fury of revolution, was advertising for sale his farm "at the Queen's Head tavern near Newtown Landing" on Long Island. No asking price was mentioned and no sale was recorded, but within a few days of the notice of sale the Bertons were boarding ship and leaving New York.

Disposing of homes, businesses, and farms was the largest problem for property-owners in the city, but the advertising columns of John Rivington's *Royal Gazette* recorded a thousand other mundane details and minor crises. Peter Rogers of London was eager to find his mother, thought to be aboard a naval frigate in the harbour. John Michel and Daniel Wright each announced their imminent departure for the River St. John; creditors and customers were invited to settle their accounts. John Le Chevalier Roome was also about to sail; he wanted only the return of the books he had loaned. A charitable society requested "contributions for the help of needy persons leaving for Nova Scotia", and Lieutenant Thomas Coffield wanted it known "that his wife Martha is conveyed from him and concealed by her mother of Queen's County to prevent her leaving New York City with her husband to Nova Scotia." Shadrack Furman wanted his runaway servant, a free black named George Scribens, returned to him; he would pay a reward either in the city or at Port Roseway. Patrick Murphy simply wanted his friends to know he was sailing with the first fleet for Port Roseway.

The publisher of all these notices was one of the very few New Yorkers preparing to stay in the city. John Rivington, whose newspapers had been printing loyal editorials and propaganda against the revolution since the earliest disputes, had hedged his bets near the end of the war by sending secret intelligence reports to the Continental Army outside New York. This service, unsuspected by his readers and advertisers, would save him. Though his newspaper was closed, he was permitted to remain in New York, and he ran a bookshop there for the rest of his life.

As the departure dates arrived, the docks grew chaotic. Carleton had secured no fewer than 183 vessels for the evacuation of the city, and many of the ships would make several journeys that summer and fall. From the military stores, his staff provided enormous quantities of tents, tenting linen and cloth, axes, spades, and other supplies that would travel with the refugees. Most of the goods to be loaded and shipped, however, were the personal effects of the individual loyalists and their families, often in surprising forms. Alexander Dobbins, who had spent much of the war serving in the Commissary-General's Department in New York City, "in 1780 built a two-storey house there which he had taken down in order to take it with him if he could obtain room in any of the transports." Dobbins's optimism was soon disabused. There was "no possible means of getting it on board" he was curtly informed, and one more loyalist house had to be abandoned to the victorious Patriots.

In April 1783 the first of the Associations of civilian loyalists began to board ship. Walter Bates, a Connecticut loyalist who had spent much of the war on Long Island, had attended a parish meeting where he learned "that the King had granted to all Loyalists who did not incline to return to their homes and would go to Nova Scotia, two hundred acres of land to each family and two years provisions." During the meeting "it was resolved by all present and mutually agreed to remove with all their families into the wilderness of Nova Scotia and settle all together." Bates's party boarded the transport *Union* about April 11, 1783, and sailed from Staten Island on April 26 with the first fleet destined for the River St. John. About a month later another large fleet departed from New York with more companies of loyalists. In June, Peter Berton's 21st Company of Associated Loyalists, 31 men, 20 women, 51 children, and 30 servants, boarded a transport called *Littledale*, of 250 tons, commanded by Captain Kelsick. Each vessel left in a fleet of a dozen or more ships carrying up to two thousand loyalists, and the migration out of New York continued as quickly as the ships could return to the city to take on new loads of passengers.

Among the loyalists most eager to be gone from New York City were the several thousand blacks who had gathered there during the war. In the preliminary treaty of peace, Britain had promised to restore captured property to the victorious Americans, and George Washington insisted that "property" included slaves who had used the revolution to escape from their masters. Boston King, the escaped slave from Charleston, reported that the news caused "inexpressible anguish and terror" among the black loyalists, until General Carleton guaranteed their freedom. Boston and Violet King sailed for Port Roseway in July 1783. Thomas Peters and his wife went aboard a ship that sailed to Bermuda and then north to Annapolis Royal, Nova Scotia.

About 32,000 civilian loyalists left New York City for Nova Scotia that summer. Thirteen hundred sailed to Quebec, more than a thousand to the Bahamas, and perhaps a thousand to Britain. In September, soldiers of British and provincial regiments were dispatched to their new homes in the Maritimes, and finally in October, with his city clear of civilians, Carleton began sending away his British regiments, some to Halifax and some to Britain. In November the last companies of troops in the city boarded ship. Carleton withdrew to Staten Island while General Washington prepared a triumphal entry into an abandoned city, and on December 5, Carleton and the last British garrison of the Thirteen Colonies sailed from Staten Island for Britain.

One of the New York loyalists who travelled in Peter Berton's fleet of June 1783 left a detailed account of the great migration. Sarah Frost of Stamford, Connecticut, had followed her husband, William, to loyalist Long Island early in the war. Her husband's war record made it unlikely that he would be tolerated in revolutionary America, for his participation in raids against Connecticut was widely known. Though her own parents had remained in Stamford, Sarah Frost elected to go with him to Nova Scotia.

The Frosts and their two children – Sarah was pregnant with their third – boarded the transport *Two Sisters* on Long Island on May 25. They had "very fair accommodation in the cabin, though it contains six families besides our own," and found the captain "a very clever gentleman". On May 28 the ship moved down from Long Island Sound to New York City. The passengers had the opportunity to go ashore, and Sarah Frost's father managed to visit her, but she expected the ship would sail almost at once, "as soon as the wind shall favor".

To Sarah Frost's surprise, *Two Sisters* remained anchored at New York for nearly two weeks while its remaining passengers were gathered together, and gradually living conditions became more uncomfortable. "Our women with their children all came on board today," she wrote on June 9, "and there is great confusion in the cabin. We cope with it pretty well through the day but as it grows toward night, one child cries in one place and one in another while we are getting them in bed. I think some times I shall be crazy." The passengers began to become sick, and Mrs. Frost was glad when the ship moved down to Staten Island, where she was able to go ashore.

On June 15, in a hailstorm, *Two Sisters* moved to Sandy Hook at the outermost boundary of New York harbour, and the next day the ship made sail for Nova Scotia, moving slowly as the escorting naval frigate gathered the convoy of transports together. Aboard *Two Sisters* were 168 members of Sylvanus Whitney's Company of Loyalists and 136 of Joseph Goreham's, and the other ships of the convoy carried 1,300 other loyalists, including Peter Berton's company, his wife, and his children.

At first Sarah Frost found the voyage exhilarating. She was enthusiastic over the progress of the ships, the fair winds, and the fish the men caught, though she retreated to her berth each time the wind grew strong. In mid-month there was a discouraging week of calm and fog, but by June 23 the weather improved and she enjoyed a game of cribbage with her husband and the Whitneys. Finally, on the twenty-sixth, the crew and passengers saw Cape Sable and entered the Bay of Fundy, and

Captain Brown announced that Saint John was only one day's sail ahead. "Oh how I long to see that place, though a strange land," wrote Sarah Frost.

The fleet reached Saint John on June 28, a Saturday, and a pilot came out to guide *Two Sisters* into Saint John harbour. "Our people went on shore and brought on board spruce and gooseberries and grass and pea vines with the blossoms on them, all of which grow wild here," noted Sarah Frost, adding as if in disbelief, "They say this is to be our city. Our land is five and twenty miles up the river."

The next day, Sunday, she went ashore, and relief at the safe landing was rapidly replaced by disquiet. "It is, I think the roughest land I ever saw; but this is to be *the city*, they say!"

PART THREE

Settlement

1783   1783

Preparing the Way

NO ONE IN THE CANADIAN COLONIES HAD BEEN EX-
pecting to make room for fifty thousand refugee loyalists.

Despite the loyalists' sense that they were going into a hostile wilderness, the territories in which they would remake
their lives were neither barren nor empty. Colonial societies
and colonial governments already existed in the great sweep of
territory curving around the northern flanks of the new United
States. During the Revolutionary War, the colonies governed
from Halifax and Quebec had resisted American invasion,
smothered internal dissension, and supported the British military efforts. Now these Canadian colonies faced another challenge of equal dimension, for suddenly they were confronted
with refugees who, by their numbers alone, promised to transform the societies they were coming to join. Forced to respond
to this crisis, the governors of Nova Scotia and Quebec had
to plan and implement decisions and actions that went far
beyond the everyday scope of colonial administration. Both

the loyalists and the colonies to which they came would be permanently marked by the consequences.

Nova Scotia, destination of most of the refugees sailing from New York in 1783, had long seemed something of a backwater compared to the now-independent colonies further down the seaboard. Though its domain stretched from the Nova Scotian peninsula all the way to the borders of Quebec and Maine far to the west, Nova Scotia still had barely twenty thousand settlers, when many of the Thirteen Colonies had hundreds of thousands each. Yet in 1783 many believed Nova Scotia was not so much unpopulated as close to the maximum population it could support. Small communities of fishermen and traders sheltered in coves and inlets along the rugged Atlantic coast, and New Englanders had occupied the fertile Fundy-side lands cleared and diked by the Acadians before their deportation in 1755. Cape Breton Island had been almost without settlement since the exiling of its French population in 1758, and the St. John River valley was still a remote frontier where Micmacs and Malecites, barely outnumbered by white settlers, still defended their territorial rights, and where both whites and natives had flirted with the American Congress during the war. Even the capital, Halifax, had only a few thousand people, and it often seemed turned more toward its global strategic responsibilities than toward the needs of the colony.

Only one great surge of development fever had been seen in Nova Scotia since the foundation of Halifax in 1749, and its outcome had helped to create scepticism about the region's potential. In the early 1760s, peace, the removal of the French rivalry, and the prohibition of expansion from the Thirteen Colonies westward into Indian territory had created a brief land boom in Nova Scotia. In a few years millions of acres had been granted in vast, vaguely measured tracts. The land grants, however, went not to labouring settlers but to land promoters, who acquired their enormous grants in exchange for a promise to promote future settlement. Halifax merchants who joined the land rush blithely predicted that the colony would soon support a million people, and in a brief flurry of speculation all the good land of the colony – and much of the rest of it as well – was turned over to private owners. In 1765, three million acres were granted in seventeen days.

The most enterprising of the promoters who acquired Nova Scotian land was a Virginian Irishman named Alexander McNutt, who, on his own and in a web of partnerships, eventually acquired no less than 2,500,000 acres scattered across every part of Nova Scotia. McNutt worked longer and harder and invested more than almost all his competitors, travelling restlessly from Nova Scotia to Europe to New England, first to promote his campaign for the land grants, then to make them profitable by peopling them with immigrant settlers. Unfortunately, McNutt proved no more successful than his less energetic competitors. New Englanders moved north to take advantage of the fertile Acadian farmlands and to exploit the trading opportunities of the Atlantic coast, but once they had chosen the best spots, the supply of settlers dwindled. By the time the American Revolution began, most of McNutt's vast domains, and most of the other estates granted in the 1760s, had only a meagre scattering of settlers. Nova Scotia's extraordinary land rush – and its failure to attract settlers – had done little but leave observers convinced that prospects for settlement there were dim. It had only one lasting consequence: almost all the colony's useful land had passed from Crown ownership to private hands. No vast acreage of land existed for the desperate refugees coming to settle in 1783.

The consequences of land speculation had been particularly sweeping on the Island of St. John, later to be renamed Prince Edward Island. In 1767 the entire island had been divided into sixty-seven lots, averaging twenty thousand acres each, and granted to soldiers, politicians, and courtiers favoured by the

British government. Similar grants were being made on the Nova Scotia peninsula and along the St. John River valley, but the owners of the island lots protected their acquisitions by having the almost unpopulated island established as a separate colony, free from any chance of interference by the colonial government in Halifax.

The land policies of the 1760s gave the Island of St. John and many parts of Nova Scotia something like an English version of New France's seigneurial regime, under which all valuable land was owned by a propertied elite who would guide and control local settlement. As much as the English derided New France as feudal and backward, the seigneurs had accepted their obligation to bear some of the expense of developing the lands they had been given. By contrast, many of the British owners of the Maritimes land grants, though still willing to accept vast estates as due reward for their status, had no desire to take up the costly role of social benefactors on the colonial frontier. By failing to bring settlers to their estates, or even to pay the land taxes called quitrents, they were often in flagrant violation of the conditions under which they had acquired their grants, but they were well placed and very determined to defend their title against any challenge. As a result they posed an extraordinary dilemma for Nova Scotia in the 1780s. Though thirty-five thousand refugees were about to descend on a huge colony with barely half that many people, Nova Scotia had already given away most of the land where the loyalists might settle.

Solving the land problem would have vexed any eighteenth-century regime respectful of hierarchy and landed property, and the colonial government of Nova Scotia had never shown a great deal of creativity. Dominated by merchants and officers deeply involved in land speculation, the governing council of Nova Scotia seemed unlikely to begin seizing land grants merely because the owners had not fulfilled their promises. Nor was there a strong leader likely to take bold measures. Since 1776 the colony had been run by a series of naval commanders more concerned with fighting the war than with developing the colony.

In 1782, on the eve of the coming of the loyalists, Nova Scotia acquired a new governor. He was fifty-six-year-old John Parr, an ex-soldier of solid but undistinguished record with political links to the Earl of Shelburne. Shelburne had entered the British cabinet that year in the change of government provoked by the Yorktown disaster, and he soon became prime minister. In the midst of his campaign to end the war and seek reconciliation with the Americans, the Earl had also to reward the people who had helped bring him to power. The command of Nova Scotia was an appropriate reward for a minor supporter, and Parr accepted it gratefully, though he had never been in North America before. Governing the old Nova Scotia would have been an appropriate job for John Parr, but there was little to suggest that he might rise to the challenge that its new circumstances were about to provide.

Yet during Parr's tenure as governor, Nova Scotia was to solve its land problem and provide generous allotments to its thousands of refugee families. The colony would organize and distribute relief supplies and rations to the new communities over several years, and would see new institutions of government and administration established to cope with the demands of a population permanently transformed by the events of 1783. John Parr himself could hardly claim all the credit – and actually got very little – for he seems to have been a cautious administrator, who never displayed a compelling or authoritative personality. Nova Scotia's achievement seems to have been a triumph of the system rather than of the men in it. For years the distribution of land and royal supplies had been the chief preoccupations of the colonial government. The arrival of the loyalists raised both these matters with unusual urgency, but the colony seems to have achieved extraordinary results by rather routine procedures.

The first and crucial step taken to prepare Nova Scotia for the loyalists was *escheat*, the process of cancelling the land grants that had transferred millions of empty acres into private hands. It helped that Alexander McNutt, the greatest land-holder and the one who would have been best able to claim that his tireless efforts to promote settlement in Nova Scotia justified his acquisitions, had joined the American Revolution and gone back to Virginia; even before the migration of the loy-alists, McNutt's competitors had been manoeuvring to have his lands transferred to themselves. It also helped that the frenzied pace of the original grants had provoked the cautious colonial administrators to put strong warnings of the consequences of non-performance into the land deeds; some undeveloped tracts had been recovered by the Crown well before the loyalist migration was foreseen. Even the Acadian experience helped. Escheat of old French land grants had been the legal formality used to ensure that no Acadian who returned from deportation could claim his land from its new owners, and so there was a familiar precedent for the use of escheating procedures in Nova Scotia.

Despite all these incentives, actually to seize the land of powerful and distinguished men, no matter how lax their stew-ardship had been, was almost revolutionary in a world where property ownership by a small elite was recognized as a bulwark of society. Only the extent of the crisis – the absolute certainty that something had to be done quickly – overwhelmed the deeply ingrained resistance to taking property away from its owners. Urged into action by Carleton in New York and the government in London, the Halifax authorities unleashed the escheat procedures and, almost as quickly as the land had been doled out to private owners, it was now recovered. The Crown swiftly regained title to 2.5 million acres of Nova Scotia. Vast tracts in every part of the colony suddenly became available for individual grants to the American loyalists.

Only St. John's Island withstood the tide of escheat. The Nova Scotian government held no authority over that colony, and the London owners of the island's sixty-seven large tracts were too distant and too well placed to be much moved either by the refugees' need for land or by Nova Scotia's bold example of escheat for non-performance. The island remained private property, and though some proprietors offered their land on ambiguous terms, it was scarcely considered as a destination for loyalists in 1783.

The reacquisition of private lands by escheat freed Governor Parr's hands, and in the spring of 1783 his government prepared to house, feed, and settle the refugees imminently expected from New York. A series of decisions and exchanges of advice between New York, London, Halifax, and Quebec had established that every loyalist household head who arrived in the remaining British colonies would receive a free grant of a hundred acres of land, with fifty more acres for each member of his family and additional acres according to his seniority if he had held military rank. Land alone was not enough, however, and the British government committed itself to providing food rations for several years, and materials and tools to help the refugees shelter themselves and begin clearing their lands. In the fall of 1782, the Nova Scotia government promised to provide up to four hundred thousand board feet of lumber to the refugees, and thereby initiated the program of support of the new settlers.

During the spring of 1783 Parr began ordering food, lumber, and equipment in enormous quantities, stimulating a boom that helped reconcile old Nova Scotians to the prospect of a mass of Americans suddenly descending upon them. Timber-cutters all over the colony, who had been producing timber for export for years, now discovered a new local market and began arranging to supply thousands of feet of lumber under government contracts. Mills in all the farming communities were soon grinding all the wheat they could acquire. Halifax businesses furnished hardware and clothing and foodstuffs, and schooner crews prepared to haul all these products to the loyalists at their landing places.

Vital as the food and equipment were, all these efforts would be wasted if the loyalists were not quickly placed on land where they could begin providing their own support. The heavy burden of allocating land fell on Charles Morris, who had recently succeeded his father as surveyor-general of the colony. Morris was a competent surveyor, but the demand was no longer for roughly delineated ten-thousand-acre tracts, barely inspected even by their owners. Now that small grants were urgently needed for thousands of individual families who expected to clear and develop their land at once, Morris needed help, and one of the men he drafted into service was Benjamin Marston.

Marston was a loyalist himself, a New England merchant whose loyalty had obliged him to flee to Boston and then to Halifax, where his efforts to make a new career had been spectacularly unsuccessful: he had been captured three times by American privateers and once barely survived a midwinter shipwreck on the Nova Scotia coast. Marston was living in Halifax, widowed, unemployed, without even enough money to take passage elsewhere, when Charles Morris approached him in April 1783 and engaged him to go to Port Roseway to assist in laying out a new township for the loyalists. One of twenty-three deputy surveyors Morris hired that spring to see the loyalists settled, Marston left almost immediately and was at Port Roseway to see the first great fleet of loyalists arrive on May 4, 1783.

Port Roseway was one of Alexander McNutt's failed colonizations, a fine harbour near the southern tip of Nova Scotia that had been bypassed by earlier waves of settlement. Both loyalist agents and Nova Scotian officials had identified it in 1782 as a promising destination for the refugees, and during the winter the Port Roseway Associates had recruited thousands of settlers from the beleaguered loyal community around New York City. It was the vanguard of this mass migration that Benjamin Marston described in his diary for May 5, 1783: "Last night the fleet got in below, upward of thirty sail in all, in which there are three thousand souls."

To the people of this fleet, newly arrived from one of the largest cities in North America, Port Roseway naturally seemed a wilderness, but it was at least one with a plan and with authorities to implement it. Marston and William Morris, the surveyor-general's son, were there to lay out a town according to plans already approved by Governor Parr. A detachment of troops and military engineers had come with the fleet to help establish the town. Already on the site was commissary Edward Brinley, who began issuing the rations, tools, and building materials that had been assembled for the loyalists.

Port Roseway quickly took shape. After consultation with the captains of the loyalist companies, Marston confirmed the location of the townsite on May 9, and by May 24 the surveyors had enough streets, blocks, and lots marked out to begin distributing town plots to the refugees. "Many are pleased," wrote Marston. "The idea of owning land is somehow or other exceedingly agreeable to the human mind." By the end of June the town had been charted and its properties allocated, and on July 2, Marston distributed the first lands outside the town.

Governor Parr visited the new town in July and was greatly

impressed with what had been achieved. He appointed civic officials – Marston was one – and announced that Port Rose-way, which was already as large as Halifax, would be renamed Shelburne in honour of his patron, the Earl. Then Parr re-turned to Halifax, reporting confidently, "From every appear-ance I have not a doubt but that it will in a short time become the most flourishing town for trade of any in this part of the world, [as] the country will for agriculture."

Shelburne, however, had just begun to grow, for in New York the Port Roseway Association had done its recruiting work well. The three thousand loyalists for whom Marston had been surveying a comfortable town in May proved to be only an advance guard for the many more who followed. A regular traf-fic of ships brought more companies of civilian loyalists, includ-ing fifteen hundred black loyalists. Three thousand soldiers from the New York garrison arrived in the fall, and at the end of 1783 Parr estimated that Shelburne might have twelve thou-sand inhabitants.

The Shelburne loyalists sheltered in tents, makeshift huts, and ships' holds, while Benjamin Marston was kept surveying until "so full of triangles, squares, parallelograms, trapezias, and rhomboids that the corners do sometimes almost put my eyes out." It was Marston and the settlers who were left to face most of the problems of the new city, because Shelburne had not attracted all the loyalists and Governor Parr had many other preoccupations. Halifax, until 1782 a city of barely two thou-sand, had taken in several thousand refugees. Annapolis Royal had grown from two hundred to six hundred people with the first influx of loyalists late in 1782, and by 1783 the local Angli-can missionary found that "the increase is so great that I am unable to make a proper computation." Similar landings were occurring all over the Nova Scotia peninsula: at Digby, Yar-mouth, Windsor, Antigonish, Chedabucto, and many other places, substantial towns arose overnight as companies and families unloaded their possessions and made a start at settlement. Everywhere, Governor Parr's overworked surveyors, engineers, and clerks – including several newly appointed loyalists – struggled to organize muster-lists of all these arrivals, to grant roughly surveyed lands of the appropriate acreage, and to provide supplies and equipment to the newcomers, all the while striving to respond to the special pleadings of both the well-connected and the utterly destitute and to avoid any expense which the Colonial Office might later condemn as needless or over-generous.

While twenty thousand loyalists were landing in peninsular Nova Scotia to create Shelburne and transform many of the established communities, almost as many had headed instead for "continental" Nova Scotia. The decision to travel up the Bay of Fundy toward the St. John River had been taken in New York the previous winter, when the loyalist agents' enthusiastic reports reached the city. General Carleton supported loyalist settlement on the St. John as a bulwark against the nearby Americans, and planning for the new community was directed from New York much more than from Halifax, where the western parts of Nova Scotia were still considered a remote frontier.

Governor Parr tolerated the loyalists' plan to populate the St. John River and the Fundy shores, but he could not entirely share their enthusiasm over the most distant part of his colony. By the time of his visit to Shelburne in July 1783, Parr was learning to discount glowing reports about sparsely populated and barely explored frontiers – and the St. John River became the focus of his doubts. "I greatly fear the soil and fertility of that part of the province is overrated by people who have explored it partially," he wrote. "I wish it may turn out otherwise but have my fears." By that time, however, the first fleet of three thousand loyalists had been ashore at Saint John for two months, and the second fleet – Sarah Frost's – had been there for nearly a month. Several more expeditions were forming up at New York, and General Carleton was preparing to send a mass of disbanded troops after them. The town at the mouth of the St. John was growing as rapidly as Shelburne.

The St. John, in fact, would justify the loyalists' optimism more than Parr's caution. Over the centuries, the floods of the big river had created broad tracts of fertile intervale land all along its banks. Parts of the Bay of Fundy coast might be as rugged as Parr feared, but agricultural land of high quality lay for hundreds of miles along the navigable St. John and its tributaries. There were rich timber resources, not only along the river but in bays like Passamaquoddy by the new American border. Already a small population of farmers, timber-cutters, and shippers had discovered the riches of the region. At the mouth of the St. John, where a small trading centre had grown to supply the upriver farmers and to export masts and timber, a small outpost called Fort Howe had ensured British control of the river and provided a measure of government in a territory ripe for large-scale settlement.

As the loyalists arrived at the mouth of the river in the summer of 1783, it was Fort Howe's commanders who had to receive and place them, much as Marston was doing at Shelburne. Even had Parr been more enthusiastic about the migration to the St. John, the governor's hands would have been full at Halifax. As things were, with Parr sceptical about Saint John and the loyalists there unconcerned about the priorities of the colonial capital, it was easy and practical for the governor to deputize his authority to his officers on the scene. Major Gilbert Studholme, an Irish-born regular officer who had commanded Fort Howe since its construction, and Lieutenant Samuel Denny Street, a London-trained lawyer doing war service in a provincial regiment, found themselves taking charge of a migration of thousands.

During the summer and fall of 1783 some fourteen thousand loyalists arrived at the mouth of the St. John and a few other landing sites along the Fundy shore. Relying for help on the leaders of the migration, Studholme and Street supervised the surveying of hundreds of plots of land, the distribution of supplies by the ton, and the establishment of civil authority in the new community. As in peninsular Nova Scotia, there was an air of confusion as thousands of fearful and ambitious loyalists disembarked into what seemed a hostile wilderness, but there was also an underlying order, as the assigned officials provided food, timber, and tools, and directed the new arrivals toward their land. Some of the companies of loyalists moved up the river almost immediately to begin clearing townsites and farms. Others remained at the mouth of the river to found the trading city of Saint John, and others settled further west in the harbours of Passamaquoddy Bay.

The rapid growth of the St. John communities and their sense of isolation from the Halifax government became the impetus for the next major step in the transformation of Nova Scotia. Within months of their arrival, loyalist spokesmen were proposing that their new home should become a colony in its own right, independent of Nova Scotia. Halifax was distant, and its governor cool if not hostile to the Saint John settlement. The loyalist leaders there had come with a sense of mission and opportunity, intending to build a great new loyal society, not merely an appendage to little Nova Scotia. They wanted influence and authority, and soon the links to Britain that they had forged during the war were being put to good use as they campaigned for the separation of the Saint John loyalist community from Nova Scotia.

John Parr's position in the face of this challenge was weak. Even in peninsular Nova Scotia, loyalists were now as numerous as old inhabitants, and their arrival had created political problems for Parr. Loyalists who had once been leaders and officials in the lost colonies looked for positions of influence as well as for land grants, and inevitably they saw the established Nova Scotia officials as rivals. Many of them thought one of their number – most likely John Wentworth, the deposed royal governor of New Hampshire – should replace Parr. Parr, whose own patron, Shelburne, was falling from power, could not counter the lobbying of the Saint John loyalists and their British supporters.

Quickly, almost without discussion, the British government moved toward the division of Nova Scotia, and in June 1784 the colony of New Brunswick was created. Thomas Carleton, brother of the commander at New York, was appointed governor, and the best-placed loyalists at London and Saint John were rewarded with titles, salaries, and responsibilities for the administration of their new colony.

After the establishment of New Brunswick, a series of administrative changes completed the reshaping of the Maritimes colonies. When a belated migration of loyalists into Cape Breton Island began in 1784, that island also became a colony in its own right. In Nova Scotia and New Brunswick, legislative boundaries were redrawn to give representation to the new communities. In 1785 elections in both colonies gave leading loyalists seats in their colonial legislatures.

Only on the Island of St. John did the coming of the loyalists to the Maritimes fail to achieve a transformation. The fertile island might soon have become a thriving colony, particularly when farm families began to search for alternatives to Shelburne's rocky surroundings, but all such possibilities were choked off by the lack of available land. Nova Scotia had quickly recovered its undeveloped lands by escheat, but the Island of St. John remained the fiefdom of its absentee landlords. Loyalists who went to the island could get few guarantees from the authorities in Charlottetown or from the land agents, and when generous land grants were available elsewhere, few were inclined to become only tenants. Only a few hundred loyalists stayed on the island.

While John Parr and his officials struggled to provide an orderly reception for the thirty-five thousand seaborne refugees who reached Nova Scotia during 1783, Governor Haldimand at Quebec faced problems of a different order. Most of the loyalists for whom his government had to find room were already in the province – and had been for several years.

Governor of Quebec since 1777, Frederick Haldimand had been a soldier for more than forty years. Swiss-born – christened François-Louis-Frédéric, he preferred French to English in his private correspondence all his life – Haldimand had served in Italian, Prussian, and Dutch armies before being recruited by the British in 1755. After that, he served almost continuously in North America, becoming a British subject as he rose to general's rank and military governorships.

Military habits shaped Governor Haldimand's attitude to civil administration at Quebec during the Revolutionary War. Fearful of disaffection in both the French-speaking majority and the Anglo-American merchant community, Haldimand ran an austere, autocratic regime, readily assuming that his critics were either insubordinate or actually disloyal. Not much loved, he was generally successful in a difficult period by treating government as a problem of military administration.

Throughout the war, the problem that preoccupied Haldimand as much as keeping his subjects loyal was maintaining his colony's defences against a series of threatened attacks from the American rebels and their French allies. As military commander, Haldimand faced the same challenge as the French defenders of Canada in earlier wars: holding the populated valley of the St. Lawrence both against seaborne attack from the

Gulf and against land invasion from New York. But defending the heartland where virtually all the 150,000 Canadians lived was only part of the problem. More important in this war than ever was the thousand-mile-long curving line of outposts on the upper St. Lawrence and the Great Lakes. These posts were still important to the administration of the fur trade (when the Americans briefly occupied Montreal in 1775-76, there were Montreal fur-traders in the upper country who did not learn of the invasion until it was over), and still vital for relations with the native nations, but they were more than ever crucial to counter American expansion that threatened to cut the chain of posts and leave Haldimand's colony boxed in by the expanding American power.

Short of regular troops and obliged to concentrate those he had around Montreal, Haldimand found that the key to strengthening and holding the upcountry posts lay with his loyalist troops. Loyalist corps had been forming at Montreal and Quebec ever since Allan Maclean's retreat there from the Mohawk Valley in the summer of 1775, and they grew steadily larger, better organized, and more reliable as the war dragged on. As the contest for control of the northern frontiers of New York, Pennsylvania, and Vermont grew more heated, the hard-pressed loyalists of those regions found it prudent to retreat across the border to regroup and resupply before pushing back into their home territories. As a result, a kind of civil war was fought throughout northern New York during the years of the Revolutionary War, with the weaker loyal side using Canadian bases and royal support, yet retaining their ties and commitment to their homes over the border.

From 1776 to 1783, the loyalists in Canada fought a successful war against the American Revolution's northern and western frontier. They never regained control of their homes in the Mohawk Valley or elsewhere, but they decisively checked every American attempt to advance against the Canadian line of defences. Their constant threat pinned down revolutionary armies that might have been used elsewhere, and by their raids and sabotage they were frequently able to burn, capture, or even prevent the planting of food crops badly needed by the Continental Army further south. Haldimand's professional scepticism about amateur soldiers and militia corps had initially been strong, and he frequently sent regular army officers to stiffen the provincial regiments, but by the end of the fighting he could hardly deny that the provincial troops and their native allies had played a vital role all along his colony's frontiers.

As the loyalist commanders based in Canada – men like Sir John Johnson and John Butler, both prominent Mohawk Valley landlords and social leaders, and Ebenezer Jessup, an important Vermont settler – discovered they could raid, visit, and spy on their former homes but never securely remain there for any length of time, they began to bring their supporters and dependents back to Canada with them. Some of these were rescued from rebel confinement and taken back to Canada by loyalist raiding-parties. Others fled on their own initiative and successfully crossed the no man's land to loyal territory. Some were freed or exchanged under flags of truce and sent north to be less of a burden to their revolutionary masters. All through the war, groups of loyal Americans from the northern frontier of the Thirteen Colonies passed into British-held Canada. By the end of the war Canada had acquired an extra population of nearly ten thousand, mostly soldiers and their families hoping to make temporary use of Canada as a base from which to reconquer and return to their homes to the south. Some more loyalist refugees would come in after the peace in 1783, but most of the loyalists in Haldimand's jurisdiction had been there for years, actively serving in the dual campaign to preserve Canada and regain the Thirteen Colonies.

As the loyalist corps became increasingly valuable to Governor Haldimand, they also educated him about the frontiers of his domain. Loyalist rangers based around Lake Champlain reported not only on rebel activity in Vermont and northern New York, but also on the land in the lightly settled territory between the Canadian and the American frontiers. Even more interesting were the reports that came in from the upcountry posts. As the loyalist corps built and expanded military posts all along the Great Lakes route from Montreal to Michilimackinac, their reports increased the governor's awareness of the potential value of all the land bounding the lakes.

In March 1779, Captain Walter Butler, of the Niagara-based corps of rangers commanded by and named for his father, John Butler, travelled from Niagara to Montreal in a small boat that hugged the north shore of Lake Ontario. In a report he presented to Haldimand the following month, Butler described the rich resources of the shoreline, noting where a sawmill might prosper, where the salmon ran in greatest numbers and the ducks fed, where hayfields awaited cultivation and harbours awaited ships. Four years later, early in 1783, Sergeant John Hay of Allan Maclean's Royal Highland Emigrants, dispatched with supplies for the garrison at Michilimackinac, compiled another diary of the upcountry. Leaving Montreal early in May, Hay and his crew proceeded in an open *bateau* up the St. Lawrence, then rowed and sailed carefully along the stormy south shore of Lake Ontario to the fort at Niagara. Portaging their cargo past Niagara Falls, they next boarded a schooner to travel west to the little post at Detroit and north across Lake Huron, reaching Michilimackinac late in July. John Hay's diary was a personal record, not an official report, but he too noticed the developing lake trades and the agricultural potential of the upcountry shorelines. By the end of the war, military service in the western posts enabled many loyalist refugees from northern New York and Pennsylvania to discover the potential of the land bounding the Great Lakes. Governor Haldimand's eyes had also been turned west.

As the terms of the peace became known, Governor Haldimand first considered the upper country as a refuge for a special group of loyalists, the Six Nations, or Iroquois, Indians. Haldimand was vividly aware that the natives allies had been at least as valuable as the loyalist corps in the successful campaign in the west. "By their allegiance we have hitherto with a handful of troops kept possession of the Upper Posts," he wrote shortly before the peace, "and without their cordial assistance it will be impossible to maintain that country." But the war had not gone well for the Iroquois, and Haldimand knew his government owed them much for their sacrifices.

In the war, the Six Nations Confederacy had at first sought to preserve their traditional neutrality and to avoid the hostility of either side, but events rapidly drew the natives into the quarrel. A section of the confederacy made an alliance with the American Congress, but the larger part, led by the Mohawk tribe and Joseph Brant, supported the British cause, arguing that an alliance with the Crown would be the natives' best shield against white encroachment. This disagreement split the Six Nations permanently, but most of the Iroquois came to share the view that the American colonists were the greater threat to Indian independence and territorial control. So Iroquois fighting men stood alongside British regulars and loyalist rangers in all the frontier campaigns, and their skills and fearsome reputation became vital assets in Haldimand's efforts to keep the rebel frontier aflame.

Right down the western frontier of the Thirteen Colonies, native nations had fought in alliance with British troops. Brant's Mohawks, closely supported by loyalist militia from northern New York, fought campaigns from Vermont to Ohio. Vivid tales of Brant's ferocity made him a legend among terrified Patriots of the western frontier.

Blue Jacket of the Shawnee, with Little Turtle of the Miami and the Cherokee Dragging Canoe, was one of many native leaders who used British arms to fight Patriot forces *and* encroaching settlers throughout the Revolutionary War. The war helped them to forge a partnership among all the native nations most threatened by the expansion of the United States. Nearly all these leaders were later founders of a native alliance that would fight the United States over land – first on its own in the 1790s, then with British support and the Shawnee Tecumseh's great leadership in the War of 1812.

Just as the Loyalists had been forced out of their homes by the fighting, the native nations were forced into retreat during and after the Revolutionary War. Blue Jacket's town in the Ohio Valley was destroyed in 1778, and his new home was burned by American raiders in 1786. The Iroquois too found their home territories west of the Mohawk Valley becoming a prime target of the revolutionary armies. In 1779 a Continental army invaded the Iroquois territory to neutralize the native fighting forces by devastating their homelands. This summer-long scourging of the Iroquois towns destroyed thousands of homes, burned acres of productive farmland, and killed scores of men, women, and children. "I flatter myself that the orders with which I was entrusted are fully executed, as we have not left a single settlement or field of corn in the country of the [Six] Nations," reported the American commander, John Sullivan. Sullivan's invasion actually had little impact on the fighting strength of the Iroquois, for already the war parties were being housed and supplied by the British forts, but the territorial base of the Six Nations was nearly destroyed. British, loyalist, and Iroquois raids continued to batter the frontiers of rebel territory, but the rebel counterstroke, unable to reach to Canada, had smashed the heartland of the Iroquois. They became a refugee nation, and by the end of 1779, five thousand Iroquois were encamped close by Fort Niagara.

Haldimand understood both the debt owed to the Iroquois and the need to retain their friendship, but such considerations meant little to the British government, eager to end the war quickly and almost completely unaware of the fundamental white-native alliances by which Canada had been built and defended. The peace treaty of 1783 ceded at a sweep all the territory south of the Great Lakes to the newly independent United States. Not only did the concession give the revolutionaries the forts at Oswego, Niagara, Detroit, and Michilimackinac, and all the other posts from which the British and the Canadians had defended their hold on the Great Lakes, but it also yielded all the Iroquois land to the Americans without a word of discussion with the Iroquois themselves. The Iroquois, who considered themselves "a free people subject to no power upon Earth", were shocked to discover that Britain's king could pretend to cede to America what was not his own to give.

Haldimand and his councillors were dismayed. Within weeks of receiving details of the preliminary treaty of peace, Haldimand wrote to Britain, "The minds of the people are much alarmed at the idea of abandoning the posts in the upper country, which are no less necessary to their security than to their commerce." His letter made it clear to the British government that the concession of the upcountry posts would mean the end of the western fur trade, and the placing of the enemy securely on Canada's western flank. Delicately hinting at his superiors' thoughtlessness, Haldimand continued: "My own anxiety at present arises from an appreciation of the effects which the preliminaries will have upon the minds of our Indian allies, who will consider themselves abandoned to the resentment of an ungenerous and implacable enemy."

Haldimand's evidence that the treaty, as written, was nearly a death sentence for Canada convinced the British government. Despite the treaty, the transfer of the western posts was postponed. Britain would retain Niagara and Detroit for nearly fifteen more years, citing as justification the Americans' broken promises to respect the rights of the loyalists. But the Iroquois lands were gone. Burned, devastated, and abandoned by 1779, they were already being claimed by land-hungry settlers. Before the end of May 1783, Governor Haldimand had sent his surveyor-general, Major Samuel Holland, to survey the north side of Lake Ontario, explaining that "I will endeavour to prevail upon the Mohawk to settle there, provided the country contiguous to it should prove propitious."

The north side of the lakes did prove propitious, and soon Haldimand recognized that it could serve his loyalist refugees as well as the refugee native allies. Haldimand would soon have nearly ten thousand loyalists on his hands – soldiers in the western posts, soldiers and families in the St. Lawrence and Richelieu valleys, and refugees arriving overland from northern New York and even by sea from New York City. "I wait with impatience for the further instructions relative to the royalists," he wrote when he reported his plan to offer land in the upper country to the Six Nations. "I feel much for the distress of these unfortunate people. Next to the obedience and submission which I owe to the pleasure of my royal master, the hopes of being by my command in this country instrumental in alleviating their distress are the greatest consolation which I promised myself in my present station."

In his search for permanent homes for the refugees, Haldimand rejected some of the most obvious locations. Like all the commanders of Quebec since its conquest, Haldimand recognized that the fundamental needs of the French-Canadian population had to be respected, if only to ensure secure British control over them. To minimize the disruption of conquest and to win over the traditional leaders of the society, the British commanders had safeguarded French religion, civil law, and land-tenure traditions, and had rejected English settlers' petitions for legislative reform that would inevitably favour the

English minority. In this vein, Haldimand recognized the impossibility of successfully mingling 10,000 loyalists with 150,000 *Canadiens*, for the newcomers would never accept the French institutions any more than the old settlers would welcome the English-speaking invasion. Looking elsewhere, Haldimand soon rejected the Lake Champlain area. Many loyalist soldiers had spent the whole war there and wanted to remain, but the governor feared it was too close to the new American border, at a time when future relations between loyal and rebellious Americans remained unpredictable. Haldimand also considered the Gaspé peninsula and Chaleur Bay, but they seemed unable to support so many settlers, especially ones unfamiliar with fishing and other maritime livelihoods. The upper country, first considered only as a shelter for the Iroquois, suddenly loomed large as a potential home for thousands of loyalists. Quickly, almost casually, Haldimand made the momentous decision that would create an English-speaking Ontario beside the French-speaking Quebec. That summer he began sending out teams of scouts and surveyors to build on the partial reports on the upper country that his soldiers had compiled during the war.

Through the summer and fall of 1783, Haldimand's explorers began to comb the upper country for the best possible settlement sites. Lieutenant David Jones of Edward Jessup's Loyal Rangers examined both sides of the Ottawa River. His fellow officer, Gershom French, travelled up the same river, then struck out to explore the Rideau River. Reaching its headwaters, he and his guides crossed to the Gananoque River, which brought them back to the St. Lawrence. Meanwhile, a Connecticut loyalist officer, Justus Sherwood, and Haldimand's deputy surveyor, John Collins, were examining the northern bank of the St. Lawrence from Montreal to the Quinte peninsula on Lake Ontario. Butler's Rangers, already comfortably ensconced on both sides of the Niagara River, reported on the quality of the lands between lakes Ontario and Erie, and the commander at Detroit was ordered to survey the ground across the river from his post. From all along the rivers and lakes, enthusiastic reports came in, perhaps summed up in Justus Sherwood's succinct recommendation: "The climate here is very mild and good, and I think the loyalists may be the happiest people in America by settling this country."

The country which Haldimand was about to populate with its first sizeable communities of permanent white settlers had already seen several stormy centuries of war and change. One hundred and fifty years before, the Huron-Iroquois wars had destroyed the Huron confederacy, the largest and most powerful native nation in the area, but the Iroquois had been unable to replace their rivals, and the Hurons' old Algonkian allies from northern Ontario pushed south to occupy the shores of Lake Ontario and Lake Erie. These newcomers from the north, formerly only a fragment of the Algonkian nation, now defined themselves as the Mississauga. A hunting and gathering culture, the Mississauga were never as numerous as their predecessors, but by the time of the American Revolution their title to southern Ontario was unchallenged. Walter Butler's 1779 reconnaissance along Lake Ontario had encountered family groups and small bands of Mississauga living at every river mouth and cove along his route.

Because the British had since 1763 recognized native ownership of all the land bordering the Great Lakes, the exploration and surveying of the territory had to proceed hand in hand with a series of negotiations with the Mississauga chiefs and councils. Living lightly upon the land and valuing the potential benefits of increased trade with white settlers, the Mississauga proved amenable to treaties, and during 1783 a series of land surrenders – usually bounded by such vague terms as "one day's travel back from the lakeshore" – provided Haldimand's government with all the property it would need for ten thousand loyalists and Iroquois. Late in 1783, surveyor John Collins began marking out the new townships, and Governor Haldimand advised the Iroquois and the white loyalists to prepare for the migration to their new homes in the spring of 1784.

Frederick Haldimand and John Parr had little contact with each other, and the loyalist migrations their colonies faced were very different, yet their responses proved similar. For each the crucial issue was land. Parr's government managed to break the artificial shortage that earlier granting policies had created. Haldimand found land for the loyalists in the upper country while preserving the seigneurial society of his French subjects in Lower Canada. Each governor presided over the opening of the western frontier of his colony — Haldimand very deliberately, Parr almost against his will – and prepared for the division of his colony to reflect its changed composition.

Both Parr's and Haldimand's administrations struggled with the task of distributing food and equipment to thousands of refugees, and tried at the same time to maintain the accurate accounts that would permit a fair and economical allocation of property and supplies. Such efforts went far beyond the usual responsibilities of the administrative corps of these small colonies. Though each governor drafted many loyalists and others to help with the task, it was inevitable that neither would be entirely successful. Inequities in land distribution were rife. Shortages in supplies were frequent. Recriminations proliferated among the officials, suppliers, and claimants. Many loyalists settled in their new homes bearing grudges for real or imagined grievances, and many of the Crown officials believed themselves unfairly blamed for problems that had arisen.

Yet measured against what might have happened, the achievement of the two governors and their colonies was immense. In the midst of the migration, John Parr admitted that he feared there would be "great mortality" among the loyalists, and it was not an unreasonable fear. The mass migration of 1783 was unprecedented, and many observers and participants must have doubted whether their small colonial societies, with limited administrative systems, scant medical expertise, and tiny reserves of wealth, could manage the movement of some 50,000 people without a catastrophe. Both in Parr's jurisdiction and in Haldimand's, the challenge was met – a great achievement by the loyalists themselves, but also a notable accomplishment for the Canadian societies that received and accommodated them.

There was another similarity between John Parr and Frederick Haldimand – neither received much credit. Vividly aware of how much they had lost, how little they seemed to be getting in return, and how much responsibility for their future still rested on their own shoulders, the loyalists were never effusively grateful to the governments that had made room for them in Canada. And neither Parr nor Haldimand had the personality that might have won the affection of their subjects or of historians. Haldimand retired to Britain in 1784, almost as soon as the loyalists reached their lands, and was soon eclipsed by his successor, Guy Carleton. Parr died in office in 1791, still criticized by rivals in both New Brunswick and Nova Scotia, and was soon overshadowed by his successor, loyalist John Wentworth.

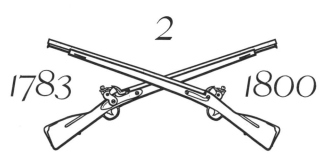

2
1783   1800

Edward Winslow's New Brunswick

FEAR OF THE HOSTILE WILDERNESS SPRANG EASILY TO Sarah Frost's mind in June 1783 when her ship anchored in Saint John harbour, amidst what she called "the roughest land I ever saw". That mix of fear and doubt was a common emotion of the loyalist landings, and it remained a well-remembered one. Sixty years later, Walter Bates recalled the St. John River homesite that he discovered in May 1783 as "nothing but wilderness before our eyes. The women and children did not refrain from tears." Another aged loyalist told her grandchildren how she had "climbed to the top of Chipman's Hill and watched the sails disappearing in the distance, and such a feeling of loneliness came over me that, although I had not shed a tear through all the war, I sat down on the damp moss with my baby in my lap and cried."

That memory of arriving in Canada to confront hardship, wilderness, and isolation was preserved in the loyalist communities for generations. Little wonder: Sarah Frost was not unusual in having abandoned most of her relatives to accompany her husband to the St. John River. She brought two small children with her and was pregnant with a third, and she had no certainty where her family would settle or how they would live. Both the Frosts and the Bateses had left behind a comfortable town not far from New York and a hundred and fifty years past its pioneering days. Now they were being set down on a frontier that in the same century and a half had never managed to attract and hold a settled population of any size.

Walter Bates's statement implied that, unlike the women and children, the men of his party did refrain from tears, but even behind such phlegmatic descriptions as Peter Berton's terse "After 15 July 1783 lived or resided at a place on the River Saint John called Pointe au Chene or Oak Point, distant from the mouth thereof twenty-five miles," one can guess at the apprehensions of family heads and company captains as they led their followers into the unknown with only the roughest notions of what the civil and military authorities could or would do for them.

Yet fear of the hostile wilderness was not the only emotion running through the loyalist landing fleets. Particularly among well-placed loyalists who knew something of the resettlement plans, there was a surge of optimism and ambition at least as strong as the tremors of doubt. Though their destination resembled a wilderness, it would be an unusually organized one, where royal officials and loyalist leaders would be distributing land, providing rations and equipment, and setting up systems of law and government for thousands of skilled, motivated settlers. With such aid, some loyalists realized, the pioneers might quickly turn thick forests and rocky shorelines into prosperous farms and trading ports. Instead of fearing to be first into an undeveloped wilderness, there were ambitious loyalists who had perceived an opportunity to lead a new society on to the world stage – and to prosper by doing so.

No one expressed this other side of the loyalist landings better than an articulate, ambitious young leader of the migration named Edward Winslow. A Harvard graduate raised in a mansion in Plymouth, Massachusetts, Winslow had been poised to continue a tradition of public office and social prominence that went back to his *Mayflower* ancestors. The revolution – which Winslow saw as a malevolent conspiracy of the corrupt and the ill-bred – destroyed his family's influence in Massachusetts, but it provided young Winslow with a chance to shine among the loyalists. After volunteering for service with the British in the first fighting around Boston, he spent most of the war at the commander-in-chief's headquarters. As the keeper of the records of all the burgeoning loyalist corps, Winslow worked closely with the most senior British commanders and all the leading loyalists who raised troops or contributed to the war effort. By 1783 he was a thirty-six-year-old lieutenant-colonel with an unmatched knowledge of loyalist plans and personalities.

Winslow first went to Halifax as one of the loyalist agents who preceded the mass migration of 1783, but the colonial establishment there seemed to offer little scope for his ambitions, and in July 1783 he joined the mass of settlers who had already landed on the River St. John. As the representative of the loyalist regiments that were preparing to leave New York, and as the newly appointed secretary to the military commander of Nova Scotia, Winslow found himself in a position in which "it is as much in my power to assist my friends as any one man in the province," and from his first landing there he became the visionary and the promoter of a loyal society on the St. John. Stiffly convinced of the natural authority that went with breeding and rank, Winslow was also a gregarious companion and a lively correspondent, and his New Brunswick letters ranged from fond instructions to his wife to detailed reports for his colleagues and descriptions of the new country his loyalists were about to colonize.

Winslow was not blind to the kind of hardships that had provoked tears from the women and children of Walter Bates's party. He urged his own elderly parents to head for comfortable Britain rather than endure the rigours of Saint John, and he complained openly about the crowding, expense, and lack of amenities that prevailed in the summer of 1783. But from the start Edward Winslow kept his eye on the big picture, and that picture excited his ambition.

In July, after his first reconnaissance up the St. John River, Winslow wrote, "A number of young bucks and myself have explored this grand river one hundred and twenty miles from its mouth and we have returned delighted beyond expression." By August he was convinced "the River Saint John's is the pleasantest part of this country" and "the land is better than any I have ever seen." Correspondents around the country were sending him equally enthusiastic reports about all the prime areas of loyalist settlement in what would soon be New Brunswick. William Paine, a doctor from Massachusetts, described the harbour at Passamaquoddy Bay as "decidedly the best in America". At Saint John, merchant William Donaldson promoted the country's "noble prospects" for timbering, fishing, and farming, and he even found the winter "by no means so cold as I expected it – it is more steady and I think not so cold as at New York." After leaving Shelburne, surveyor Benjamin Marston wrote of the country along the upper St. John: "though I have seen it only wrapped in the hoary garment of winter, I am charmed with the grandeur of its prospects."

With his own judgment reinforced by opinions such as these and by "much conversation with merchants and other well informed gentlemen on this subject" during his first year there,

Winslow found his optimism growing into an ambitious vision of the development of the St. John River. Lumber industries were sure to thrive, for "the fund of timber is literally inexhaustible," while the forests and rivers were ideal for cutting and moving the lumber. If thousands of houses and several entire towns had been created from local materials in a single year, Winslow argued, how could a firmly established lumber industry fail to prosper? He felt the potential of the fishing industry scarcely needed a description, "because it must occur to every man of common sense that if the New England traders could find a profit in sending their vessels to this coast for fish, those who inhabit its borders can carry on the business to much greater advantage." He was equally keen on agricultural prospects, reporting that "beef and pork are produced in great abundance," and he felt that one could hardly imagine "a more delightful grass country, better cattle, or better grain, or more abundant crops."

Now that the loyalists had provided a population to exploit these resources, there seemed no limit to what could be achieved. As one of Winslow's correspondents told him, the real American revolution might yet prove to be the transformation of the British American colonies settled by the loyalists. All these colonies, Winslow read, "will in all probability and at no very distant period become of infinite advantage to Britain and, rising in proportion to the decline of the neighbouring American states, be in a condition to overawe them." With his own opinions mirroring these, Winslow saw the loyalists' migration not as a flight into wilderness exile, but as a golden opportunity to build a better New England – and to grow rich in the process. "There are assembled here," he wrote triumphantly, "an immense multitude, not of dissolute vagrants such as commonly make the first efforts to settle new countries, but gentlemen of education, farmers formerly independent, and reputable mechanics, who by the fortune of war have been deprived of their property. They are as firmly attached to the British constitution as if they never had made a sacrifice. . . . By Heaven we will be the envy of the American states."

A vital part of Winslow's vision of a colony the world might envy was the separation of the new St. John River communities from the colony of Nova Scotia. He was the first to propose the division, and he promoted it vigorously to all his influential contacts. Seeing the confusion, competition, shortages, and delays that had intimidated ordinary settlers landing at Saint John, Winslow had become convinced that a separate government would attack these urgent, complex tasks with greater ease and efficiency than the distant Nova Scotian authorities ever could. The settlers' difficulties had already aroused resentment against the Nova Scotians, whom in any case Winslow considered slack and much too sympathetic to the American rebels. He believed that a division of responsibilities would ease these tensions and eliminate friction. Winslow did not doubt that peninsular Nova Scotia also had a bright future, particularly now that it had received an infusion of loyalist energy, but creating a separate government for the St. John Valley was the keystone of his grand design.

Winslow's advice was hardly disinterested. Accustomed to leadership, he intended that the creation of a new colony would produce positions of responsibility for his friends and himself. That, in fact, was central to his plan, for Winslow's sympathy for the ordinary loyalists and their difficulties was paternal, and he fully expected them to turn to leaders like himself. "Here they stand," he wrote of the loyalists he saw on the St. John, "with their wives and their children looking up for protection, and requesting such regulations as are necessary to the weal of society. To save these from distress, to soothe and comfort them by extending indulgences which at the same time are essentially beneficial to the country at large, is truly a noble duty." In the new colony he foresaw, Winslow intended to be one of those granting rather than requesting indulgences. When his proposal was adopted and the colony of New Brunswick established in 1784, Winslow received several senior appointments, and his place among the leading men of his colony was given royal approval.

The sense that the new community and its settlers needed powerful, paternal leadership gave the impetus to another plan that complemented Winslow's vision. In June 1783, fifty-five loyalists at New York City, many of whom had been landowners or community leaders in various parts of the Thirteen Colonies, sent a petition to General Guy Carleton. The object of this petition was land: the fifty-five wanted Carleton to recommend that each one of them be granted 5,000 acres of land, for a total grant of 275,000 acres, in the new regions of loyalist settlement.

Among the fifty-five were individuals who had lost much or had served valiantly during the war, but their petition hardly stressed their need or right of compensation. Rather, the petitioners suggested that the new colony was going to need an elite to lead and organize the mass of poorer loyalists who were now heading out of New York. The fifty-five saw themselves as likely candidates for the role of the elite, and title to land was all they needed to fulfil their responsibilities. By opening their new estates to scores of tenants and by providing roads and mills and community leadership in general, the fifty-five would create the social structure that the new country and its leaderless people needed, and the rents they earned would provide them with the investment capital they would need. Edward Winslow, already entitled by his military rank to a land grant of five thousand acres, was not one of the fifty-five petitioners, but his close friend Ward Chipman was, and the attitude behind the petition meshed with Winslow's. Winslow wanted a new colony established on the St. John so that a paternal leadership could more effectively lead the settlers toward the successful creation of a new society. By proposing that great landed estates should dominate that society, the fifty-five were indicating where the leaders would come from.

The petition of the fifty-five clearly foresaw a society of landlords and tenants in the new colony. The 5,000-acre grants would be useless without labour, and the allocation of 275,000 acres of prime land to fifty-five owners was likely to mean that thousands of others would not acquire good land of their own. The petitioners saw no reason to be defensive about this. New York's Hudson Valley and Mohawk Valley had thrived and would continue to prosper as tenant societies, the Island of St. John had been divided into great estates, and the wartime system that entitled military officers to vastly enlarged land grants was built on a vision of a society where land and leadership went hand in hand. The petition of the fifty-five may not have been very practical – many thousands of ordinary soldiers had already been promised land of their own – but the land-holding system it proposed was traditional and familiar. The petitioners foresaw a highly organized and structured society that gave both privileges and responsibilities to a landed elite. Winslow and the fifty-five petitioners doubtless felt that the challenge of creating a new society out of nothing demanded such a system, and they were ready to accept both the privileges and the responsibilities.

This plan to create in New Brunswick a strict hierarchy of owners and tenants did not go unchallenged. Soon after the petition of the fifty-five became public, six hundred loyalists presented a counter-petition. Denouncing not so much the social hierarchy proposed as the pretensions of those who had appointed themselves to lead the new society, the counter-petitioners refused "to be tenants to those, most of whom they consider as their superiors in nothing but deeper art and keener policy." The intention of Winslow and the fifty-five petitioners to provide leadership for the thousands of loyalist refugees had always depended on the consent of those who would be led, and the counter-petition revealed the extent of resistance to such dependence. In effect, there were many loyalists who felt entitled to be landlords, and very few who were ready to be tenants.

The counter-petitioners' aims were sustained by British policy. Even before the separation of New Brunswick from Nova Scotia, orders were given entitling every loyalist household to one hundred acres of land, with extra acres for each family member and as rewards for military service. The vision of an ordered hierarchical society based on landed estates faded. When every individual was receiving more land than he could put to use, the value of the larger holdings granted to the elite became less certain, and a society of massive landed estates farmed by tenants became impossible. Though Edward Winslow had acquired both land and the titles of public leadership, his plan for a powerful, prosperous New Brunswick, humbling the Americans by its successes in industry, commerce, and trade, would be pursued by a society of small, independent proprietors rather than by an organized hierarchy of leaders and those they led.

Winslow had hoped that the loyalist soldiers would settle on large tracts under the direction of their officers, but instead, much of the colonization of New Brunswick was undertaken by smaller groups – sometimes even by single families. With two-hundred-acre lots standard, no family lacked for land. Twelve or fifteen acres was about the maximum that a single family could plant and harvest each year, and simply to clear that many acres required several years' work. The land grants were generous: even with pasturage, woodlots, timber-cutting operations, and hunting preserves, few families would find they needed all of their allotments. With such expanses of lands to exploit, and with the river providing easy communications, farmers were not obliged to live close to their neighbours, and soon isolated single farms began to appear all along the river.

Not all of these were small. At the mouth of the Nerepis River, not far above Saint John, Major John Coffin acquired a six-thousand-acre property from a pre-war settler and began to clear, plant, and fence an estate he called Alwington Manor. On the Kennebecasis, Gilbert Studholme tried to develop a comparable estate when he retired from the command of the Saint John garrison. But each of these men found difficulty in hiring labourers, for most of the loyalists turned to smaller properties they could call their own.

Many settlers went inland in groups self-selected out of the larger regiments and associations. The first to venture inland in New Brunswick were civilian loyalists who had arrived in the first fleets from New York, and it was often the better organized and more cohesive groups that headed past Saint John to take up land. Captain Peter Berton, who arrived with the second fleet from New York in June 1783, led a party directly upriver and established a permanent settlement at Oak Point by July. Slightly further on, where Belleisle Bay joins the main river, Walter Bates's group had set itself down in a promising corner of the New Brunswick wilderness and named it Kingston.

Bates's group of Kingston settlers had more than a shared migration to unite it. Most of Walter Bates's party had been neighbours in Stamford and adjacent Connecticut towns, and they had spent the war years together on Long Island, often co-operating in raids against their old homes across Long Island Sound. These associates were also united by their Anglican faith, which had brought them together on Long Island and which seems to have grown in importance as the other structures in their lives disintegrated. It was at a church meeting on Long Island that Bates's group "mutually agreed all together to remove with all their families into the wilderness of Nova Scotia and settle all together in such situation as we might enjoy the comforts of a church and school in the wilderness."

Shared religious faith and shared experience united the Kingston settlers. When they chose a settlement site and landed, men of the group resolved to set aside a part of each of the central lots of the settlement as the site of a church. After an official surveyor ratified the group's decisions and laid out the town of Kingston in July 1783, the settlers continued to work co-operatively, "clearing places for buildings, cutting logs, carrying them together by strength of hands, and laying up log houses." By November 1783 every family was adequately housed, and a town had been born. Years later, Bates still remembered the July landing as a time of tears and apprehension, yet he reported that by November "a happier people never lived upon the globe." Bates himself, who acquired a lot adjacent to the church, spent the rest of his life in the town he helped to found in 1783.

A number of smaller Kingstons were founded in 1783 by enterprising settlers such as New Jersey farmer Isaac Perkins. Perkins, who had served most of the war in James DeLancey's Westchester Volunteers, "arrived in the harbour of Saint John 13 May 1783, proceeded up the river immediately, built a house on Swan Lake back from the main river," and soon had a farm under development in previously unsettled territory along the Kennebecasis River, another tributary of the St. John. Despite such examples of initiative, however, many of the civilians who headed up the St. John in 1783 looked for a more secure wintering site. These people often headed for Maugerville, the principal town of those who had settled on the St. John before the American Revolution. Until their land grants were surveyed and made official, many careful loyalists found it prudent to wait in sizeable, centrally located Maugerville, where provisions, trade goods, and information were readily available. As the largest upriver community, with twenty years' success as a farming and wood-cutting centre, Maugerville seemed likely to

become the key town of the interior of the new colony, but settlement decisions taken late in 1783 created a rival town that
soon supplanted Maugerville.

The loyalist military regiments, held back to garrison New
York City while the civilians departed, did not reach New
Brunswick until the fall of 1783. There, the hard-pressed surveyors and administrators, struggling with the demands of
thousands of earlier arrivals, aimed to reduce the overcrowding
of Saint John – and to increase inland settlement – by sending
the troops upriver, beyond the areas of civilian settlement, to
settle on a series of large river-front tracts that had been designated for them. Regimental commanders cast lots to see which
tract each unit would take, and during the fall, boatloads of
troops were moved rapidly up the St. John to inspect and, it was
hoped, to settle their new properties.

The move was less than wholly successful. Once the regiments were disbanded, officers and men were free to settle
where they chose, and many individuals drifted away to join a
friend, escape a disliked officer, or seek their fortune elsewhere.
Private John Billea of the King's American Regiment arrived in
Saint John in October 1783 with his unit, but as his father had
already settled on the lower part of the river, Billea left the regiment when he was discharged and travelled no further than
Oak Point, where he joined the community that Peter Berton
and other civilians had begun four months earlier. Some of
Billea's regimental officers also remained in the civilian-settled
areas of the lower St. John Valley: Ensign Henry Nase settled
on the Nerepis River a few miles from Billea's small farm, and
Captain Abraham de Peyster of the same regiment preferred
Maugerville.

Nevertheless, many of Billea's fellow soldiers and their families joined in the military migration to the upper parts of the
river. Though some of the military units found their twelve-
mile-by-twelve-mile regimental tracts acceptable, settled in,

and began to clear and build, the King's Americans judged their particular allotment too remote and infertile, and they became one of several corps that rejected their designated lands. Instead, Sergeant Benjamin Ingraham, a dozen of the King's Americans officers, and many more officers and men from other regiments discerned an opportunity to settle with their families at St. Anne, just below the first rapids and shallows that inhibited navigation further upstream. These settlers – there may have been two thousand all told – struggled through the first months with many families wintering in tents, beset by early snows and sometimes unable to secure the provisions promised to all the loyalist settlers.

The following spring, those who remained at St. Anne laid out a town, and their choice of site soon proved astute. St. Anne became Fredericton, and Fredericton soon became the market town and lumbering centre of the growing upriver population of the St. John Valley. In 1784 the new governor of New Brunswick, Thomas Carleton, gave the town a vital boost. Fearing that a concentration on Saint John would leave New Brunswick with no more than a thin strip of coastal settlements, Governor Carleton was determined to place his capital inland, and in choosing a site he bypassed flood-prone Maugerville in favour of Fredericton. With a garrison, government offices, and eventually a cathedral church and college to supplement its commercial role, the growth of Fredericton was assured, and the officers of the King's Americans and other regiments who had persevered there found themselves well placed to acquire militia commissions, minor appointments, and other marks of the governor's favour.

As the families of civilians and soldiers scattered out along the length of the St. John and its tributaries, planting the fertile valley and harvesting the hardwood and evergreen trees from the surrounding hills, other communities grew with equal speed along the coast. Outside Saint John itself, the fastest-growing coastal communities were those of Passamaquoddy Bay, already hailed by Edward Winslow's correspondents as some of the finest country in America.

Passamaquoddy Bay's first loyalist settlers came from nearby Penobscot, just down the coast in Maine. Penobscot had been occupied by British troops in 1779 and had become a wartime centre for the re-establishment of loyal refugees, who were assured that the region would remain royal territory. Instead, peace and the treaty terms of 1783 forced a second evacuation upon Penobscot loyalists like Colin Campbell. Originally from Virginia, where he had represented a firm of Glasgow tobacco traders, Campbell had been driven out at the beginning of the rebellion. He and his family returned to Scotland, but after a Caribbean venture the indefatigable merchant began a business at Penobscot about 1780 and soon brought his family to join him. "Extremely mortified" by the cession of the town in 1783, Campbell joined the Penobscot Association, which planned to move the townspeople and their enterprises east to Passamaquoddy. When the time came to leave, Colin Campbell left little behind. He even dismantled his house and took it with him to the new town called St. Andrews, where the reconstructed building joined several others that had gone into exile with their owners.

In Passamaquoddy's tangle of inlets, the fine harbours and resources of timber and fish seemed to promise quick prosperity, and the Penobscot Association was joined by civilian and military groups and by many fortune-seeking individuals who abandoned land grants along the St. John in favour of St. Andrews. Gathering in businessmen, woodsmen, sailors, and farmers, St. Andrews soon had more sawmills and ships than any other part of New Brunswick and, with two thousand settlers, one of the largest populations in the new colony.

Although the Penobscot refugees sailed directly to Passamaquoddy Bay, the vast majority of the fifteen thousand loyalists who arrived in New Brunswick between May and December 1783 arrived at Saint John, and they permanently transformed the tiny community below Fort Howe. Though many of the civilians moved up the river or along the coast, and though the military regiments were encouraged to do the same in the fall, thousands remained in the port city, whether from mercantile ambitions, from a desire to remain at the centre of events, or simply from fear and hesitation over pushing any further into the unknown.

New Jersey loyalist Robert Campbell, who led a company of one hundred and ninety civilian loyalists to New Brunswick, was one of those who chose to remain in Saint John. Perhaps because he had commanded a work detachment of Guides and Pioneers during the war, Campbell was quickly drafted to help in the establishment of the town, and from his arrival in Saint John on August 25, 1783, he was "closely employed in drawing and distributing His Majesty's donations to the people under his command, and sending such up the river as chose to go, and laying out lands in the city for those who chose to stay until land could be found for them up the river."

When Campbell arrived in August, he found Saint John growing chaotically and beset by disputes. Though the local authorities had been preparing since May to distribute land and supplies and had actually issued the first lots before the end of June, the continuing rush of thousands of refugees soon outstripped all predictions and overwhelmed the original allocation of property. Competition for land and supplies became fierce among refugees who urgently needed food and shelter and were eager to establish themselves in new homes. Factional disputes quickly arose. Edward Winslow blamed the Halifax authorities for their failure to prepare, but many New Yorkers were ready to accuse New Englanders like Winslow who had arrived early and acquired favoured positions. Memories of the fifty-five and their petition remained vivid, and lawyer Elias

Hardy soon became the spokesman for loyalists who felt they had been unfairly treated by a well-placed and self-aggrandizing elite. Robert Campbell seems to have fallen victim to tensions over property allocations, for in November, in a fight that may have arisen from his surveying activities, he "lost part of his left arm from a stroke of a cooper's knife by an assassin" and was left unable to work for the rest of the winter.

Amid the chaos, the town grew rapidly. Fifteen hundred houses had been framed and finished by the end of 1783. Construction trades flourished as new commercial houses built wharves, warehouses, and ships to supply the growing community with goods. Town meetings were held, a newspaper opened, and church services began. In fact, Saint John was quickly fulfilling the hope that it would be a major port, a centre of mercantile activity, and the supplier of all the new towns and farms of the loyalist communities on the St. John River and the Fundy shore. In the early years, farms, timber mills, and shipyards consumed capital and equipment shipped in through Saint John, and the merchants there were also positioning themselves to control the future exports of all these businesses. Businessmen and artisans well-placed to benefit from this commerce had reason to be optimistic for their future and that of Saint John.

Saint John was also crowded with less successful immigrants who had neither the skills nor the aptitudes to carve out livelihoods in New Brunswick. Loyalists who were surviving on royal supplies and trying to build homes and careers had little disposable income, and their poverty limited the prospects of professional men who hoped to practise in the city. Dr. Azor Betts, "a well known practitioner of physic in New York and noted for his success in inoculation", arrived in Saint John in May 1783. He soon had a large practice in the growing city but, "on account of the poverty of the people finding it quite insufficient to support his numerous family," he also turned to the land and began raising vegetables. Betts was philosophic about his changed circumstances: he took pleasure in the success of his crops and hoped "he may yet live contented and his children be comfortable and happy." Lawyer Filer Dibblee, whose brother Frederick was the first Anglican clergyman in Walter Bates's Kingston settlement, was much less able to adapt to his changed circumstances. Crowded into a small house with his wife and six children, living mostly on potatoes, Dibblee grew depressed over his limited prospects and his war losses, and he committed suicide before the end of the first winter.

Edward Winslow did better than Betts or Dibblee. The establishment of colonial government in New Brunswick had ensured that he and his friends acquired power and position. Winslow was a member of the governing council from 1784, and for many years he served as secretary to the governor. He became a county magistrate and later a judge, and he briefly administered the colony when its senior officials were absent. Between terms of work at Fredericton, he managed his estate in Kingsclear successfully enough that by 1788 he could write, "I am in the midst of as cheerful a society as any in the world." He mocked American predictions of disaster for New Brunswick: the loyalists were not "in the least danger of starving, freezing, or being blown into the Bay of Fundy". His wife bore him fourteen children, and gradually he secured British military commissions for the sons and appropriate marriages for the daughters.

Over the years, however, Winslow developed some ambivalent feelings about the progress of his colony. Always firmly committed to the vision of a landed agricultural society in which the superiority of the social elite would go unchallenged, he was pleased to see farms spread out along the river front for more than one hundred miles, and delighted to read of English visitors charmed by the vista of a loyalist farmhouse or a "pretty cottage with a fine sloping lawn from the door to the river". Still, he regretted what he considered a reckless granting of patents of property to loyalists of every sort: "A great proportion of the original patentees were idle, dissipated, and capricious," he eventually decided, for "as soon as they were fairly in possession of their lands and had expended the bounty of government, they sold it for a trifle." Where farming communities languished and towns declined, Winslow was apt to find the cause in the fecklessness of the settlers, and he clearly regretted the loss of the firmly defined hierarchy that would have given the elite of the loyalists authority to direct and dictate the progress of the colony.

Even the authority he and his friends did possess was frequently challenged by New Brunswick's fractious legislature, but the lack of greater power probably saved Winslow from greater disillusion, for his vision of New Brunswick had been excessively optimistic. Even unlimited responsibility for the colony would not have enabled him to fulfil all his hopes for it. Despite its resources, New Brunswick could not in a few years surpass the American states in all the fields it had entered. Coastal towns that tried to outdo New England in timber and fish saw their sawmills closing and their people forced to move away, while Saint John eventually traded as much with New England as with any British colonial port.

Despite his continued defence of the agricultural prospects of New Brunswick, Winslow's own farm never made him rich, and he was sorry to see the loyalist elite tied to its farms while less distinguished men moved toward wealth and power in other pursuits. "Our gentlemen have all become potato farmers and our shoemakers are preparing to legislate," he wrote mournfully. His wish to see a settled and prosperous farming society made him doubtful of Saint John, for despite his pride in its growth he deplored how the wrong kind of people too often succeeded in trade: "Our metropolis is wonderfully increased and is really a very beautiful town; our shoemakers have all turned merchants and appear to have made their fortunes."

Winslow lived long enough to see the future powers of New Brunswick emerge from the loyalist foundation. In 1808 he reported to a friend how Napoleon's blockade of British trade in Europe, which forced Britain to rely on North American timber, was pushing up the price of New Brunswick's wood. Eventually the timber trade would dominate New Brunswick's nineteenth-century growth, and timber wealth would make the new elite of the province, but Edward Winslow remained true to his vision of 1783. Though he visited the United States, he was not reconciled. "Their government has not existed long enough to acquire either character or consistency," he wrote in 1811, anticipating the Americans' "chastisement" if the war that seemed about to break out between Britain and the United States actually occurred.

Troubled by gout and other ailments, and finally unable even to maintain the correspondence he had delighted in, Winslow remained steadfastly devoted to the society he had done so much to create. In 1807, when a judgeship had brought him a small but steady income, he had written, "I should prefer an income of four or five hundred a year here to double the sum in any other place." He had not made New Brunswick the uncontested envy of the American states, and his conservative vision of a society dominated by an aristocratic elite had foundered, partly on the competition of too many claimants to the highest places, partly on the impossibility of preserving that hierarchical mindset in late-eighteenth-century North America. Yet when he travelled along the hundreds of miles of settled riverfront along the St. John, where Walter Bates, Sarah Frost and her children, and many more of the loyalists of 1783 had succeeded in making homes and lives out of New Brunswick's wooded river banks, he could be permitted to reflect that his optimism had been borne out at least as strongly as the fear and doubt that the others had expressed.

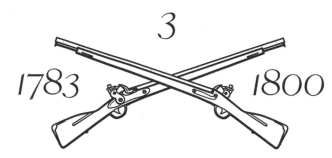

3

1783 ✕ 1800

Gideon White's Nova Scotia

MARY JESSUP REPORTED NO TEARS OR APPREHENSIONS
when she and her family landed in Shelburne, Nova Scotia, in
September 1783, but neither had she come with a confidence-
inspiring master plan such as the one Edward Winslow had
constructed for New Brunswick. Mrs. Jessup and her husband, a
barrelmaker from Hackensack, New Jersey, had never been part
of the loyalist high command, and throughout the war most of
their decisions had been made for them. At Shelburne, too,
their future would depend on what other loyalists could create.

Daniel Jessup had been sympathetic enough to the British
cause in 1776 to aid and guide British troops when they entered
New Jersey, and the subsequent British withdrawal from his
town brought Patriot reprisals that forced the family to take refuge in New York City. To earn a living, if for no stronger reason,
Daniel Jessup had joined the New Jersey loyalist regiment
raised by Dr. Abraham Van Buskirk and, "although pretty far
advanced in years" (he was actually in his mid-forties), he
served in the ranks throughout the war. His military service

ensured that he would not be welcomed home when the war ended, and at the evacuation of New York, the Jessups and their four children had little choice but to follow Colonel Van Buskirk to Shelburne.

Though Daniel Jessup's woodworking skills were likely to be in demand in a city just beginning to be built, the Jessups still depended on the leadership of others. They had arrived at Shelburne as part of a migration of ten thousand loyalists, most of whom had no savings and few possessions and urgently needed to work if they were not to depend on charity. If Shelburne were to support them all, the refugee camp would have to be made quickly into a thriving city, one where humble barrel-makers, as well as farmers, sailors, clerks, lawyers, former plantation-owners, former plantation slaves, and thousands more from every level of society, could find places for themselves and their dependents.

The Port Roseway Associates who had started the great migration to quiet Port Roseway intended to provide for all these settlers – and to ensure their own futures – by making Shelburne into a great city. They believed the wooded territory around Shelburne was waiting to be logged, quarried, and cleared for farms. They knew its fine, deep harbour was ready to shelter a trading fleet that could range the whole Atlantic, and they had calculated that the fish and the whales in the coastal waters would support a thriving industry. Above all, they considered the new people of Shelburne a unique resource. Already crowded with settlers, Shelburne would never have to struggle to increase its numbers by later immigration or natural increase, and in the eyes of Shelburne's promoters the quality of the population was as significant as its size. It was a New Brunswick loyalist who described Halifax's founding population as "the refuse of the jails of England and America", but Shelburne's pioneers might have agreed. They felt that by comparison their own city was uniquely favoured in the range of talents and abilities its first settlers had brought.

From all these elements – the varied resources and the equally varied settlers – the leaders of the Shelburne migration intended to found a city that would prosper in agriculture, industry, fishing, and trade. The ambition was bold, but it was not utopian. At St. John's in Newfoundland, at Louisbourg and Halifax, and at Saint John in New Brunswick, the rise of new societies in Atlantic Canada had always fostered the growth of major ports. As the loyalists revitalized Nova Scotia, it seemed that Shelburne was poised to rival or outdo any of its predecessors.

One latecomer drawn to Shelburne by all this promise was Gideon White, a Massachusetts loyalist who had not been part of the great migration from New York to Port Roseway in 1783. Late in the war, White, then an officer in a loyalist regiment, had been sent to do garrison duty in Jamaica, and he came from there to Halifax at the end of 1783. In the spring of 1784 most of the soldiers who had come with him went to found a settlement on a remote bay at the other end of Nova Scotia, but White and a few others preferred Shelburne.

Gideon White was thirty-two and a bachelor when he landed in Shelburne in May 1784. Already well acquainted with Nova Scotia, he made a likely citizen of the commercial city that Shelburne aspired to be. Trained for the merchant trade in Plymouth, Massachusetts, White had been among the loyalists who had retreated to Halifax in 1776, and in the first years of the war, trading voyages had taken him to many of the little communities along the Nova Scotian coasts. His subsequent military service in South Carolina and Jamaica entitled him to military half-pay, so he came to Shelburne with an income, and his pre-war experience in New England's commerce had prepared him for the similar enterprises by which

Shelburne hoped to rival trading centres like White's home town of Plymouth. White had connections among the mercantile circles of Nova Scotia and New Brunswick, and also in Britain and Jamaica, where contacts forged during military service would soon produce orders for Shelburne timber and fish. He also had useful social and political ties among New England loyalists now becoming prominent in the affairs of Nova Scotia and New Brunswick, including his relative Edward Winslow. With his training, his assets, and his connections, White seemed the kind of man who could help build Shelburne into a city able to support all the loyalists who had come to settle there.

The Shelburne that Gideon White discovered in May 1784 had grown mightily since another Massachusetts merchant, Benjamin Marston, had arrived a year earlier to survey a town. Waves of migration that had continued from May through December 1783 had upset all Marston's calculations of the size of the town and the number of lots it would need, and his surveying had been interrupted by frequent quarrels and several redistributions of land. As the population continued to grow, Marston ceased to share the Port Roseway Associates' high estimation of the settlers. "These people are the very worst we've had yet," Marston wrote of one party that arrived in September. "They seem to be the riff-raff of the whole." But he could also sympathize with the refugees' plight. Even when men sought special preference in his allocation of land, each seeking "to go first to be nearest the town and to have the best land," he admitted "'tis very natural," considering their dire need. On a snowy day early in November 1783, Marston noted how the southerners among the refugees were "much frightened at the weather; poor people, they are to be pitied."

Despite fears such as these and despite the overcrowding that left many loyalists sheltering in huts, cellars, and ships' holds, Shelburne was an impressive place by the end of 1783.

Governor Parr described it as "the most considerable, most flourishing, and most expeditious" of all the new towns in his colony. "Eight hundred houses are already finished, six hundred more in great forwardness, and several hundred lately begun upon, with wharves and other erections. There are upwards of 12,000 inhabitants, about 100 sail of vessels, a most beautiful situation, the land good, and the fairest and best harbour in the world. I have not a doubt of its being one day or other the first port in this part of America."

Parr may have been exaggerating Shelburne's population a little – no census reported more than eight thousand residents, and a population much over ten thousand seems unlikely – but even in the midst of his difficulties, Benjamin Marston could share Parr's enthusiasm, reporting in admiration that by February 1784 nearly 250 substantial frame buildings stood among the 800 log houses that had been thrown up for quick shelter. By the summer 300 more buildings were up, and Marston observed that "these later buildings are altogether framed houses and most generally large, commodious, and some of them elegant buildings."

Six miles away, at Birchtown, the fifteen hundred free blacks who had been part of the migration to Shelburne were also building a town. Since the Nova Scotian authorities – and white Shelburne – expected the blacks to become menial labourers and household servants, they had given few of the Birchtown settlers substantial plots of land, and many black loyalists were obliged to seek work in Shelburne. Still, Birchtown, the largest community of free blacks anywhere in North America, established its independent character. In the first winter, a religious revival there had created strong and enthusiastic Methodist, Baptist, and Anglican congregations led by black preachers and reaching out from Birchtown to blacks and whites in Shelburne and the rest of loyal Nova Scotia. Boston King and his wife, Violet, were among the first converts to

Methodism. King was then working as a carpenter in Birch-town, but he would eventually be a leading lay preacher among the black Nova Scotians.

In Shelburne, sawmills, shipyards, and fishing businesses had been started before the end of the first year. Bakers, black-smiths, and shopkeepers were busy, though the royal stores were still the prime source of supply and ration tickets were still a vital currency. Marston thought the royal provisions were "very good of their kind, particularly the bread", though one loyalist later complained of having nothing but "His Majesty's rotten pork and unbaked flour".

James Robertson, a printer from Connecticut, had begun publishing Shelburne's first newspaper, the *Royal American Gazette*. Regular courts held session; the city soon acquired a gallows, a whipping post, and a pillory, and an early ordinance prohibited "negro frolics and dances" in the city. Several churches had begun offering services within days of the first landing, though the Anglicans were embarrassed by two rival clergymen who fought a long and public battle over the rector-ship of Shelburne.

The refugee camp was growing into a sometimes stylish town. Though Marston was undoubtedly correct in his slightly disdainful observation that many of the Shelburne settlers "were of the lower class of the great towns" of the Thirteen Col-onies and hardly a collection of privileged aristocrats, services from wig-making to silversmithing were available for those who could afford them. The social leaders, some attended by ser-vants and slaves, enjoyed lavish entertainments. Shelburne had held its first ball – to celebrate the king's birthday – within weeks of its foundation, and a second one, in Governor Parr's honour, in July 1783. Early in 1784 Marston described a ball marking the Queen's birthday, where fifty guests "danced, drank tea, and played at cards in a house which stood where six months ago there was an almost impenetrable swamp – so great have been the exertions of the settlers in this new world." Abraham Van Buskirk, as a colonel, a doctor, and now one of Shelburne's magistrates, was probably among the invitees. James Bruce, once a plantation-owner and a member of the governor's council in far-off West Florida, could also have expected an invitation. Considering the crowd of Shelburnites equal to these – successful merchants from New York and New England, former planters from the south, military officers, and displaced royal officials – Marston probably realized that only his power over land grants had gained him admittance.

By the time Gideon White arrived in this new world, however, Shelburne was entering a period of crisis. In the town's first months, the urgent need for shelter had kept everyone busy. Even Dr. Van Buskirk, whose family had spent part of the winter in Benjamin Marston's cellar, had helped to gather stone for the chimney of his own new house, and building the scores of new houses that had evoked the admiration of Governor Parr had provided steady employment for the working people who never shared in the glamorous entertainments. But this activity proved short-lived. "Many people have reduced themselves to the last shilling in building and have not at present the wherewithal to support themselves," reported one observer by the spring, and the sudden slowdown in house-building left many working people underemployed and restive. For the first time Shelburne's promise to support the huge population it had attracted was tested: in May 1784 the abrupt loss of work – and pay – triggered a riot of discharged soldiers and workmen.

The rioters' first target was the free black labourers. Though forced to work for white employers by their lack of access to property of their own, the blacks were accused of taking work from the soldiers, and in a few turbulent days the rioters forced all of them to retreat to Birchtown. Once the blacks had been evicted, the rioters turned their anger in a new direction: toward Benjamin Marston.

As the royal surveyor authorized to allocate property to the loyalists, Marston held a vitally important post in Shelburne, but his authority had always been checked by what he called the "cursed republican town-meeting spirit" among these refugees from republicanism. From Shelburne's first days, the loyalists had insisted on participating in all major decisions through the leaders of their Associations. Marston was ill at ease with such constraints, and he blamed many of the problems of the land-granting process on the greed and inadequacy of hastily appointed loyalist leaders "whom neither nature nor education intended for that rank." In return, many loyalists accused Marston of incompetence or dishonesty when land grants went against their own preferences. As the man responsible for the crucial decisions about every piece of property in Shelburne, yet lacking independent authority or respect, Marston was a natural scapegoat for the town's anxieties about its prospects. The rioters concluded that Shelburne's troubles had been caused by double-dealing in land distribution, and as his danger grew, Marston fled to Halifax, fearing for his life. Governor Parr arrived to restore order, but when he gave credence to complaints about the surveying, Marston decided to make his future in New Brunswick, "as most of the New England refugees will be there, and among them my nearest and dearest friends." These included Edward Winslow, who had recommended Marston as Shelburne's surveyor and would find him new duties in New Brunswick.

At least one New England refugee and friend of Edward Winslow was not very sympathetic to Marston's plight. Gideon White arrived at Shelburne soon after the riots with the suspicion that matters were poorly regulated there "owing to the misconduct or folly of those in power". But he evidently thought Shelburne's problems were either temporary or superficial, for he soon settled in to stay. As his friend and business colleague Nathaniel Whitworth had realized, the financial embarrassment of those who had overbuilt made it "more than probable you'll be able to purchase a store already completed" for less than the building's cost.

Profiting from these kinds of opportunities in his first months at Shelburne, White also laid the foundation for the career that would support him there for the rest of his long life. He already had a share in a vessel bringing rum, sugar, and coffee from Jamaica, and he would soon be ready to send a stock of timber and fish in return. He invested in a whaling company and moved cautiously into the fishing industry. Heeding Whitworth's advice not to be "too hasty in entering into the fishery; rather await the result of other people," he discovered that salt for the drying of cod was the most marketable commodity in the town, and he also tested the demand for beef, pork, butter, and cloth.

White also looked to the land. Fellow officers in Jamaica had authorized him to claim lands on their behalf, and in their names and his own he began to acquire tracts of land around Shelburne. Not long after his arrival he began importing seeds, livestock, and farming equipment, and soon he was employing farm families to tend his lands on a sharecropping basis. Within a few years he had a grist mill busy grinding what they produced.

Pursuing all these opportunities, establishing ties with local suppliers and clients and with business correspondents in the colonies and Britain, Gideon White was also beginning to create employment for the working population of Shelburne. His sea trades needed the help of sailors, fishermen, boat-builders, and rope-makers, all of whom were represented in the Shelburne population, and his agricultural interests supported several tenants, mostly black families, as well as millers and woodcutters. The trades White was taking up seemed precisely those that the town's founders had foreseen, and the success of more entrepreneurs of his kind was the likeliest way for

Shelburne to support the dependent workers who had come in thousands to the new city. Daniel Jessup, who might have been among the rioting ex-soldiers of early 1784, but who might also have provided barrels for White's cargoes in the following year, would have seen in the business of merchants like him the surest source of his own eventual security.

Shelburne was supporting Gideon White adequately if not yet richly. He began to acquire the public offices that befitted a man in his position: in 1785 he began to supervise Shelburne's shipping as an official of the Court of Vice-Admiralty. He had acquired a home, where in 1787 he was married to the sister of his friend and fellow merchant Nathaniel Whitworth. And gradually the prediction he had made for Shelburne in 1784 seemed to be borne out. "Be assured it is dam'd hard," he wrote to a friend in Jamaica who was considering a move to Nova Scotia, "though in the course of a few years it will be a very eligible situation."

Shelburne's trades were never conducted in isolation. Gideon White was as likely to complete a ship's cargo at Halifax or Passamaquoddy as in his own port, and both his correspondence and his own travels kept him closely informed of the progress of loyalists all over Nova Scotia.

From Annapolis Royal across the Nova Scotia peninsula, Thomas Millidge wrote almost hopefully to ask if the "most horrid accounts" he had heard of hardships at Shelburne were true. Millidge, the ex-major of a New Jersey loyalist corps, had his own tale of hardships to share, for after settling at Annapolis with his wife and five children he admitted, "the great expenses of my family and having a house to build for a covering for them has drained me entirely of cash." Fortunately other loyalists who had settled there could give happier accounts of that community.

The Annapolis district, long settled by French and then by

English, attracted many loyalists, who settled in the town of Annapolis Royal, in the valley behind it, and also at the other end of the basin, where a crowd of loyalists founded the town that became Digby. Brothers James and Stephen DeLancey, heirs of the wealthy New York family long prominent in colonial politics and each a high-ranking officer in a loyal regiment, chose Annapolis Royal as their new home. Acquiring large tracts of land in the vicinity, the brothers were soon joined by their brother-in-law, Major Thomas Barclay. Barclay had been one of Edward Winslow's companions in the exploration of New Brunswick, but despite his praise for the St. John, he joined his in-laws at Annapolis Royal and soon established an estate. Even Winslow, the great promoter of New Brunswick, had to admire. "In my tour through the peninsula, I have been astonished at observing the improvements lately made," he wrote during a visit to Annapolis, praising "the number of houses built and above all the increase of sawmills – no less than nine have been erected in a few months." Timothy Ruggles, another high-ranking loyalist with a ten-thousand-acre estate at nearby Wilmot, boasted of the neighbourhood's fruit and vegetable crops and was particularly pleased when a visitor "drank the best cider here he ever drank in his life."

Annapolis Royal, a busy town since Acadian days, was able to accommodate most of the loyalists landing there. Jacob Bailey, the local Anglican clergyman and himself a loyalist who had escaped from Maine in 1779, correctly surmised that "many of these families . . . will remove at some distance, upon the lands they have received." When they did take up lands, Annapolis's road and sea links helped them to acquire supplies and to market their produce, and the result was substantial growth in the Annapolis Valley.

The Annapolis Valley had also attracted groups of black loyalists. Thomas Peters, the big, forceful ex-sergeant of the Black

Pioneers, became their unofficial leader. Peters, by then in his mid-forties, laid out a black township near Digby. With another ex-sergeant, he petitioned Governor Parr, demanding that black loyalists be given the same acreages and supplies that white loyalists were receiving. Getting no satisfaction from Parr, Peters made the same demands and got the same response in New Brunswick. He would spend the next several years seeking justice for the black loyalists – and discovering that loyalist communities had little intention of granting equality to black fellow refugees.

From the mouth of the Sissiboo River, where loyalists were beginning the town called Weymouth, Gideon White received another report on the progress of farmers around Nova Scotia from a friend named Stephen Jones. "God knows I am from habit as little acquainted with settling new countries as any loyalist now in Nova Scotia," wrote Jones. "Nevertheless I have not been the most negligent. . . . I have cut down and cut up twenty-odd acres, half of which is fit for immediate improvement. I raised this summer two acres of wheat and as much of oats and potatoes, and in a few days I shall put into the ground four acres of wheat and rye."

White's most frequent letters came from the fellow officers and men of his old regiment who had settled in a group around Chedabucto Bay in northeastern Nova Scotia. These friends had expected White to accompany them there, and even when he was well established in Shelburne, they continued to send him enticing reports of the progress of towns called Guysborough and Manchester. Guysborough, actually the second loyalist town of that name in Nova Scotia, had succeeded an ill-advised attempt at settlement begun near Liverpool in October 1783 by twenty-five hundred refugees from New York. In May 1784, when a forest fire destroyed what little the settlers there had been able to build during the harsh winter, most of the settlers resolved to try their luck elsewhere, some at Passamaquoddy, some at Digby, some at the new Guysborough on Chedabucto Bay. Here, too, conditions were scarcely welcoming. Carolina plantation-owner Frederick Feltmate, who came to the Guysborough area with his regiment of South Carolina loyalists, soon described himself living "at Country Harbour in an unhappy situation, having had the misfortune of being frost-bitten and losing the use of his feet."

Manchester proved little more welcoming, and several of White's friends drifted off to other places, but years later some who had persevered still thought their Shelburne friend might be persuaded to join them. "As you complain so much of the badness of your lands, would it not be better for you to remove here?" asked Thomas Cutler. "I assure you this place is thriving fast, and we should be very happy to have you to add to our society, which God knows is none of the best."

The difficulties faced by the Chedabucto Bay communities also confronted those who hoped to create agricultural towns in the rugged interior of Nova Scotia, and few proved less fortunate than the men of Alexander MacDonald's battalion of Royal Highland Emigrants. Captain MacDonald had spent the whole of the war in Nova Scotia, and gradually he had become reconciled to a posting far from the front lines. When he brought his wife, Suzanna, and their children to be with him in Halifax, he wrote plaintively, "How long we are to be stationed in this place, God only knows," but when at the age of fifty he found himself about to become a father again, he laughingly reported, "the vast quantity of fish got in this place has a wonderful effect on old gray-haired people," and henceforth his views of Nova Scotia became more enthusiastic. He decided to sell his Staten Island property, and when his cousins Allan and Flora MacDonald and their grown sons were released from rebel custody, he urged them to join him, for "bad as this place was always reckoned, this is certainly the most peaceable place now in America." In 1778 all the MacDonalds were united at his new posting, Fort Edward, at Windsor, Nova Scotia.

But Flora MacDonald soon became ill and returned to Scotland, and in 1779 Alexander MacDonald suffered a shattering blow when his wife, Suzanna, died "and left me behind a miserable wretch with five children much at a loss which way to turn." Her death seems to have ended MacDonald's budding enthusiasm for Nova Scotia. In 1784 his commander, John Small, secured a tract of land not far from Windsor for the men of the regiment. MacDonald, however, was thinking of retirement, and in November 1784 he took ship for Britain, where he had not lived since the 1750s, politely leaving behind a notice in Halifax's *Nova Scotia Gazette* to thank the people of the colony for nearly ten years of hospitality. His cousin Allan also returned to Britain.

Their men, meanwhile, confronted harsh prospects on their new land. Evan McPhee, Finlay McMillan, and Christian Hennigar, who had been among MacDonald's original recruits for the regiment, reported years later that when they were discharged, "they were settled in the interior part of the country, that they had neither roads nor water carriage, that they underwent very great difficulties before they had any roads or horses, and were forced for several years to carry seed and potatoes on their backs through the woods with only the help of blazed trees." Most of the veterans recognized that farms could not prosper under these conditions. Many left to join larger Highland settlements elsewhere in Nova Scotia, and gradually the regimental settlement dwindled to a tiny remnant.

Other loyalists around Nova Scotia were also being forced to accept that simply clearing the forest would not render their land fertile. Jesse Hoyt, whose wife, Mary, had been brutally driven from their Connecticut home when he became a British naval pilot in 1776, was soon discouraged by the difficulty of farming at the little loyalist community on the Sissiboo River. Hoyt soon made a sensible analysis of how he could improve his prospects. "It is a very hard country to get a living in," he wrote late in 1787, "but I yet hope to see better times. Shipbuilding seems to be carrying on in all parts of the province and especially at this place. We have one fine ship nearly ready to launch, but as the season is so far advanced, we have concluded to let her stand in the stocks until the spring. But when launched I expect to have the command of her."

Jesse Hoyt's assessment predicted the future of the loyalists in Nova Scotia. Many of the farms the American loyalists founded so enthusiastically in 1783 proved unprofitable, and the amount of Nova Scotian land under cultivation actually declined for several years thereafter. Like Hoyt, adaptable loyalists were turning to other trades that were probably better suited to their own skills and were certainly better suited to Nova Scotia. As they made their adaptations, they consciously or unconsciously followed the example of the pre-loyalist settlers of Nova Scotia, the "bluenose" woodcutters, shipbuilders, and traders who had previously learned how to make the best of Nova Scotia's hard but not always unpromising conditions. In the small coves and towns of Nova Scotia, loyalists and bluenoses who were now neighbours began to work together.

This convergence of the two groups began despite many loyalists' disdain for the earlier inhabitants of Nova Scotia, which Edward Winslow had expressed in his vivid way when he claimed that the loyalists' efforts at Annapolis Royal had "excited something like emulation in the languid wretches who formerly inhabited the country". It continued despite lingering tensions between old settlers and loyalist refugees. Jacob Bailey thought his loyalist background was a "principal foundation of that aversion and illtreatment I receive from the former inhabitants", and the distinction between old settler and newcomer was maintained. Yet the loyalists beyond Shelburne gradually came to resemble their Nova Scotian neighbours. By their numbers as well as by their skills and their determination, the loyalists were making an indelible contribution to the colony, but in the process they were assimilated into the local population.

Even Shelburne, where the Nova Scotian loyalists seemed most likely to create something unique and new, could not remain immune to its surroundings. The founders of Shelburne had promised to build a loyalist capital for ten thousand people. Governor Parr had expected it to be the leading port of his colony, and even when Jacob Bailey happily described Annapolis Royal's remarkable progress, he had to admit, "we cannot pretend to vie with the mighty Shelburne." But soon Shelburne began to encounter renewed difficulties, against which Gideon White's mercantile successes were almost too small to be noticed.

The hundreds of Shelburne settlers who moved to Benjamin Marston's laboriously surveyed country lots to support their families by farming and stock-raising soon shared Jesse Hoyt's disillusionment, for they were attempting to cultivate a rocky and infertile woodland. Merely to cut a road across the peninsula to Annapolis Royal proved an enormous task, and the valuable expanses of wheat, oats, and hay that the Port Roseway Associates had foreseen never appeared. The number of customers for Gideon White's grist mill dwindled rapidly, and though in 1792 he could still say that there were some "loyal industrious husbandmen who have for nine years been contending with this unfriendly soil to gain a subsistence," no one would any longer speak of Shelburne as a farming centre to rival New York or Pennsylvania.

Shelburne's ambitious sea trades suffered as well. Gideon White was only one loyalist entrepreneur who had invested in whaling ventures there, but the whale population of the Nova

Scotia coast could only support a sizeable industry for a year or two, and the enormous costs of outfitting vessels that could follow the whales to Arctic and Antarctic waters far outstripped the means of the heavily burdened founders of the industry. The cod resource was more reliable, but every Nova Scotian port had a fishing fleet, and none had supported more than a few hundred people by that means.

Gideon White had already shown that Shelburne could be the home port of an enterprising merchant, but in aspiring to become a major port with a population of thousands, Shelburne was trying to take up Halifax's role on Halifax's own coast – and Halifax proved more resistant to the challenge than some confident loyalists had expected. Though Shelburne had attracted businessmen with skill and money, Halifax already had a corps of merchants who had learned the local conditions, developed their supply lines, and cultivated the support of the local officials. Many of them had prospered in 1783 by providing the goods the Crown had distributed to the refugee loyalists, and they intended to continue being the suppliers, traders, and moneylenders for all of the new and more populous Nova Scotia – including Shelburne.

As Halifax maintained its place as Nova Scotia's great trading port, many who had hoped to make Shelburne a great city, even Nova Scotia's capital, moved away to the older city to share in its commerce, to seek patronage from the officials there, or simply to enjoy the more glamorous society of the governor's circle and the military garrison, which in the 1780s and 1790s included two sons of George III. With its trading ambitions blocked, its industries struggling, and its agriculture almost extinct, Gideon White's town was proving unable to support and hold the mass of refugees who had depended on its prosperity to provide them with work. Shelburne was shrinking fast by the time the royal provisions ceased in 1787.

The black community of Shelburne and nearby Birchtown

remained only a few years longer, for Nova Scotia had proved a dubious refuge for black loyalists. Freedom had been the incentive that drew slaves to the British, and Nova Scotia undoubtedly offered them greater freedom than revolutionary America, but white attitudes and the difficulties of making a living in Nova Scotia conspired against the ambitions of the blacks of Shelburne. Expected to be useful and docile labourers who would demand little in return, the former slaves rarely received the supplies and land grants to which they were entitled. When Gideon White was striving to develop farms outside Shelburne, he found that landless black workmen were ready to become sharecropping labourers on his estates, and he probably thought that was the normal and proper place for them.

Both dire necessity and a determination to gain real freedom drove the black loyalists to protest. Thomas Peters managed to travel to Britain to present their grievances. In London his story brought a quick response. An anti-slavery society that had been promoting a colony in Sierra Leone as the best refuge for poor blacks living in Britain saw in Nova Scotia more settlers who might revitalize their struggling colony in Africa. Peters soon returned to Nova Scotia, carrying a promise of support for black loyalists who chose to go to Sierra Leone.

The response was astonishing. In their years in Nova Scotia, many blacks had bound themselves to long-term employment, and few who were still free to travel knew anything of Africa. The Nova Scotia government worked to dissuade the blacks from leaving, and the official efforts were supported by whites unwilling to lose their labourers and fearful that only the destitute and sickly would remain. Yet despite all disincentives, at least twelve hundred black loyalists, almost half of those who went to Nova Scotia in 1783, sailed from Halifax early in 1792.

Boston King and his wife, Violet, were among those recruited for the migration to Africa. King's decision swayed most of his Methodist congregation in Preston, Nova Scotia, to go with him, and they all arrived in newly founded Freetown, Sierra Leone, in March. Fever soon ravaged the new settlement. By mid-summer both Thomas Peters and Violet King were dead. The Nova Scotian loyalist community endured, however, to become one of the founding populations of modern Sierra Leone. Boston King, Carolina-slave-turned-Nova-Scotia-loyalist-settler, spent the last ten years of his life there, a hard-working, much-revered Methodist preacher in Africa.

Gideon White estimated that eight hundred left Shelburne and Birchtown in the exodus to Sierra Leone, "a serious loss but more so to me than anyone. I had eight Negro families as tenants, which had each a quantity of my land and allowed me rent. Each had his house, etc. These are all gone."

By 1792 it was clear that Shelburne's destiny was to be a small fishing port with a limited commerce in timber, ships, and local carrying trades. Like scores of other loyalist communities, Shelburne had been forced to accept and adapt to the realities of Nova Scotia, though the men who had originally founded it still sought scapegoats for its decline. When John Parr died in 1791 and was succeeded as governor by loyalist John Wentworth, James Dole, one of the original Port Roseway Associates, offered a vindictive epitaph. "Now the enemy of Shelburne is moved to his grave," he wrote to Gideon White, "and its friend to the helm." But Governor Wentworth did not move his capital from Halifax, and though he gave official appointments and favours to many loyalists, neither his patronage nor wartime prosperity in the 1790s could reverse Shelburne's decline, which Parr had not caused and Wentworth could not prevent.

By that time thousands of Shelburne's founders had drifted away to other parts of the Maritimes, to Upper Canada, or even to the United States. Abraham Van Buskirk, doctor, landowner, and half-pay colonel, stayed in Shelburne for several years, but he described himself as "reduced from affluence to poverty and distress". James Bruce, who had hoped Shelburne would replace his extensive plantations and colonial appointments in West Florida, described himself fallen "from a state of affluence and ease to very low circumstances – and that at a period of his life when he can have little hope of a sufficient length of days to enable him to retrieve himself."

Shelburne proved as hard on Mary Jessup as on anyone, despite the limited aspirations she and her husband had brought along as they followed the migration there. Daniel Jessup, whose wife thought he had been too old for his arduous military duties during the war, had flung himself into the no-less-demanding work of building a city and remaking a career. He saw the town established and witnessed its initial strivings, but no more, for just after New Year of 1786, Daniel Jessup "died suddenly, age fifty, and left a widow and four children almost destitute." With Shelburne's decline, the hope for something great and special for loyalism in Nova Scotia faded, and Mary Jessup's story faded along with it. She left no record of where she went, but she did not even stay long enough to register a claim to any of the now-vacant lots that Shelburnites had fought so hard to acquire in 1783.

As Shelburne became a fishing and trading village of a few hundred people, Gideon White stayed on. The town's great prospects were gone, and he admitted both his nostalgia for New England and his wife's occasional discontent. "Madam had rather be envied than pitied, and the fact is our situation here during the war is by no means the most eligible," he wrote in the 1790s, but he persevered with all the opportunities he could find.

As White became a judge and a member of the Nova Scotia legislature, he and his wife travelled regularly to Halifax, and occasionally to New England and to Britain. In the wartime conditions of the 1790s, he was concerned enough about his income to seek a new military appointment, but he and his wife managed to raise nine children in a handsome three-storey frame house that one of Shelburne's founders had built and abandoned in the town's first year, and eventually he saw his sons established in his own trade. Shelburne had not been able to become the loyal metropolis that the Port Roseway Associates had imagined in 1783, but by adapting his ambitions to the kind of opportunities Nova Scotia could provide, Gideon White and the other loyalists of 1783 who had been equally adaptable had recovered from the disasters that made them refugees, and learned to be Nova Scotians.

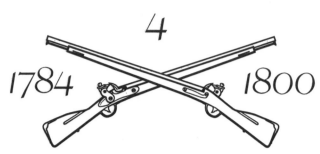

4

1784   1800

Samuel Farrington's Upper Canada

IN THE SPRING OF 1784, AT THE FORTIFIED POST OF Carleton Island near the Lake Ontario entrance to the St. Lawrence River, Samuel Farrington was completing the last months of almost a decade of service and preparing to rendezvous with the family members and other loyalists with whom he was about to found one of the new communities of Upper Canada.*

Born and raised in the Mohawk Valley of northwestern New York, Samuel Farrington had been young and single in 1775, and it was probably this freedom from responsibility to family or land that had enabled him to become an early recruit for the loyalist forces. Farrington had enlisted in Allan Maclean's Royal Highland Emigrants near the start of the conflict. He

---

* For decades before 1784, "Upper Canada" or, more commonly, "the upper country" was used to describe the territory up the St. Lawrence west of Montreal, though the colony of Upper Canada was not officially established or named until 1791.

may even have been one of Alexander MacDonald's eager volunteers of late 1774, and he served in Maclean's Canadian battalion of the Emigrants throughout the war. Finally he and the whole battalion had been gathered at Carleton Island late in 1783 to await an order to disband.

Samuel Farrington's father, Stephen, had evidently remained longer in the Mohawk Valley, tied to land and family. Of Stephen's wife, Charity, there is no record beyond her name, but there were two other children, Robert and Deborah, and there was certainly the house and barn, the livestock, and the twenty cleared and planted acres of the three-hundred-acre property that the Farringtons leased from one of the Mohawk Valley landlords.

Gradually, as the fighting spread, the revolution had threatened even older, settled loyalists, and Stephen Farrington had followed his son into uniform. By the time he enlisted, the most influential of the Mohawk Valley landlords were raising regiments of their own. Instead of joining Samuel in the Royal Highland Emigrants, Stephen Farrington, and eventually Robert as well, had enlisted in the King's Royal Regiment of New York, formed and led by the greatest landlord of the region, Sir John Johnson.

The three Farringtons in their two regiments had probably all served in the Upper Canadian posts that protected the Great Lakes waterway, but by the beginning of 1784 only Samuel remained in Upper Canada. The First Battalion of Johnson's regiment, in which both Stephen and Robert had served, had taken part in several raids and invasions into their home territories of northern New York, but halfway through the war it had been assigned to garrison duties around Montreal, where it was disbanded soon after the peace treaties were signed. By then Stephen Farrington had already left active service. During the war he had "lost the use of his legs by sickness" and had retired to the camp for refugee loyalists that

Governor Haldimand had authorized at Yamachiche, near Trois-Rivières.

Samuel Farrington, the first to enlist, had remained on duty. Confirmation of the peace had reached Quebec too late in 1783 to permit immediate disbanding of the loyalist regiments in the distant and contentious upper country of Canada. Farrington and the other men of Maclean's battalion of the Emigrants had remained on duty at Carleton Island. Meanwhile, the one remaining battalion of Johnson's King's Royal Regiment had been gathered nearby at Cataraqui. This new post was intended not only to replace Carleton Island but also to become – under the name of Kingston – the centre of the loyalist settlements along Lake Ontario's north shore. Another unit of Mohawk Valley loyalists, Major John Butler's Corps of Rangers, had mustered at Fort Niagara, its base of operations for most of the war. During the spring of 1784 Governor Haldimand ordered that all three corps, the last loyalist troops to be released from active service, should be formally disbanded on the same day, June 24, 1784.

By the spring of 1784 the Farrington family was scattered among all the places where the loyalists under Governor Haldimand's jurisdiction had gathered. Samuel was one of more than a thousand soldiers and officers, mostly from northern New York and adjacent territories, waiting in the Upper Canadian posts for their discharges. Robert was among the larger number of loyalist soldiers who had been discharged at the disbanding of the regiments in Lower Canada late in 1783. Most of these men had been permitted to spend the winter in their quarters at Montreal, at Quebec, and at several Richelieu River posts between Sorel and Lake Champlain. Stephen Farrington, disabled and ageing, had joined a still larger group, the civilian loyalists who had fled to Canada or followed soldiers north, and who probably included his daughter, Deborah. About three hundred civilians like them shared the camp at Yamachiche, where the local seigneur had been given royal funds to provide them with housing, schools, and a mill. Thousands more lived at Sorel and the other Richelieu River communities, close to garrisons where loyalist troops had served throughout the war, and a substantial number had settled in Montreal. Some of the civilians had been in Canada for several years, often as dependents of soldiers in the loyalist corps, while others had come across the border since the peace. One large group had come even further: by sea from New York City.

Some of the New York City loyalists simply considered Montreal a better business prospect than the new settlements in the Maritimes. William Mooney, for instance, had been a butcher in New York before and during the war, and he soon re-established his trade in Montreal. The leaders of the seaborne migration, however, had set their sights on Upper Canada. One of them, Peter Van Alstine of Albany, had spent part of the war in Canada and had relatives in Johnson's King's Royal Regiment. The other leader, a Mohawk Valley tanner named Michael Grass, had known Cataraqui, which was soon to be Kingston, when the French had had a base there and called it Fort Frontenac. Grass said he had been impressed by the lands around the fort while a prisoner of the French during the Seven Years War. When New York City was being evacuated in 1783, he recruited several hundred loyalists and won General Carleton's support for a migration "to the District of Frontenac in the Province of Canada". Grass, Van Alstine, and about thirteen hundred loyalists from New York City arrived in Canada in the summer and fall of 1783, to discover that the plan for settling Upper Canada that they thought was their own had become official policy for the growing number of loyalists already in Canada.

As regiments were disbanded and civilian loyalists reached Canada in small groups or large associations, the loyalist population in Lower Canada grew toward ten thousand. Refugees rather than settlers, they remained without permanent homes through 1783, while Haldimand's officials explored the upper country and awaited final confirmation of the peace. The enthusiastic reports he had received about the upper country during 1783 convinced Haldimand that the loyalists' future lay there, and during the winter of 1783-84 royal officials worked to persuade the loyalists to move up the St. Lawrence in the spring. At the same time, however, resistance to the upper country developed among the loyalists in Lower Canada.

At first doubts about the governor's plan grew out of a simple fear of the unknown. In February 1784, after the people of the Yamachiche refugee camp had spent several months discussing the prospect of Upper Canada, Josiah Cass, their school-teacher, informed the governor that there were "as yet but about twelve or fifteen families that seem anyways inclined that way." The Yamachiche refugees stressed the distance they would have to travel and the "bad passes" that impeded navigation up the St. Lawrence, but they also underlined their need for a guarantee of assistance. As Cass put it, "I am very confident that a considerable number of good people here would agree to go to Cataraqui if there was encouragement held out to them equal to the undertaking."

Those who feared Cataraqui's remoteness seem to have been converted or at least silenced, as government officials and loyalists who had seen the upcountry lands stressed their quality and the relative ease of communication with Montreal. The "encouragement" Cass had mentioned was a more serious problem. Both the loyalists and the officials knew Cass was right to insist that "a people who have lost their all, destitute of cattle, of farming tools or money to purchase them" would not be able to develop new lands or even to feed themselves during the initial work of building and clearing. Like the loyalists of Nova Scotia and New Brunswick, those going to Upper Canada could not succeed without a steady supply of equipment and provisions over several years. Haldimand recognized the need for such aid. He intended to grant it, but at the time of Cass's letter he had received no authorization to do so, and he cautiously refused to commit the British government to projects it might not complete. Finally, in March 1784, due authorization arrived from Britain. Assurances of aid were quickly circulated among the refugees, and almost at once the number of volunteers for Upper Canada rose reassuringly.

In the interim, however, another concern about Upper Canada had surfaced, one that focussed on the loyalists' title to the lands on which they would live. Governor Haldimand had favoured the settlement of the upper country partly as a way to maintain distance and reduce friction between the loyalists and the French *Canadiens*, but all of Upper and Lower Canada remained part of the one colony of Quebec, and British rule had reaffirmed that the seigneurial tenure that had been the basis of landholding in New France would remain the law of the land. Landlord-and-tenant relationships were hardly unfamiliar to the loyalists in Canada: the Johnsons, the Butlers, and many other loyalist leaders had managed great estates in the Mohawk Valley, and most of the men who followed them to Canada had, like the Farringtons, been their tenants. Britain's promises to the American loyalists, however, entitled each of them to land of his own, and this legal contradiction had forced Haldimand to work out a compromise. There would be seigneuries in the upper country, he decided, but no landlords. Or, rather, the king would be the loyalists' landlord, creating a symbolic tenancy to the Crown that would preserve the forms of Canadian law without restricting any loyalist's use of his land.

This plan to create seigneuries-without-seigneurs, though ingenious, was complicated. Since it made no one a landlord, it had few enthusiastic advocates, and loyalists who were already uncertain about going into the wilderness that was being recommended to them soon expressed doubts about a project that seemed about to make them tenants in a foreign and seemingly feudal fashion, subjects to a distant king who could perhaps demand not only allegiance but personal subservience. A fear began to grow that the military commanders who had ruled the loyalist soldiers were ready and willing to exercise equal power over the loyalists who became civilian settlers.

Doubts about Upper Canada encouraged the appearance of rival plans for the loyalists. Some of the loyalists who had spent most of the war years in Lower Canada were unwilling to be uprooted, and nearly eight hundred of them acquired property around the garrison towns of Sorel, Chambly, and Fort St-Jean on the Richelieu River. Owners of seigneuries also courted some refugees. They had begun to see the loyalists as potentially valuable tenants, and they offered seigneurial lots as an alternative to land in the wilderness. Few seigneurs attracted many tenants, however, if only because none of them could match the Crown's offer of both land and aid. Other loyalists, preferring sea-coast homes to ones far inland, sought land on the Gaspé peninsula, and eventually three hundred loyalists sailed from Quebec to found small English-speaking towns at Chaleur Bay and Gaspé. A more distant alternative was promoted by Abraham Cuyler, a loyalist from Albany, New York, who used political influence in Britain to have Cape Breton Island removed from the Nova Scotian government and established as a separate colony. Cuyler claimed that three thousand loyalists would join him from Lower Canada, but barely one hundred and fifty actually sailed in 1784.

Despite his enthusiasm for Upper Canada, Governor Haldimand had encouraged the Gaspé proposal and tolerated those of Cuyler and the seigneurs. He was less tolerant of another group, principally Vermont loyalists and veterans of Jessup's Rangers, who had settled in the border country east of Lake Champlain. The land around Lake Missisquoi was good, but

Haldimand feared that loyalists there would be too close to the United States. If there were not conflict between them, there would be smuggling instead, and Haldimand wanted neither. The promoters of the Missisquoi venture were not cowed, however, and they declared they were determined "not to move off from that land for the general's order or any other, nor to be drove off except by a superior force, for by Lord North's declaration they had a right to settle on any of the King's land they should choose." Despite Haldimand's annoyance, a few managed to settle in this territory, though it would not be until after 1791 that their settlements were officially recognized and organized into the Eastern Townships.

Though Montreal, the Richelieu towns, Gaspé, and Missisquoi together had persuaded a substantial number of loyalists to remain in Lower Canada, the main body of refugees was looking toward the western townships, the lands that Haldimand's surveyors had prepared along the upper St. Lawrence and Lake Ontario. Against the Missisquoi settlers' rumours and allegations, the royal officials had shown that the settlements around Cataraqui would actually have easier access to Montreal than Missisquoi would, that there was nothing sinister in the complicated land-tenure system, and that settlers going to Upper Canada would have active assistance from the Crown during the pioneering years. Declaring that he had "no predilection for Cataraqui but from his wish to establish permanent and happy settlements," Haldimand stressed again that no better site for loyalist settlement existed, and he was supported by the most influential loyalist leaders. Edward Jessup, in whose corps of rangers most of the Missisquoi group had served, reported that he himself was "every day more convinced" that the loyalists should settle in regimental groups, officers and men together, and that the place to do so was Upper Canada. Since regimental loyalties provided the only communities most

of the loyalists still had, the sense that the regiments should settle in Upper Canada helped to commit many waverers to the
new territories.

In May 1784, as soon as the river began to clear of ice, at
least three thousand loyalists gathered at the town of Lachine,
at the foot of the rapids just west of Montreal. At Lachine, Captain Jacob Maurer had been busy all winter, chartering river
boats normally used by fur-traders, requisitioning tents and
cloth, ordering thousands of hoes and axes from the military
smiths, and stockpiling provisions and seed. With these preparations, the westward movement proceeded quickly. Despite
the "confused and crowded manner" of the gathering at
Lachine, Maurer was able to begin sending the loyalists upriver
before the end of May. Flotillas of a dozen boats began departing, with each boat carrying four or five families, a ton or two of
provisions and household effects, and a crew of five experienced boatmen. By the end of June, Maurer could report in
relief that the last of his charges had gone from Lachine. The
loyalist exodus from Lower to Upper Canada had begun.

As the flotillas of loyalists worked their way up the turbulent
St. Lawrence, Samuel Farrington confirmed his own settlement
plans at the garrison post on Carleton Island. His choice to stay
in Upper Canada had been influenced as much by associations
he had formed in his Mohawk Valley youth as by his years of
military service. Rejecting the choice made by most of his fellow soldiers, Farrington was following the lead of an old
Mohawk Valley acquaintance, one who was now about to
acquire a major influence on the future of the Farrington family.

Forty-one-year-old Archibald MacDonell was a junior
member of a large Highland clan that had migrated en masse to
northern New York shortly before the revolution to acquire
vast tracts of Mohawk Valley land from the Johnson family. In
1776 many of the MacDonells received commissions in Sir
John Johnson's King's Royal Regiment, but for some reason

Archibald MacDonell did not, even after accompanying John-son on his retreat from the Mohawk Valley to Montreal. Instead, MacDonell became an officer in Maclean's Royal Highland Emigrants and served with them throughout the war.

As an American settler, Archibald MacDonell was slightly unusual in Maclean's regiment, a corps that had drawn most of its officers from among Highlanders in Canada or from Maclean's kinsmen in Scotland. MacDonell became more unusual still in 1784, for as most of the officers of the Emigrants prepared to return to homes in Lower Canada or in Scotland, Archibald MacDonell was one of only three Emigrants officers, all lieutenants with a Mohawk Valley background, who chose to settle in Upper Canada.

By June 24, 1784, when Major John Adolphus Harris mus-tered the Royal Highland Emigrants at Carleton Island and for-mally disbanded the battalion, it was clear that the officers' nearly unanimous decision to leave Upper Canada at the end of their duty would greatly influence the choices made by the five hundred men being freed from military service along with them. In all the new Upper Canadian settlements, the loyalists were settling in a military fashion, with former officers proceed-ing at the head of each group, and providing the money, author-ity, and leadership the new communities would need. Without such leadership, wilderness settlement seemed daunting to all but a few, and as the officers of the Emigrants chose to depart, so did the ordinary soldiers. Some soldiers would attach them-selves to communities founded by groups from other regiments – the Farringtons were not the only family with members in more than one loyalist corps – but the only soldiers from the Emigrants who settled as a group were those who cohered around Archibald MacDonell. Instead of five hundred men fol-lowing the officers of the Emigrants, only about fifty followed Lieutenant MacDonell to attempt a settlement in the new Upper Canadian townships. One of these followers was Samuel

Farrington, who may have served under MacDonell in the regiment, but who surely knew him as part of the large, prosperous, and respected MacDonell clan of the Mohawk Valley.

Samuel Farrington's decision to follow MacDonell's lead proved decisive for all of his family. His father and brother decided to forgo their opportunity to settle with their former comrades of Johnson's King's Royal Regiment in order to settle with Samuel, and they waited in Lower Canada to hear of his location while the main migration set off up the St. Lawrence.

Events now moved quickly in Upper Canada. As regiments were disbanded and flotillas of civilians reached Lake Ontario on their upriver migration, the lands that had been roughly surveyed the previous fall were allocated. Archibald MacDonell's party, along with an assortment of discharged soldiers who had joined the loyalists from several British regiments and one German regiment, received their land in what was then simply called Township Number Five west of Cataraqui, but which its residents would soon call Marysburgh. By the seventh of July 1784, three hundred loyalists and soldiers had landed there, and in a month surveyor John Collins could report that he had "completed the survey and settlement of the Fifth Township, situated on the peninsula between Lake Ontario and the Bay of Quinte."

Unlike most of the townships occupied that year, Marysburgh was not a simple rectangle of roughly one hundred square miles but a long, narrow strip of high land on the Quinte Peninsula, bordered to the south by Lake Ontario and looking north across a small channel to Peter Van Alstine's Township Number Four, the future Adolphustown. Marysburgh was smaller and less regular than most of the townships, and it was perhaps for that reason that Collins had been able to survey it so rapidly. Collins went on to report that each man had "taken the oaths agreeable to the King's Instructions, signed the book, received his certificate, and is now in possession of his land, with which I am persuaded they will be well pleased, as the lands in general appear to be of good quality."

Samuel Farrington, one of those who had sworn, signed, and received his land, may have been expecting that his family would soon be joining him, but he was still the only Farrington there in October 1784 when a muster of Marysburgh settlers was taken. His father, brother, and sister probably came up from Lower Canada to join him in the spring of 1785. As they in their turn arrived at Lachine to find passage in the big multi-oared boats, Robert, Deborah, and Stephen Farrington became part of a second migration that ensured that the foothold gained in 1784 would be maintained and enlarged. Women, children, and dependents of the first settlers now felt confident enough to venture upriver toward the pioneer communities. John Stuart, once a missionary to the Six Nations Confederacy in New York and since 1784 the Church of England minister in the Cataraqui townsite that would soon be Kingston, reported happily on the "new accessions of strength" arriving every day, and he guessed that by the summer of 1785 there were five thousand settlers in the lakefront townships alone.

As they travelled up the rapids of the St. Lawrence, a jour-ney John Stuart was already describing as "easy and frequent" just a year after the loyalists' first venture, the three Farringtons had a chance to observe the progress the loyalist settlements had made in one year. On the north bank of the St. Lawrence, eight 100-square-mile townships had been surveyed in 1783 and populated by the boat flotillas of 1784. The soldiers and families of the King's Royal Regiment had settled the first five of these townships, so as they moved past the newly established townsites at Cornwall, Williamstown, and Lancaster, and past the clearings being opened all along the river front, Robert and Stephen Farrington should have seen many of their fellow vet-erans from Johnson's corps, now settled in communities care-fully apportioned into Catholic and Presbyterian sections.

Johnson himself, an Anglican, lived with neither group, having returned to live in Montreal after seeing his troops settled.

Further upriver, the travellers ascended more series of rapids, each of which obliged the passengers to climb ashore while the heavy boat was towed with ropes. Here Vermont and Connecticut loyalists led by Edward Jessup were settling three riverfront townships in the region where Brockville and Prescott would soon be founded. Surveyor John Collins, who made the upriver voyage in 1785, reported that these loyalists appeared well satisfied, having "made much greater improvements than could be expected in so short a time. They have all comfortable houses and their cleared fields sown." Collins had to admit, however, that here where the maps showed neat rows of lots running twelve miles back from the river, settlement was still in reality no more than a strip of clearings along the shore.

Where the river passed among the Thousand Islands, the travellers encountered a break in settlement where the surveyors had judged the rugged, rocky ground too barren for immediate occupancy. Then the river boat, which was probably hauling freight and correspondence as well as passengers, moved into Lake Ontario and reached Cataraqui.

Kingston township – Cataraqui Number One in the dry official parlance – had been granted to Michael Grass's party of New Yorkers, who with the support of additional settlers had already established farm lots on five rows of property running far into the countryside. The little town that was growing into Kingston was an even more impressive achievement. Around the permanently garrisoned post of Fort Cataraqui, more than two hundred town lots had been granted, and framed houses, "some of them very elegant", were rapidly giving form to the town plan. Wharves and warehouses proliferated along the shore to serve the growing trade that linked Kingston downriver to Montreal and along the lake to Niagara and the west. A sawmill and a grist mill, both built by the Crown to assist the loyalists, were active. "We are a poor, happy people, industrious beyond example," wrote the Reverend Mr. Stuart. "Cataraqui will certainly be the capital of all the new settlements and is very conveniently located."

At Kingston, already home port to a growing fleet of lake vessels, the Farringtons probably exchanged their river boat for a sailing craft and completed their journey with a short voyage west to Marysburgh. Skirting the edge of another series of small lakeshore townships, passing the newest public sawmill at Millhaven, and finally entering Quinte Bay, they landed at Marysburgh to greet their son and brother on the lands he had acquired for them a year earlier.

In their ten-day or two-week voyage from Lachine to Marysburgh, the Farringtons had seen at close hand the main line of loyalist settlement stretched out over one hundred and fifty miles of the river front and the lakeshore, but there were several thriving centres of loyalist settlement which they did not visit. Well to the west of them, along the west bank of the Niagara River, the officers and men of Butler's Rangers had since 1780 been building homes and growing crops, and in 1784 they had formally established the town of Butlersbury, soon to be Newark and eventually Niagara-on-the-Lake. A few men from Butler's Rangers had also made a tentative settlement at the other end of Lake Erie, taking lands opposite Fort Detroit, another place of wartime service now in American territory. But the largest of the mass migrations on Lake Erie during the summer and fall of 1784 had involved not John Butler's Rangers but their wartime allies of the Six Nations Confederacy.

Moving from their homelands along the south side of Lake Ontario had been profoundly difficult for the people of the Six Nations after they found to their horror that the United States had laid claim to all the Iroquois land and that Britain had let the claim go unchallenged. One British Indian agent, Daniel Claus, expressed some sense of the disturbance that exile caused when he described the Iroquois's sense of themselves as "a people who lived at their ease on a rich tract of country left them and possessed by their ancestors from time immemorial." Claus went on to explain how the Confederacy felt itself to be rooted in the soil of its territory. "By the natural monuments of that country, such as rivers, woods, hills and rocks in its environs, they chiefly preserve the thread of the general history of their race." Any Iroquois could identify in his homeland not only his ancestors' burial places, but also the place where Dekaniwideh had founded the Confederacy and delivered its laws hundreds of years before.

The land on the other side of the lakes, by comparison, was "a country inhabited by a nation they do not understand", the alien Mississauga Indians, and Claus reported that the Iroquois had "a contemptible opinion" of it all. Nevertheless the exile could not be avoided. Thayendanegea, or Joseph Brant, led about eighteen hundred of his followers to a vast tract of property along the Grand River in 1784, while Deserontyon, another war leader, and a small group of Mohawks acquired a township-sized reservation on the Bay of Quinte just west of Marysburgh.

The settlement of these Iroquois fragments in Upper Canada confirmed the wartime shattering of the Six Nations Confederacy, for the largest part of the Iroquois population had remained in New York State to make treaties with the new American authorities. Despite Brant's efforts in the following years to weld the Six Nations and the other tribes of the Great Lakes into a larger confederacy that could withstand white encroachment and adopt the best of the white man's ways, the now scattered holdings of his people were never successfully reassembled, though the groups that had made the difficult trek into Upper Canada were able to rebuild much of the traditional culture and society of their people and to invest new landmarks with the significance of the abandoned ones.

At Marysburgh, the newly arrived Farringtons found that Samuel Farrington had brought them to a community preparing to thrive. The founding population of three hundred had not increased, for many single men had drifted away, some to Kingston, some to Niagara, and some right out of Upper Canada. Despite these losses, Marysburgh became a more balanced community, as women and children joined the men who had taken land in 1784. In 1787 there were still just three hundred settlers, but by then the number of women had grown to fifty and there were eighty-four children. As proof of the ferocious activity of the settlers, nearly eighty houses had been built and nearly six hundred acres of rich, fertile land was ready for planting. Mills for timber and grain were operating nearby, and regular lake traffic linked the rural community to the commerce of Kingston. John Stuart came occasionally to preach, marry, and baptize, and in the following year there would be a Methodist preacher and schoolteacher at nearby Adolphustown.

For the Farringtons the great benefits of Marysburgh were security after a decade of disruption – and land. Instead of twenty arable acres rented from one of the Mohawk Valley landlords, the four Farringtons, as loyalists and soldiers, had become the proprietors of several hundred acres of land. They were no longer tenants, except in a theoretical sense, to the king as their seigneurial landlord. And their land was as favoured, for lake frontage, stream water, and sod quality, as anyone's, because in 1784 Governor Haldimand had ordered that, while officers were entitled to more land than private soldiers, they were not to pre-empt the most advantageous properties. Everyone participated in the distribution, and if the wealthy or powerful wanted a specific lot, they had to attempt to buy it from the grantee. On these terms, the three hundred settlers of Marysburgh had become the proprietors of twenty-five thousand acres of land by 1787.

Despite the fairness of the original land distribution, Marysburgh and the other rural townships that were growing along with it remained rather traditional societies with a strong sense of social hierarchy. Almost everywhere in Upper Canada, former military officers, who had been landlords and leaders in the Thirteen Colonies, had retained their elite status even as their tenants and soldiers became landowners beside them. At Marysburgh, Samuel Farrington's former Mohawk Valley neighbour and regimental officer, Archibald MacDonell, was no exception, and events in his community during its first months had proven how important such leadership was.

All the Upper Canadian loyalists of 1784 had settled on their lands too late in the year to raise crops, and they had depended heavily on provisions shipped up from Montreal for them. Samuel Farrington and the other Marysburgh pioneers, however, had found that their location exposed them to particular difficulties: frequently provisions ran out before they reached the little community at the western end of the supply line that ran from Lachine via Kingston. The men turned to MacDonell, who, with his settlement close to collapse, wrote urgently to Sir John Johnson, his former Mohawk Valley patron, who was now living in Montreal. Johnson passed the request for aid to Governor Haldimand, adding his own warning that "if their wants are not attended to, the settlements will be for the greatest part broken up." Haldimand personally ordered his officials to see Marysburgh's plight remedied. Provisions sufficient to see the settlers through the winter were distributed, and the following spring Farrington and the others were able to plant their first crops and bring their families to join them.

MacDonell played down his own influence in this crisis,

explaining that he took the initiative on the men's behalf because "I am settled among them and you were pleased to direct me to hear their representations." In fact his success in exploiting the networks of influence on his men's behalf had been crucial to Marysburgh's survival. This kind of ability, used in many smaller ways throughout the loyalists' first years in Upper Canada, inevitably enhanced the prestige and authority not only of MacDonell but of all the ex-officers who were now unofficial "heads of townships". MacDonell, who in 1784 was merely the unofficial (but very effective) representative of the township settlers, was soon a magistrate, a member of the board that issued land grants, and the social leader who invited the people of Marysburgh into his home when John Stuart came to preach.

The role of men like Archibald MacDonell was economic as well. By 1787 Marysburgh's most important assets were the planted acres and the livestock that the settlers were tending, for Crown rations were ending, and the loyalist townships would have to become self-supporting. Marysburgh's farmers had easy access to grist mills and potash works, the first vital industries of the agricultural society, but they needed trade as well. MacDonell, who owned a town house in Kingston and had probably been able to invest in lake vessels as well, became an important intermediary between his farmers at Marysburgh and the merchants of Kingston, particularly one who was becoming increasingly prominent in Upper Canadian affairs, Richard Cartwright.

The well-educated son of a leading Albany merchant, Cartwright had headed for Canada as a loyalist in 1777. His father's connections had enabled the son to travel north comfortably and peaceably, protected by a passport from the Albany committee of safety, and Cartwright was equally successful in finding his way in Canadian society. After a stint of military service, he turned to trade, and for the rest of the war he was an upcountry merchant of a familiar kind, shipping goods from Montreal to supply the Great Lakes garrisons and fur-traders, and sending furs back in exchange. These were the long-established trades of the "empire of the St. Lawrence", and at first Cartwright seemed no more than another apprentice to a trade that went back more than a century. In 1784, however, Cartwright proved himself the most adept at transforming his business to accommodate the loyalist farmers who were settling east and west of his new headquarters at Kingston and around the base of his partner, Robert Hamilton, on the Niagara River.

Soon Cartwright and Hamilton were supplementing their fur-trade activities and military provisioning by selling food, clothing, housewares, and rum to the loyalists, and taking wheat, corn, potash, and pork in return, shipping some to Montreal and selling the rest to their old clients in the fur-trade posts and military garrisons. In a few years Cartwright had become the owner of a fleet of lake traders, proprietor of several mills, and the major exporter of Upper Canadian produce. He dealt regularly with Archibald MacDonell, his Kingston neighbour, fellow magistrate, and land-board colleague, and almost certainly it was Cartwright who purchased, milled, packed, and shipped much of the Farrington family's farm produce.

Marysburgh's new farms were already producing saleable crops in a small way by 1787, and as more land was put to use, its production would increase, despite a drought and crop failure in 1788 that temporarily made the loyalists once more dependent on Crown rations. Marysburgh was going to remain a small rural community, with few amenities beyond a church and a mill, but even by 1787 its farmers had grasped where their opportunities lay. Richard Cartwright's most marketable export after wheat was salt pork, and in 1787 the three hundred people of Marysburgh were already the proprietors of no less than two hundred and nineteen pigs.

The successful linking of small loyalist communities like the

Farringtons' Marysburgh to the lively trade of Kingston and the larger Great Lakes trading system underpinned the rapid rise of Upper Canada. More than any of the other loyalist communities in British America, Upper Canada prospered in its early years, and prosperity established it as a landed, agricultural society where merchants and proprietors with wealth, education, and social connections successfully acquired the positions of leadership that they had previously had from military command and from their status as landlords in the Thirteen Colonies. The Farringtons had become landowners rather than tenants, but they still looked up to the social and economic leadership of men like MacDonell and Cartwright, just as they had done in the Mohawk Valley before the revolution.

In 1785 Archibald MacDonell had been one of a group of ex-officers who petitioned the government of Quebec to make the Upper Canadian townships self-governing and to abolish the curious technicalities of landholding that the rule of seigneurial tenure required. It was a petition that seemed democratic in philosophy and American in origin, but the influence of men like MacDonell throughout Upper Canada ensured that should the new settlements take charge of their own affairs, these men would be the ones to control any new levers of power that were created. Despite hints of opposition to military officers who sought to retain "the shadow of former power", the influence of the former officers who had become leaders of the new communities was real, and most of it was tolerated. Given the prosperity and security that Upper Canada was providing, there was little reason for the Farringtons and other humble exiles of limited expectations to object.

Ironically, the only challenge to the authority of the re-established elite over the comfortable prosperity of loyalist Upper Canada came from the speed with which the new communities' success attracted further waves of settlement. The fewer than ten thousand loyalist refugees who had settled in

Upper Canada in the first years were not long to be left alone. By 1791 there may have been thirty thousand people living in Upper Canada, and Upper Canada was being transformed to accommodate them.

Some of the new immigrants were loyalists from Nova Scotia or New Brunswick, settlers who had become discouraged at Shelburne or the St. John River. They migrated to Upper Canada in numbers large enough to provoke Edward Winslow to complain that "Niagara fever" was tearing away the settlers of his colony. There were also American loyalists, who had supported the British cause during the revolution but had stayed for several years in the United States: typical of these was a former sergeant in a loyalist cavalry regiment, John May, who finally immigrated to Upper Canada in 1792 but was able to make a successful claim for land as a loyalist. Another group who arrived in Upper Canada at about the same time honestly admitted that during the war they had "stood by their property and wished to keep themselves neutral as much as possible." Such neutrality was not always well received in the United States; sanctions directed against the Pennsylvania Mennonites for their desire to avoid civic office and military duty helped to create the Mennonite migration into Upper Canada in the 1790s.

Many of the newcomers to Upper Canada had no strong loyalist or anti-loyalist sentiments. They were attracted simply by the settlement prospects of Upper Canada. These were the largest group, and as they poured into Upper Canada, the original townships multiplied. Townships like Marysburgh did not always grow in population, for they remained rural communities, and most of their arable land had been claimed. Instead, surveyors and land boards were kept busy laying out and granting new townships. As the Niagara peninsula, the Kingston–Bay of Quinte shore, and the lands along the St. Lawrence River were allocated and filled, settlers moved rapidly into new areas: the harbours and inlets of Lake Ontario and Lake Erie, the shores of navigable rivers from the Rideau in the east to the Thames in the distant west, and anywhere that settlement prospects seemed good.

In 1791 the sheer size of the Upper Canadian population brought about the fulfilment of the first settlers' desire to be separated from Lower Canada. That year a revision of the colonial constitution created Upper Canada as a colony in its own right. The new Lieutenant-Governor of Upper Canada, John Graves Simcoe, was not a loyalist but a British officer. He had commanded loyalist troops in the Revolutionary War, and he soon brought some of his former officers from New Brunswick to join him, but his plans for Upper Canada far outstripped those of the small loyalist society founded in 1784.

Simcoe was determined to develop and govern the whole territory of Upper Canada, not just the parts of it pioneered by the loyalists. Less than a decade after the loyalists had debated whether Kingston was too remote to be successfully settled, Simcoe was planning to make his capital at London in the far-off interior of western Upper Canada. While the loyalists had depended on water travel and had valued river- or lake-frontage above all, Simcoe planned major highways to run hundreds of miles through the Upper Canadian woods. Determined, like the loyalists, to build a better society than the American one by working from British models of government and society, Simcoe believed that his colony would be successful enough to command the allegiance even of former rebels. Richard Cartwright was one of several loyalists to express dismay at finding former enemies settling in what he had always seen as a special refuge for the loyal victims of the revolution, but his protests failed to shake the governor's confidence. Loyalists and late loyalists could claim special respect, but anyone willing to swear an oath of allegiance could acquire land in Simcoe's Upper Canada.

After 1792 the loyalists were not so much overruled as out-numbered, for Upper Canada had outgrown them. New leaders were as likely to come from recent immigrants or the governor's circle of friends and associates as from the small original elite of the loyalists. There were still places for capable and well-connected loyalists, of course. In 1792 Richard Cartwright was appointed to Simcoe's Legislative Council, and Archibald MacDonell continued to acquire titles of responsibility and respect. When his township of Marysburgh was incorporated into the newly created county of Prince Edward, the former lieutenant was soon able to style himself Colonel MacDonell of the Prince Edward County Regiment of Militia. But loyalists no longer dominated the running of Upper Canada. With Simcoe's coming, the colony had ceased to be the exclusive domain of the refugee loyalists.

Nevertheless, Upper Canada continued to build on founda-tions the loyalists had laid in 1784. All of the astonishing acre-ages of land granted in Upper Canada after 1792 were divided and subdivided into simple rectangular township grids in rows called concessions, just as Haldimand's surveyors had esta-blished in 1783, and the mix of agriculture, industry, and com-merce that the Farringtons, MacDonells, and Cartwrights had created in those townships during the 1780s became Upper Canada's hallmark throughout its nineteenth-century growth.

If a uniquely loyalist Upper Canada had been overwhelmed by Simcoe's plans and the sheer weight of numbers, Samuel Farrington was probably not much dismayed, for the secure and probably quietly prosperous life he had built since 1784 was barely changed. After 1791 his titular subservience to George III as seigneur of Marysburgh ended when freehold land tenure replaced the conventions of seigneurial law, but the settlers of Upper Canada in 1784 had never doubted that their land was their own. Farrington acquired a vote for Upper Canada's new Legislative Assembly, but he and his neighbours continued to elect leaders much like those they had followed since 1783, and he and his brother were almost certainly mustered in Colonel MacDonell's militia regiment.

For Samuel Farrington, the personal consequences of 1792 outweighed the political changes heralded by the arrival of John Graves Simcoe. The life of Marysburgh, one of the small, productive agricultural communities that had sprouted around the busy town of Kingston, went on, not much affected by the ceaseless expansion of the colony of Upper Canada. But that year, with his personal estate secured by almost a decade of clearing and planting on his new land, Samuel Farrington was able to seal his status as an adult and a landholder. In 1792 he married Katherine Brown, a more recent arrival in Marysburgh, and they began the family of four sons who would ensure that one tiny and far-from-famous loyalist estate would survive and prosper in Upper Canada.

5

Taking Root

AFTER ALL THE FIGHTING ENDED, SAMUEL CURWEN went back to Salem, Massachusetts.

The now elderly gentleman who had left Salem in 1775, disgusted by the collapse of peace and order there, had spent the war years in London, but he never grew fond of Britain, and though he moved in the same social circles as many of the leading loyalists there, he acquired no ideological fervour against the revolution. In the fall of 1784, when the new United States seemed as likely to keep Salem in peace and order as the old Colony of Massachusetts had done, Samuel Curwen took ship and returned to his home.

Salem did prove orderly, and the man once harassed and threatened as a "tory" found himself tolerantly received, but this return home proved brief. Discovering that, after their long separation, he and his wife had grown totally estranged, Curwen returned to Britain, and only after learning that she had died did he return to live permanently in Salem. Without her, Salem offered all the peace and order Curwen desired, and he lived there until his death in 1802, aged eighty-seven.

Samuel Curwen's unopposed return to his home, an experience so contrary to that of all the loyalists who had been abused, beaten, shot at, and driven into exile in 1783, marked a sudden change in the Americans' attitude to their defeated fellows. In 1783 victory had unleashed a paroxysm of triumphant violence against the loyalists, and Congress's treaty commitment to protect loyalists and their property had been ignored in every state. This implacable hostility certainly convinced some wavering loyalists to choose the risks of Canada over the brutality and persecution of the successful revolutionaries.

Yet that hostility – the tyranny of the majority that the loyalists had always seen at work in the revolution – proved surprisingly short-lived. Many of the wealthy, powerful, and influential leaders of the American struggle, though committed to replacing imperial authority with American self-rule, had always been conservative revolutionaries, with no patience for the tyranny of the majority or anything like egalitarian democracy. In the midst of the revolution against British authority, John Adams had asserted, in a phrase Edward Winslow might have applauded, that "there must be a decency, and respect, and veneration introduced for persons of authority of every rank, or we are undone." After the war, Adams was one of the political leaders who began to link respect for authority with respect for the law, and as the initial anti-loyalist hysteria faded, these Americans began to argue that decency and the honour of the republic required that the national treaty obligation to the loyalists take precedence over vindictive anti-loyalist state laws.

A hard practical spur also moved the United States along the path of virtue. When the United States had ignored its treaty obligations, Britain had refused to evacuate its long

chain of military posts on the American territory bordering
Canada. As long as forts like Niagara, Detroit, and Michilimackinac remained British, they preserved Britain's native
alliances and the influence of the Montreal fur-trade brigades
in the west. To expand westward, the United States needed the
forts; but to claim the forts, the new nation had to abide by its
promises to the loyalists.

National interest, national honour, and a dawning sense
that the republic was secure and would not be threatened by
the return of loyalists, quickly combined to change both laws
and attitudes hostile to the loyalists. Samuel Curwen was one of
the first to discover the consequences: by 1784 it was becoming
possible for a loyalist to return to the United States without fear
of persecution.

Many loyalists did return. Shelburne's rapid transition from
the loyalist capital with ten thousand citizens to Gideon
White's hardworking little port was accomplished by the quiet
return of many discouraged settlers to the United States. Some
of those who left Shelburne made their way elsewhere in Nova
Scotia, on to Upper Canada, or away to Britain or the Caribbean, but many simply accepted the tacit amnesty developing
in the United States. In New Brunswick at least a tenth of those
who had sailed in the loyalist fleets to Saint John returned
whence they had come. It was the same in Upper Canada: as
early as June 1784, Major John Ross reported that "the men are
changeable in their opinion since they have heard that the
Americans persecute the Loyalists not so violently as formerly."
Some of Samuel Farrington's fellow settlers, who were soon
recorded under the heading "Quitted his land and gone off",
surely found their way back to the United States.

The return of loyalists was not a sign of their political con-
version, and many committed opponents of the revolution
returned to the United States. Christopher Sower, who had
been arguing and fighting for the British cause since his days

as a German-language publisher in pre-revolutionary Pennsylvania, had become a publisher, postmaster, and King's Printer
in New Brunswick, but he eventually moved with his printing
business to Baltimore. Dr. William Paine, who in 1784 had fed
Edward Winslow's optimism with his glowing predictions of the
loyalists' future at Passamaquoddy Bay, was one of many settlers
there who went back to New England after a few disappointing
years. Such men were not obliged to change their beliefs or
acknowledge any error or crime in their loyalty when they took
advantage of the surprising tolerance that soon developed
between Britain and the United States. Most of the returning
loyalists were putting practicalities ahead of politics. Some of
the most convinced and thoughtful loyalists, in fact, had the
most difficulty adapting to the small societies and sometimes
limited opportunities of the new loyalist settlements, and found
themselves obliged to sacrifice political preferences for the
material security of the American cities.

But while some went back to the United States, the vast
majority of loyalists did not. For some it remained a matter of
principle. In 1776 Massachusetts-born loyalist Jonathan Sewell
had told Edward Winslow, "As to Massachusetts Bay, I wish
never to see it again 'til I return at the millennium – no, believe
me, Ned, the mad conduct of my countrymen has given me a
dose I shall never get over." Sewell often saw Samuel Curwen
during their London exile, but after Curwen went home,
Sewell remained true to his pledge. He went with his family
to New Brunswick and lived all his life there. Even Sewell visited New England, however, and most loyalists stayed in their
new Canadian homes neither out of stiff-necked obstinacy nor
out of inability to return if they chose.

Rather, most of the loyalists had discovered Canada, and
they had discovered it was not a howling wilderness in which to
eke out an exile for the sake of loyalty, but a place of promise.
Perhaps their success was not the sort that would compel the

American states to envy – republican America did not crumble
or New Brunswick prosper to quite the extent that Edward
Winslow had predicted in 1783 – but the perilous migrations of
1783 and 1784 had given birth to societies that refused to fulfil
the predictions of disaster the revolutionaries made for them.
Even as some loyalists limped back to the United States, equal
numbers of Americans, disenchanted with the fruits of the revolution, chose to join the loyalists north of the border. Some of
these had quietly supported the British cause. Some simply
liked Canada's prospects or came to join a relative or friend.
These "late loyalists", like the pioneers of 1783 or 1784, often
discovered in New Brunswick, Nova Scotia, and Lower or
Upper Canada places where satisfying and secure lives could
be made.

For most of the loyalists, the Canadian colonies worked in
precisely the way that revolutionary America had not. Where
the American Revolution made loyal colonials feel like exiles
in their own homes, the successful loyalists in Canada soon felt
at home in what may at first have been only a place of exile.
They quickly put down roots. Rather than remaining or
becoming a cohesive group, they adapted to the parts of Canada they lived in, so that soon there were several very different
and rather competitive loyalist colonies in British North
America.

Canadian circumstances eroded the master plans some of
them had brought, but loyalists who adapted to their new situation made vital contributions to the development of their communities. From the decline of Shelburne, Gideon White
emerged as a hardworking merchant of a kind well known to
Nova Scotia, typical of those who would bring Nova Scotian
society to its nineteenth-century "Golden Age" of global shipping trade and domestic prosperity. In New Brunswick, loyalist
names – not always those of the original leaders – appear all
through the history of the province, and in Upper Canada the

mix of agriculture, industry, and trade first established by the Farringtons, MacDonells, and Cartwrights has remained the basis of Ontario's wealth and power.

Adaptations to Canada were likely to include political evolutions. All the loyalists had taken a stand for the Crown and the British Empire, but even in the revolution their commitment had ranged from a rigorous toryism to some vague sense that royal government was hardly so evil as its enemies claimed. In Canada this diversity was preserved. The loyalist communities were rarely unanimous – or placid – in their politics.

Nevertheless, adaptations to small and fragile Canadian colonies often reinforced loyalties forged in the revolution, for all the Canadas of which the loyalists and their children became part needed the empire the loyalists had fought to preserve. In 1775 the loyalists had believed not only in the British Crown and the British government, but also in the British Empire of which they felt a part. They had held that Pennsylvania, New York, and South Carolina needed the empire and would not prosper without the imperial tie. The revolutionaries had proven them wrong, for the Thirteen Colonies continued to thrive and grow when they became the United States. But in Upper or Lower Canada or in any of the Maritimes colonies, the empire was not only esteemed but needed. Perhaps Pennsylvania could survive independently in 1783, but New Brunswick could not. The small, fragile, new colonies of British North America needed imperial assistance, imperial trade, imperial government.

In that world the loyalist commitment to the British Empire – all the stronger for their sufferings on its behalf – added a faith to a practical necessity. The commitment to empire that had made them exiles and victims in the Thirteen Colonies matched the needs of the infant colonies of British America precisely. And the survival and subsequent triumphs of the

British Empire, and the loyalists' share in them – from the shipping trades of New Brunswick and Nova Scotia to Upper Canada's victories in 1812 – vindicated their faith.

Could the loyalists themselves, the loyalists of 1783 and 1784, have predicted the astonishing ascendency of the nineteenth-century British Empire? Probably not, any more than they could have foreseen the distant and gradual diminishing of Canada's imperial ties. But the loyalists themselves had not come to Canada for the future glories of Trafalgar or the British Raj, and most of the world had not yet been coloured imperial pink. In 1783 and 1784 Gideon White and Sarah Frost and Samuel Farrington and most of fifty thousand others had settled in to make lives for themselves in particular corners of a much smaller empire. In Shelburne or Saint John or Marysburgh, the enduring loyalist achievement can be found in two hundred years of a Nova Scotia fishing port, a New Brunswick urban centre, or a rural Ontario farm, communities that could hardly have been born without both the loyalty and the labour of the loyalists.

Notes

These notes give the sources for quoted statements and for information on specific individuals. The bibliography that follows gives complete references for works briefly cited in the notes and lists other works that influenced various sections of the text.

ABBREVIATIONS USED:

AO:	The Audit Office papers of the Public Record Office, London
Haldimand:	The Haldimand papers in the British Museum Additional Mss
PAC:	Public Archives of Canada, Ottawa
PANS:	Public Archives of Nova Scotia, Halifax
OA:	Ontario Archives, Toronto
DCB:	*Dictionary of Canadian Biography*
MG:	Manuscript Group
RG:	Record Group

Preface

p. 8 "when we push" – Maier, *Old Revolutionaries*, xv.

The Eve of Revolution, 1774-75

pp. 13-15   Thomas Hutchinson – Bailyn, *Ordeal*.

pp. 15-17   Bart Stavers – AO 13/52/547; Egerton, Royal Commission, 29.

pp. 17-23   Alexander MacDonald – MacDonald, *Letterbook*; PAC, MG 23
         B1, #7583.

pp. 23-26   James Allen – Allen, *Diary*.

pp. 26-33   Nicholas Cresswell – Cresswell, *Journal*.

p. 31   Robert Jardine – AO 13/30/634.

p. 31   Mary Douglass – AO 13/39/374.

p. 33   Blue Jacket – DCB V, 852.

pp. 34-35   Thomas Peters – DCB IV, 626.

pp. 35-38   Moses Kirkland – AO 13/36/260.

p. 37   Thomas McKnight – AO 13/122/236.

p. 37   Lewis Johnston – Johnston, *Recollections*.

The Language of Liberty, 1763-76

p. 41   John Adams – Bailyn, *Origins*.

p. 53   William Smith – Upton, *Loyal Whig*.

p. 58   William Pitt – Simmons, *American Colonies*, 33.

The Crisis of Loyalty, 1775-76

pp. 65-69   Samuel Curwen – Curwen, *Journal*.

pp. 69-70   Samuel Hale – AO 13/52/268.

p. 70   Thomas Hutchinson – Bailyn, *Ordeal*.

p. 70   Jonathan Sewell – Raymond, *Winslow Papers*, 14.

p. 70   Isaac Hubbard – AO 13/41/476.

p. 70   Bart Stavers – AO 13/52/547.

p. 71   Daniel Leonard – AO 13/47/216.

p. 72   William Smith – Upton, *Loyal Whig*.

pp. 72-74   James Allen – Allen, *Diary*.

p. 73   John Smith – AO 13/72/55.

p. 73   Hugh Stewart – AO 13/72/139.

p. 74   Christopher Sower – AO 13/72/107; DCB IV.

pp. 74-76   Alexander MacDonald – MacDonald, *Letterbook*.

p. 75   Luke Bowen – AO 13/11/312.

p. 75   Donald Cameron – AO 13/11/442.

p. 75   Derby Lindsey – AO 13/19/104.

p. 76   Zaccheus Cutter – AO 13/53/37.

pp. 76-77   Samuel Bliss – AO 13/22/11.

p. 77   Thomas Gilbert – AO 13/24/199.

p. 77   William Cross – AO 13/24/94.

p. 77   Archibald Cunningham – AO 13/24/97.

p. 77   John Joy – AO 13/47/97.

pp. 77-78   John Jeffries – AO 13/47/40.

p. 78   Abraham Savage – AO 13/80/424.

p. 78   Allan Maclean – DCB IV; Haldimand 21762, p. 190.

p. 79   Richard Lechmere – AO 13/47/113.

p. 79   John McRae – AO 13/122/285.

pp. 79-80   Torquil MacLeod – AO 13/122/115.

p. 80   Allan MacDonald – AO 13/122/28; Vining, *Flora*.

p. 82   Moses Kirkland – AO 13/36/260.

pp. 80-81   Richard Lechmere – AO 13/47/113.

p. 81   Robert Campbell – AO 13/21/74.

The King's War, 1776-81

pp. 85-86   Alexander MacDonald – MacDonald, *Letterbook*.

p. 86   George III – Mackesy, *War for America*.

pp. 89-91   Guy Carleton – Stanley, *Canada Invaded*.

p. 90   Samuel Prenties – Prenties, *Narrative*.

p. 91   Allan Maclean – Historical Section, *Military and Naval Forces*;
             Wurtele, *Blockade of Quebec*, 179.

pp. 91-92   Six Nations – Graymont, *Iroquois in American Revolution*.

pp. 92-93   Thayendanagea – DCB V.

p. 92   Konwatsi-tsiaienni – DCB IV.

pp. 94-95   General Howe – Long Island Historical Society, *Memoirs*, II,
             407.

pp. 95-96   Francis Blackburn – AO 13/21/27.

p. 96   Jesse Hoyt – AO 13/41/406.

p. 96   Ichabod Oliver – AO 13/19/282.

p. 96   Abraham Van Buskirk – AO 13/19/323.

p. 96   Gabriel Van Norden – AO 13/19/418.

p. 97   Daniel Jessup – AO 13/25/216.

p. 97   Margaret Thomson – AO 13/24/151.

p. 99   George Boyle – AO 13/11/318.

p. 99   George Brenner – AO 13/11/344.

p. 99   Samuel Anderson – AO 13/11/48.

p. 99   Grace Clarke – AO 13/25/110.

pp. 101-102   Torquil MacLeod – AO 13/122/115.

p. 102   Moses Kirkland – AO 13/36/260.

p. 102   James Cassells – AO 13/127/332.

p. 103   "The Whigs and Tories" – Nadelhaft, "Havoc of War".

p. 103   "solemn assurances" – AO 13/127/332.

pp. 104-105   James Cassells – AO 13/127/332.

p. 105   Michael Egan – AO 12/127/421.

p. 105   Moses Kirkland – AO 13/36/260.

p. 105   Silas Deane – *Deane Papers* IV, 424.

The Loyalists' War, 1775-81

p. 108   Mather Byles – Brown, *King's Friends*.

pp. 108-109   Thomas Barker – AO 13/11/205.

p. 109   Azor Betts – AO 13/11/275.

pp. 109-10   Robert Campbell – AO 13/21/74.

p. 110   Benjamin Garrison – AO 13/24/193.

p. 110   Alexander MacDonald – MacDonald, *Letterbook*.

p. 111   Bartholomew Crannell – AO 13/12/117.

p. 111   Alexander Grant – AO 13/13/109.

p. 111   Samuel Moore – AO 13/19/192.

p. 111   Daniel Begal – AO 13/11/237.

p. 111   Lemuel Goddard – AO 13/24/201.

pp. 111-12   Mary Hoyt – AO 13/41/406.

pp. 112-13   John Cummings – *Calendar of N.Y. Historical Mss.*, 672-76.

pp. 113-14   Samuel Martin – *Calendar*, 349.

p. 114   Whitehead Hicks – *Calendar*, 347.

p. 114   John Willett – *Calendar*, 360.

p. 114   William Free – AO 13/12/511.

p. 114   Samuel Dickenson – AO 13/13/272.

p. 114, 115   Alexander Fairchild – AO 13/22/80.

pp. 114-15   Azor Betts – AO 13/11/275.

p. 115   Paul Gardiner – AO 13/24/190.

p. 115   Samuel Jarvis – AO 13/42/2.

p. 115   William Bustis – AO 13/22/26-32.

p. 115   John Anderson – AO 13/22/1.

pp. 115-16   Thomas Barclay – AO 13/11/169.

p. 116   Luke Bowen – AO 13/11/312.

p. 116   John Bates – AO 13/11/222.

p. 116   James Bruce – AO 13/25/7.

pp. 116-18   James Allen – Allen, *Diary*.

p. 119 Isaac and David Bennett – AO 13/11/301.

p. 119 Thomas Haycock – AO 13/13/205.

p. 119 Bartholomew Crannell – AO 13/12/117.

p. 119 Joannis Ackermann – AO 13/25/1.

p. 120 John Johnson – Fryer, *King's Men*.

p. 120 Abraham Van Buskirk – AO 13/19/323.

p. 120 James DeLancey – Longley, "DeLancey Brothers".

pp. 120-21 Timothy Hierlihy – AO 13/41/382; MacGillivray, *Hierlihy*.

p. 121 John Eagles – AO 13/12/353.

pp. 121-22 Alexander MacDonald – MacDonald, *Letterbook*.

Refugee Routes, 1777-83

pp. 124-25 Peter Berton – AO 13/11/235; OA *Report 1904*, 862; Scott, *Rivington's New York Newspaper*.

p. 125 Thomas Farrar – AO 13/24/193.

p. 126 Christopher Sower – AO 13/72/107.

p. 126 Robert Fowles – AO 13/52/234.

p. 126 William Frost – Raymond, *Kingston*.

p. 126 William Bates – Raymond, *Kingston*.

p. 126 Joseph Thorne – AO 13/20/220.

p. 126 Filer Dibblee – AO 13/41/257.

p. 127 "six hundred square-rigged . . ." – Cresswell, *Journal*.

p. 127 Thomas Gilbert – AO 13/24/199.

p. 127 James Van Emburgh AO 13/19/368.

pp. 127-28 Thomas Hazard – AO 13/68/311.

p. 128 "Money is here" – Cresswell, *Journal*.

p. 128 Charlotte Sergent – AO 13/72/99.

p. 128 Samuel Stearns – AO 13/80/460.

pp. 128-29 *Royal Gazette* – Scott, *Rivington's New York Newspaper*.

pp. 129-33 Nicholas Cresswell – *Journal*.

p. 133 Associated Loyalists – Tebbenhoff, "Associated Loyalists".

p. 134 Guy Carleton – Jones, "Guy Carleton"; Smith, "Guy Carleton".

p. 135 Southern loyalist population – Jones, "Guy Carleton".

p. 135 Moses Kirkland – AO 13/36/260.

p. 135 Thomas Farrar – AO 13/24/193.

p. 135 John Hardey – AO 13/31/105.

pp. 136-39 Black loyalists – Walker, *Black Loyalists*.

p. 136 Boston King, DCB V, 468. Quarles, *The Negro in the American Revolution*.

p. 137   Washington's slaves – Freeman, *Washington*, 465.

p. 138   Thomas McKnight – AO 13/122/236.

pp. 138-39   William Knox – AO 13/36/348.

p. 139   James Kitching – AO 13/36/309.

p. 139   Thomas Fenwick – AO 13/178/22.

p. 140   Moses Kirkland – AO 13/36/260.

p. 140   Thomas Edgehill – AO 13/127/330.

pp. 141-42   Bahamas – Craton, *History of Bahamas*.

p. 141   John Shoemaker – AO 13/80/433.

pp. 141-42   William Moore – AO 13/122/401.

pp. 142-43   Guy Carleton – Jones, "Guy Carleton".

pp. 143-44   Loyalists in Britain – Norton, *British Americans*.

pp. 143-44   Enoch Hawkesworth – AO 13/30/583.

p. 144   Samuel Curwen – Curwen, *Journal*.

p. 144   Archibald McCall – AO 13/31/136.

pp. 144-45   Christopher Carter – AO 13/22/44.

p. 146   Loyalist Associations – Wright, *Loyalists*.

p. 147   Amos Botsford – Wright, *Loyalists*.

pp. 147-48   anti-loyalist sentiment – Jacobs, *Treaty and Tories*.

p. 148   George Gillmore – AO 13/13/55; AO 13/41/302.

pp. 148-49   Thomas Hazard – AO 13/68/311.

p. 149   Richard Mackie – AO 13/31/306.

p. 149   John Siger – PAC, MG 23, B1, #7623(4).

p. 149   Peter Berton – Scott, *Rivington's New York Newspaper*.

p. 149   *Royal Gazette* – Scott, *Rivington's New York Newspaper*.

pp. 150-51   Alexander Dobbins – AO 13/22/67.

p. 151   Walter Bates – Raymond, *Kingston*.

p. 151   transport ships – Wright, *Loyalists*.

p. 152   Thomas Peters, DCB IV, 626; DCB V, 468.

pp. 152-54   Sarah Frost – Raymond, *Kingston*.

Preparing the Way, 1783

p. 159   Halifax merchants . . . predicted – Raymond, "McNutt".

p. 159   Alexander McNutt – Raymond, "McNutt"; DCB V.

pp. 159-60   Island of St. John – Clark, *Three Centuries*; Siebert and
         Gilliam, "Loyalists in P.E.I.".

pp. 161-62   John Parr – DCB IV; MacKinnon, "Loyalist Experience";
         MacDonald, "Memoir of Parr".

p. 162   escheat – Ells, "Clearing the Decks".

p. 164   Charles Morris – DCB V.

pp. 164-66   Benjamin Marston – DCB IV; Raymond, "Benjamin Marston".

pp. 165-66   John Parr – Raymond, "Marston".

p. 166   "the increase is so great" – PANS, MG 1/104, Jacob Bailey Papers.

pp. 171-72   Haldimand – DCB V.

p. 174   Walter Butler – Butler, "Journal".

p. 174   John Hay – PAC, MG 23 J5, John Hay Papers.

p. 175   Haldimand – Haldimand 21716/3/17, 14 Feb. 1783.

pp. 175-78   Six Nations – Graymont, *The Iroquois in the American Revolution*; DCB V, "Thayendanegea".

p. 176   Blue Jacket – DCB V, 852.

p. 177   "a free people"   Johnston, *Valley of Six Nations*, 35.

p. 177   Haldimand – Haldimand 21716/3/19v, 7 May 1783.

p. 178   "I will endeavour" – Ibid., 22v, 2 June 1783.

p. 178   "I wait with impatience" – Ibid.

pp. 178-79   Haldimand – Cruikshank, *Settlement of Loyalists*.

p. 179   surveyors – Cruikshank, *Settlement*.

p. 179   Justus Sherwood – Cruikshank, *Settlement*.

pp. 181-82   "great mortality" – MacDonald, "Memoir of Parr".

Edward Winslow's New Brunswick, 1783-1800

p. 183   Sarah Frost – Raymond, *Kingston*.

p. 183   Walter Bates – Raymond, *Kingston*.

p. 183   Chipman's Hill – Raymond, *River St. John*, 254.

p. 184   Peter Berton – AO 13/11/235.

p. 185   Edward Winslow – DCB V; Raymond, *Winslow Papers*.

p. 186   William Paine – Raymond, *Winslow Papers*, 196; DCB V.

p. 186   William Donaldson – Raymond, *Winslow Papers*, 266.

p. 186   Benjamin Marston – PANS, MG 1/1/1898, Ferguson Papers F9, 27 Feb. 1785.

p. 187   Winslow's optimism – Raymond, *Winslow Papers*, 189.

pp. 189-90   fifty-five petitioners – Wright, *Loyalists*; Gilroy, *Loyalists and Land Settlement*.

pp. 190-91   counter-petition – Gilroy, *Loyalists and Land Settlement*.

p. 192   John Coffin – Wright, *Loyalists*.

p. 192   Gilbert Studholme – DCB V.

p. 192   Peter Berton – AO 13/11/235.

p. 192   Walter Bates – Raymond, *Kingston*.

p. 193   Isaac Perkins – AO 13/19/43.

pp. 193-94   Maugerville – MacNutt, *New Brunswick*; Wright, *Loyalists*.

p. 194   John Billea – AO 13/11/277; Wright, *Loyalists*.

p. 194   Nase and De Peyster – Wright, *Loyalists*.

p. 195   Benjamin Ingraham – Wright, *Loyalists*.

p. 195   Thomas Carleton – DCB V; MacNutt, *New Brunswick*.

p. 196   Colin Campbell – AO 13/21/40.

pp. 197-98   Robert Campbell – AO 13/21/74.

pp. 197-98   Elias Hardy – DCB IV.

pp. 198-99   Azor Betts – AO 13/11/275.

p. 199   Filer Dibblee – AO 13/41/257.

pp. 199-200   Edward Winslow – Raymond, *Winslow Papers*, 356, 468.

p. 200   "pretty cottage" – Wynn, *Timber Colony*, 23.

pp. 200-201   Edward Winslow – Raymond, *Winslow Papers*, 443, 585, 669, 670.

Gideon White's Nova Scotia, 1783-1800

p. 203   Mary Jessup – AO 13/25/216.

p. 204   "refuse of the jails" – AO 13/41/218 (Polly Dibblee).

pp. 205-206, 209, 210-12   Gideon White – PANS, MG 1, White Papers; Ells, *Catalogue of White Papers*; Archibald, *Gideon White*.

pp. 206-10   Benjamin Marston – Raymond, "Marston".

p. 207   John Parr – Raymond, "Marston".

pp. 207-208   free blacks – Walker, *Black Loyalists*.

p. 208   "His Majesty's rotten pork" – Smith, "Loyalists at Shelburne".

p. 208   James Robertson – Smith, "Loyalists at Shelburne".

p. 209   Abraham Van Buskirk – AO 13/19/323.

p. 209   James Bruce – AO 13/25/7.

p. 209   Abraham Van Buskirk – Raymond, "Marston".

p. 209   "Many people have reduced" – White Papers, 310.

pp. 209-10   a riot – Raymond, "Marston".

p. 212   Nathaniel Whitworth – White Papers.

p. 212   Thomas Millidge – White Papers; DCB V; AO 13/19/177.

p. 213   James and Steven DeLancey – Longley, "DeLancey Brothers".

p. 213   Thomas Barclay – PANS, MG 1/939, Wentworth Papers, 13.

p. 213   Edward Winslow – Raymond, *Winslow Papers*, 250.

p. 213   Timothy Ruggles – Raymond, *Winslow Papers*, 107.

p. 213   Jacob Bailey – PANS, MG 1/104, Jacob Bailey Letterbook.

pp. 213-14   Thomas Peters Walker, *Black Loyalists*.

p. 214 Stephen Jones – PANS, MG 1, White Papers, 385.

p. 215 Frederick Feltmate – AO 13/24/163.

p. 215 Thomas Cutler – White Papers, 589.

pp. 215-16 Alexander MacDonald – MacDonald, *Letterbook*; Scott, *Rivington's New York Newspaper*.

pp. 215-16 Allan MacDonald – AO 13/122/28.

p. 216 *Nova Scotia Gazette* – PANS, *Nova Scotia Gazette*, 23 Nov. 1784.

p. 216 McPhee, McMillan, Hennigar – PANS, MG 100, vols. 163/10 and 184/22, 42; Gilroy, *Loyalists and Land Settlement*.

pp. 216-17 Jesse Hoyt – AO 13/41/406.

p. 217 Edward Winslow – Raymond, *Winslow Papers*, 250.

pp. 217-18 Jacob Bailey – PANS, MG 1/104, Bailey Letterbook, p. 45.

p. 218 Jacob Bailey – Ibid., p. 147.

p. 218 Gideon White – White Papers, 560.

pp. 219-21 blacks of Shelburne – Walker, *Black Loyalists*.

p. 220 Thomas Peters – DCB IV.

pp. 220-21 Boston King Walker, *Black Loyalists*.

p. 221 Gideon White – White Papers, 560.

p. 221 James Dole – Wright, *Loyalists*; AO 13/12/308; White Papers, 574.

pp. 221-22 Abraham Van Buskirk – AO 13/19/323.

p. 222 James Bruce – AO 13/25/7.

p. 222 Mary Jessup – AO 13/25/216; Gilroy, *Loyalists and Land Settlement*.

pp. 222-23 Gideon White – White Papers, 616.

Samuel Farrington's Upper Canada, 1784-1800

p. 224 Samuel Farrington – Cruikshank, *Settlement*, 110; Haldimand 21828, p. 74.

p. 225 Stephen Farrington – AO 13/12/387; OA *Report 1904*, p. 443.

p. 225 Farrington family – Reid, *Loyalists of Ontario*.

p. 225 King's Royal Regiment – Fryer and Smy, *Rolls of the Provincial Corps*.

p. 225 "lost use of his legs" – AO 13/12/387.

p. 226 Samuel Farrington – Cruikshank, *Settlement*, 110.

p. 226 Yamachiche – Siebert, "Temporary Settlement".

p. 227 William Mooney – AO 13/80/343.

p. 227 Peter Van Alstine – OA *Report 1904*, p. 445.

p. 227 Michael Grass – DCB V; AO 13/13/118.

p. 228 Josiah Cass – Cruikshank, *Settlement*, 52.

p. 229 title to land – Cruikshank, *Settlement*, 45.

pp. 230-31   rival plans – Cruikshank, *Settlement*, 61; Siebert, "Loyalist Settlements in Gaspé".

p. 230   Abraham Cuyler – Morgan, "Loyalists of Cape Breton".

pp. 230-31   Missisquoi – Cruikshank, *Settlement*, 85; Siebert, "Loyalists in the Eastern Seigniories".

p. 232   Jacob Maurer – Cruikshank, *Settlement*, 73.

pp. 232-33   Archibald MacDonell – Preston, *Kingston*, 74; Cruikshank, *Settlement*, 135; Scott, "Loyalist Family"; AO 13/80/289.

pp. 232-34   Samuel Farrington – Cruikshank, *Settlement*, 135.

p. 234   Marysburgh – Haldimand 21828, p. 40, July 1784.

p. 234   John Collins – OA A/1/1/, vol. 3, Collins, 12 Aug. 1784.

p. 235   muster of Marysburgh – Haldimand 21828, p. 74, 4 Oct. 1784.

p. 235   John Stuart – Preston, *Kingston*.

p. 236   Edward Jessup – DCB V.

p. 236   John Collins – Preston, *Kingston*.

pp. 236-37   Kingston – Preston, *Kingston*.

p. 237   John Stuart – Preston, *Kingston*.

p. 237   Butler's Rangers – Fryer, *King's Men*.

pp. 237-39   Six Nations – Johnston, *Valley of Six Nations*; Graymont, *Iroquois in American Revolution*.

p. 239   Marysburgh in 1787 – OA *Report 1905*, p. 468, 6 Oct. 1787; Preston, *Kingston*.

p. 240   MacDonell and Johnson – Cruikshank, *Settlement*, 167.

pp. 241-42   Richard Cartwright – DCB V; PAC, MG 23 H, Cartwright Papers.

p. 243   ex-officers' petition – Preston, *Kingston*.

p. 244   Edward Winslow – Raymond, *Winslow Papers*, 470.

p. 244   John May – OA, RG 1, L3/397, May petition, 14 June 1793.

p. 244   "stood by their property" – OA, RG 1, L3/327, Devant petition, c. 1793.

p. 245   John Graves Simcoe – DCB V.

p. 246   Richard Cartwright – DCB V.

p. 246   acreages of land granted – Paterson, *Land Settlement*; Blake and Greenhill, *Rural Ontario*.

p. 247   Katherine Brown – Reid, *Loyalists of Ontario*.

Taking Root

p. 248   Samuel Curwen – Curwen, *Journal*.

p. 249   American attitudes – Jacobs, "Treaty and Tories".

p. 249   John Adams – Hoerder, *Crowd Action*, p. 7.

p. 250   New Brunswick a tenth – Wright, *Loyalists*; Acheson, "Loyalist County".

p. 250   John Ross – Cruikshank, *Settlement*, 125.

p. 250   "Quitted his land" – Haldimand 21828, p. 74, Oct. 1784.

pp. 250-51   Christopher Sower – AO 13/72/107; DCB IV.

p. 251   William Paine – Raymond, *Winslow Papers*, 196.

p. 251   Jonathan Sewell – Raymond, *Winslow Papers*, 14.

Bibliography

Primary Sources

OTTAWA, PUBLIC ARCHIVES OF CANADA
PAC MG 14, Audit Office 13, Records of the Loyalist Claims Commission
PAC MG 21, British Museum, Additional Manuscripts 21670-21877, "The Haldimand Papers"
PAC MG 23, British Headquarters Papers, New York, 1782-83
    Richard Cartwright Papers
    John Hay Papers

HALIFAX, PUBLIC ARCHIVES OF NOVA SCOTIA
PANS MG 1, Jacob Bailey Papers
    C. B. Ferguson Papers
    Wentworth Papers
    White Papers
PANS MG 100, Hennigar, McPhee, McMillan Papers

TORONTO, ARCHIVES OF ONTARIO
OA RG 1, A/1/1, Surveyor-General's Letters, 1784-85
OA RG 1, L3, Upper Canada Land Petitions, 1793-97

Books, Articles, Printed Documents

Acheson, T. W. "A Study in Historical Demography of a Loyalist County."
    Histoire sociale/Social History I (1968): 53-65.

Allen, James. "Diary." *Pennsylvania Magazine of History* 9 (1885): 176-96,
    278-96, 424-41.

Archibald, Mary. *Gideon White, Loyalist*. Shelburne, N.S.: Shelburne
    Historical Society, 1975.

Bailyn, Bernard. *The Ideological Origins of the American Revolution*.
    Cambridge, Mass.: Belknap Press, 1967.

——. *The Ordeal of Thomas Hutchinson*. Cambridge, Mass.: Belknap
    Press, 1974.

Blake, Vershoyle Benson, and Ralph Greenhill. *Rural Ontario*. Toronto:
    University of Toronto Press, 1967.

Bonomi, Patricia U. *A Factious People: Politics and Society in Colonial New
    York*. New York: Columbia University Press, 1971.

Brown, Wallace. *The King's Friends*. Providence, R.I.: Brown University
    Press, 1965.

——. *The Good Americans: The Loyalists in the American Revolution*. New
    York: Morrow, 1969.

Butler, Walter. "Journal of Walter Butler." *Canadian Historical Review* I,
    no. 4 (1920): 381-91.

Calhoon, Robert McCluer. *The Loyalists in Revolutionary America,
    1760-81*. New York: Harcourt Brace Jovanovich, 1973.

Clark, Andrew Hill. *Three Centuries and the Island*. Toronto: University of
    Toronto Press, 1959.

Craton, Michael. *A History of the Bahamas*. London: Collins, 1968.

Cresswell, Nicholas. *Journal of Nicholas Cresswell*. London: Jonathan Cape,
    1925.

Cruikshank, Ernest A. *The Settlement of United Empire Loyalists on the
    Upper St. Lawrence and the Bay of Quinte in 1784: A Documentary
    Record*. Toronto: Ontario Historical Society, 1966.

Cumming, Peter, and Neil H. Mickenberg, eds. *Native Rights in Canada*.
    Toronto: Indian-Eskimo Assn., 1972.

Curwen, Samuel. *Journal of Samuel Curwen*. 2 vols. Cambridge, Mass.:
    Harvard University Press, 1972.

Deane Papers. Collections of the New York Historical Society (1889-94).

Dictionary of Canadian Biography. Vols. IV (1771-1800) and V
    (1801-1820). Toronto: University of Toronto Press, 1979 and 1983.

Egerton, Hugh Edward, ed. *Royal Commission on the Losses and Services of
    American Loyalists, 1783-85*. Oxford: Roxburge Club, 1915.

Ells, Margaret. "Clearing the Decks for the Loyalists." *Canadian Historical Association,* Annual Report for 1933, pp. 43-58.

———. "Settling the Loyalists in Nova Scotia." *Canadian Historical Association,* Annual Report for 1934, pp. 105-9.

———. *Catalogue of the White Papers.* Halifax: Public Archives of Nova Scotia, 1937.

Freeman, Douglas S. *George Washington.* Abridged edition. New York: Scribners', 1968.

Fryer, Mary Beacock. *King's Men: The Soldier-Founders of Ontario.* Toronto: Dundurn Press, 1980.

———, and William A. Smy. *Rolls of the Provincial (Loyalist) Corps.* Toronto: Dundurn Press, 1981.

Gilroy, Marion. *Loyalists and Land Settlement in Nova Scotia.* Halifax: Public Archives of Nova Scotia, 1937.

Government of Ontario, *Bureau of Archives Report,* Vol. II (1904), Vol. III (1905). Toronto: King's Printer, 1905, 1906.

Graymont, Barbara. *The Iroquois in the American Revolution.* Syracuse: Syracuse University Press, 1972.

Historical Section of the General Staff. *History of the . . . Military and Naval Forces of Canada.* 3 vols. Ottawa: King's Printer, 1919-21.

Hoerder, Dirk. *Crowd Action in Revolutionary Massachusetts.* New York: Academic Press, 1977.

Jacobs, Roberta Tansman. "The Treaty and the Tories: Ideological Reactions to the Return of the Loyalists, 1783-87." Unpublished Ph.D. dissertation, Cornell University, 1974.

Johnston, Charles M. *The Valley of the Six Nations: A Collection of Documents.* Toronto: University of Toronto Press, 1964.

Johnston, Elizabeth Lichtenstein. *Recollections of a Georgia Loyalist.* London: Mansfield and Co., 1901.

Jones, Alice Hanson. *Wealth of a Nation to Be: The American Colonies on the Eve of the Revolution.* New York: Columbia University Press, 1980.

Jones, Eldon Lewis. "Sir Guy Carleton and the Close of the American War of Independence, 1782-83." Unpublished Ph.D. dissertation, Duke University, 1968.

Long Island Historical Society. *The Battle for Long Island.* Long Island Historical Society Memoirs, Vol. II, 1869.

Longley, R. S. "The DeLancey Brothers, Loyalists of Annapolis County." *Collections of the Nova Scotia Historical Society,* no. 32 (1959).

MacDonald, Alexander. "Letterbook." *Collections of the New York Historical Society,* 1882.

MacDonald, James S. "Memoir of Governor John Parr." *Collections of the Nova Scotia Historical Society* XIV (1910): 41-79.

MacGillivray, C. J. *Timothy Hierlihy and His Times*. Halifax: Nova Scotia Historical Society, 1935.

Mackesy, Piers. *The War for America, 1775-83*. London: Longmans, 1964.

MacKinnon, Neil. "The Changing Attitudes of the Nova Scotia Loyalists, 1783-91." *Acadiensis* II (1973): 43-54.

————. "The Loyalist Experience in Nova Scotia 1783–91." Unpublished Ph.D. dissertation, Queen's University, 1975.

MacNutt, W. Stewart, *New Brunswick: A History, 1784-1867*. Toronto: Macmillan, 1963.

Maier, Pauline. *The Old Revolutionaries: Political Lives in the Age of Samuel Adams*. New York: Knopf, 1980.

————. *From Resistance to Revolution: Colonial Radicals and the Development of American Opposition to Britain, 1765-1776*. New York: Knopf, 1972.

Mason, Bernard. *The Road to Independence: The Revolutionary Movement in New York, 1773-77*. Lexington: University of Kentucky Press, 1966.

Morgan, Robert J. "The Loyalists of Cape Breton." *Dalhousie Review* LV (1975): 5-22.

Nadelhaft, Jerome. "The 'Havoc of War' and its Aftermath in Revolutionary South Carolina." *Histoire sociale/Social History* XII (1979): 97-121.

New York Historical Manuscripts: Revolutionary Papers. Albany, 1868.

Norton, Mary Beth. *The British Americans: The Loyalist Exiles in England, 1774-89*. Boston: Little, Brown, 1972.

Paine, Thomas. *Common Sense*. Philadelphia, 1776.

Paterson, Gilbert C. *Land Settlement in Upper Canada, 1783-1840*. Toronto: King's Printer, 1921.

Prenties, Samuel Walter. *Narrative*. Edited by G. G. Campbell. Toronto: Ryerson, 1968.

Preston, Richard A. *Kingston Before the War of 1812: A Collection of Documents*. Toronto: Champlain Society, 1959.

Price, Jacob M. *France and the Chesapeake*. 2 vols. Ann Arbor: University of Michigan Press, 1973.

————. "Economic Function and Growth of American Port Towns in the Eighteenth Century." *Perspectives in American History* VIII (1974): 123-86.

Quarles, Benjamin. *The Negro in the American Revolution*. Chapel Hill, N.C.: Duke University Press, 1961.

Raddall, Thomas H. "Tarleton's Legion." *Collections of the Nova Scotia Historical Society* 28 (1949): 2-41.

Rawlyk, George A. *Nova Scotia's Massachusetts: A Study of Massachusetts Nova Scotia Relations, 1630-1784.* Montreal: McGill-Queen's Press, 1973.

Raymond, W. O. "Benjamin Marston of Marblehead, Loyalist." *Collections of the New Brunswick Historical Society* 7: 79-110, and 8: 204-77.

———. "Colonel Alexander McNutt and the Pre-Loyalist Settlements of Nova Scotia." Royal Society of Canada *Transactions*, III, 5 (1911): 23-115.

———. *The River Saint John.* Saint John: New Brunswick Historical Society, 1910.

———, ed. *Kingston and the Loyalists of the Spring Fleet of A.D. 1783.* Saint John: Barnes, 1889.

———, ed. *The Winslow Papers, A.D. 1776-1826.* Saint John: New Brunswick Historical Society, 1901.

Reid, William D. *The Loyalists of Ontario: The Sons and Daughters of the American Loyalists of Upper Canada.* Lambertville, N.J.: Hunterdon House, 1973.

Scott, Kenneth. "Rivington's New York Newspaper: Excerpts from a Loyalist Press, 1773-83." *Collections of the New York Historical Society* LXXXIV (1973).

Scott, W. L. "A U. E. Loyalist Family." Ontario Historical Society *Papers and Transactions* 32 (1937):140-70.

Siebert, Wilbur H. "The American Loyalists in the Eastern Seigniories and Townships of the Province of Quebec." Royal Society of Canada *Transactions*, III, 7 (1913): 3-41.

———. "The Loyalists and Six Nations Indians in the Niagara Peninsula." Royal Society of Canada *Transactions*, III, 9 (1915): 79-143.

———. "The Loyalist Settlements on the Gaspé Peninsula." Royal Society of Canada *Transactions*, III, 8 (1914): 399-405.

———. "The Temporary Settlement of Loyalists at Machiche, P.Q." Royal Society of Canada *Transactions*, III, 8 (1914): 407-14.

———, and Florence Gilliam. "The Loyalists in Prince Edward Island." Royal Society of Canada *Transactions*, III, 4 (1910): 109-24.

Simmons, R. C. *The American Colonies: From Settlement to Independence.* New York: David McKay, 1976.

Smith, Paul Hubert. *Loyalists and Redcoats: A Study in British Revolutionary Policy.* Chapel Hill: University of North Carolina Press, 1964.

————. "Sir Guy Carleton, Peace Negotiations and the Evacuation of New York." *Canadian Historical Review* 50: 245-64.

Smith, T. Watson. "The Loyalists at Shelburne." *Collections of the Nova Scotia Historical Society* VI (1887-88): 53-89.

Stanley, G. F. G. *Canada Invaded 1775-76.* Toronto: Hakkert, 1973.

Tebbenhoff, Edward H. "The Associated Loyalists: An Aspect of Militant Loyalism." *New York Historical Society Quarterly* LXIII (1979): 115-44.

Upton, L. F. S. *The Loyal Whig: William Smith of New York and Quebec.* Toronto: University of Toronto Press, 1969.

Vining, Elizabeth Gray. *Flora: A Biography.* Philadelphia: Lippincott, 1966.

Walker, James W. St. G. *The Black Loyalists.* Halifax: Dalhousie University Press, 1976.

Williamson, Chilton. *American Suffrage from Property to Democracy.* Princeton: Princeton University Press, 1960.

Wood, Gordon S. "Conspiracy and the Paranoid Style: Causality and Deceit in the Eighteenth Century." *William and Mary Quarterly,* III, 39 (1982): 401-41.

Wright, Esther Clark. *The Loyalists of New Brunswick.* Privately published. Fredericton, 1955.

Wurtele, Frederick C. *The Blockade of Quebec in 1775-76.* Quebec: Literary and Historical Society of Quebec, 1905.

Wynn, Graeme. *Timber Colony: A Historical Geography of Early Nineteenth Century New Brunswick.* Toronto: University of Toronto Press, 1981.

Index

Abaco, Bahama Islands, 141
Acadians, 158, 162
Ackermann, Joannis, 119
Adams, John, 16-17, 38, 41, 59, 249
Adolphustown, Ont., 234, 239
Allen, Andrew, 25
Allen, James, 23-6, 53, 72-4, 116-18, 143
Allen, William, 23-6, 53, 143
American Highlanders, 78
American Revolution: Adams's view, 16-17; developments leading to, 52-60; start of, 60-1; Declaration of Independence, 63-4; challenge to Britain, 86; Iroquois, 91-3; conflict at Saratoga, 98-100; Cornwallis surrenders, 104; loyalist corps in Quebec, 172-4; treatment of loyalists, 252
Anderson, John, 115
Anderson, Samuel, 99
Annapolis Royal, N.S., 166, 212-14, 217-18

Bahama Islands, 62, 141-2, 152
Bailey, Jacob, 213, 217

Barclay, Maj. Thomas, 116, 213
Barker, Thomas, 108-9
Bates, Walter, 151, 183-4, 186, 192-3, 199, 201
Bates, William, 126
Begal, Daniel, 111
Bennett, Isaac and David, 119
Berton, Peter: merchant in N.Y., 124-5, 127, 133, 145; captain of Loyalist Association, 146; leaves N.Y., 149, 151, 153; at Oak Point, 184, 192, 194
Betts, Dr. Azor, 109, 114, 198-9
Billea, Pte. John, 194
Birchtown, N.S., 207, 209, 221
black loyalists, 136-40, 207, 209, 219-20
Blackburn, Francis, 95
Bliss, Samuel, 76, 79
Blue Jacket, 33, 176
Board of Associated Loyalists, 127, 133
Boston: Massacre, 55; Tea Party, 56; punitive acts, 57-8; battles, 60; influx of loyalists, 77; retreat, 80-1
Botsford, Amos, 147
Bowen, Luke, 75, 116

Boyle, George, 99
Brant, Joseph (Thayendanegea),
    92-3, 175, 238
Brant, Mary (Konwatsi-tsiaienni),
    92
Brenner, George, 99, 100
Brinley, Edward, 165
Brockville, Ont., 236
Brown, Capt., 154
Brown, Katherine, 247
Brown, Thomas, 38
Bruce, James, 116, 209, 222
Bunker Hill, 60, 77-8
Burgoyne, Gen. John, 99, 111
Bustis, William, 115
Butler, Maj. John, 173, 174
Butler, Capt. Walter, 174, 180
Butler's Rangers, 174, 179, 226,
    237
Byles, Mather, 108

Cameron, Donald, 75
Campbell, Colin, 196
Campbell, Robert, 81, 110, 197
Canada, 90, 252-4
Canadiens, 90, 91, 179
Cape Breton Island, 78, 158, 170,
    230
Carleton, Gov. Guy: Quebec Act,
    89; holds Quebec City, 90;
    strong stand at N.Y., 134, 145,
    149; peace talks, 142; evacu-
    ation of N.Y., 152; succeeds
    Haldimand, 182; petition for
    land, 189
Carleton, Thomas, 170, 195
Carleton Island, 224, 226, 232
Carter, Christopher, 144, 145
Cartwright, Richard, 241-2, 243,
    245, 246
Cass, Josiah, 228-9
Cassells, James, 102, 104-5
Cataraqui (Kingston), Ont., 226,
    227, 228, 231, 234, 236-7

Chaleur Bay, 230
Chambly, Que., 230
Charleston, S.C., 35, 135
Charlottetown, 62
Chedabucto Bay, 214
Chesapeake Bay, 27-8, 79, 104
Chipman, Ward, 189
Clarke, James, 99
Claus, Daniel, 238
Clinton, Gen. Henry, 101
"Coercive Acts", 58
Coffield, Lt. Thomas, 150
Coffin, Maj. John, 192
Collins, John, 179, 181, 234-5, 236
colonial assemblies, 43
committees of correspondence, 57
committees of safety, 112
Common Sense, 62-3
Concord, Mass., 60, 67
Continental Army: established
    under Washington, 61; siege in
    Boston, 77; retreat from N.Y.,
    96; retreat from Philadelphia,
    97-8; cuts off Burgoyne's army,
    99; at Yorktown, 104; invitation
    to loyalists, 114; peace treaty,
    147; enters N.Y., 150
Continental Congress, 59, 61-2,
    63, 97
Cornwall, Ont., 235
Cornwallis, Gen. Charles, 103-6
Crannell, Bartholomew, 111, 119
Cresswell, Nicholas, 26-7, 29-33,
    129-32, 133
Cross, William, 77
Cummings, John, 112-13
Cunningham, Archibald, 77
Curwen, Samuel, 65-9, 144, 248-9,
    251
Cutler, Thomas, 215
Cutter, Zaccheus, 76
Cuyler, Abraham, 230

Deane, Silas, 105

Declaration of Independence, 63-4, 94

De Lancey, James, 120, 213

De Lancey, Oliver, 120

De Lancey, Stephen, 213

de Peyster, Capt. Abraham, 194

Deserontyon, 238

Deveaux, Andrew, 141

Dibblee, Filer, 126, 199

Dibblee, Frederick, 199

Dickenson, Samuel, 114

Digby, N.S., 213

Dobbins, Alexander, 150-1

Dole, James, 221

Dominica, 141

Donaldson, William, 186

Douglass, Mary, 31

Dunmore, Lord, 79, 80

Eagles, John, 121

Edgehill, Thomas, 140

Egan, Michael, 105

escheat: obtaining land in N.S., 162

Fairchild, Alexander, 114, 115

Fanning, Edmund, 103

Farrar, Thomas, 125, 135

Farrington, Deborah, 225, 226, 235

Farrington, Robert, 225, 226, 235

Farrington, Samuel, 224-5, 226, 235, 239, 240, 246-7

Farrington, Stephen, 225, 226, 234, 235

Feltmate, Frederick, 215

Fenwick, Thomas, 139

Fletchall, Thomas, 38

Florida, East and West, 89, 102, 135

Fort Cataraqui, 236

Fort Frontenac, 227

Fort Howe, 168

Fort Niagara, 226

Fort St-Jean (later St. Johns, Quebec), 230

Fowles, Robert, 126

France, 61, 87, 100, 147

Franklin, Benjamin, 53, 60

Franklin, Gov. William, 60, 114, 133

Fredericton, 195

Free, William, 114

Freer, Joannis, 112

French, Gershom, 179

Frost, Sarah, 152-4, 168, 183

Frost, William, 126, 152

Furman, Shadrack, 150

Gage, Gen. Thomas, 58, 60, 66, 71, 78, 79, 80, 90

Gardiner, Paul, 115

Garrison, Benjamin, 110

Gaspé, 230

Gaspee, 55

George III, 59, 62, 64, 68, 86, 219, 246

Georgia, 35, 37, 59, 101, 102, 104, 135

German immigrants, 74

Germany, 88

Gilbert, Thomas, 77, 127

Gillmore, George, 148

Goddard, Lemuel, 111

Goreham, Joseph, 153

Grand River, 238

Grant, Alexander and Sarah, 111

Grass, Michael, 227, 236

Great Britain: limited westward expansion, 32, 46, 54; imperial theory, 39; voting power, 43; rights of Englishmen in colonies, 43; Seven Years War, 45-6; eighteenth-century politics, 47-8; outbreak of war, 86; German regiments, 88; sea power, 89; major European war develops, 100; Cornwallis surrenders, 104; aid to escaping slaves, 137-8; loyalists in, 144-5; peace treaty, 147; evacuation of N.Y., 150-1; landholding in Upper Canada, 229

Guysborough, N.S., 214

Haldimand, Gov. Frederick, 171-82, 226-9, 230-1, 239, 240, 246

Hale, Samuel, 69-70, 71, 72, 76

Halifax: Howe retreats to, 80; restored as military head-quarters, 93; land rush, 158-9; growth since refugees, 166; Saint John settlement wants separation, 169; hopes for Shelburne failed, 218, 221

Hamilton, Robert, 242

Hardey, John, 135

Hardy, Elias, 197-8

Harris, Maj. John Adolphus, 233

Hawkesworth, Enoch, 143

Hay, Sgt. John, 174

Haycock, Thomas, 119

Hazard, Thomas, 127, 148

Hennigar, Christian, 216

Hicks, Whitehead, 114

Hierlihy, Timothy, 120-1

Highlanders of North Carolina, 79, 80

Holland, 100

Holland, Maj. Samuel, 178

Hopkins, Ezek, 62

Howe, Richard, 94

Howe, Gen. William, 94-5, 96-8

Hoyt, Jesse, 96, 216-17

Hoyt, Mary, 111, 216

Hubbard, Isaac, 70

Hudson River, 19

Hurons, 92, 180

Hutchinson, Gov. Thomas, 13-15, 38, 70, 143

Indians: agents in Mohawk Valley, 75; treaties limiting westward

expansion, 32, 46, 54; American Revolution, 61, 91-3. *See also* Hurons; Iroquois; Mississauga Indians; Six Nations Confederacy

Ingraham, Sgt. Benjamin, 195

Iroquois, 91-3, 175, 176, 180, 237-8

Island of St. John (P.E.I.), 159, 163, 170

Jamaica, 140

Jardine, Robert, 31

Jarvis, Samuel, 115

Jefferson, Thomas, 63, 130

Jeffries, Dr. John, 77-8

Jessup, Daniel, 97, 203-4, 212, 222

Jessup, Ebenezer, 173

Jessup, Edward, 231, 236

Jessup, Mary, 203, 222

Jessup's Rangers, 111

Johnson, Sir John, 75, 120, 173, 225, 229, 240

Johnson, Samuel, 49

Johnson, Sir William, 20, 75, 92, 120

Johnston, Lewis, 37

Johnstown. *See* Cornwall

Jones, Lt. David, 179

Jones, Stephen, 214

Joy, John, 77

Kelsick, Capt., 151

Kennebecasis River, 192

King, Boston, 137, 220-1

King's American Regiment, 103, 194-5

King's Royal Regiment of New York, 120, 226, 235

Kingston, N.B., 192-3

Kingston, Ont., 199, 226, 231, 235, 236, 247. *See also* Cataraqui

Kirk, James, 29

Kirkland, Moses, 35-8, 80, 102, 105, 107, 135, 140

Kitching, James, 139
Knox, Alexander, 29
Knox, William, 140
Konwatsi-tsiaienni, 92

Lachine, Que., 232
Lake Champlain, 174, 179
Lancaster, Ont., 235
landholding: in N.Y., 19; in
  tobacco colonies, 27-8; voting
  power in colonial assemblies,
  42; speculation in N.S. and
  P.E.I., 158-60; social hierarchy
  in N.B., 188-91, 199; in Upper
  Canada, 229, 239-40, 245,
  246-7
Lawson, George, 112
Lechmere, Richard, 79, 81
Legge, Gov. Francis, 122
Leonard, Daniel, 71, 76
Lexington, Mass., 60, 67, 77
liberty, 48-55, 63-4, 68-9
Lindsey, Derby, 75
Littledale, 151
London, Eng., 144
London, Ont., 245
Lower Canada, 227-30, 245
loyalists: labelled tories, 68; influx
  into Boston, 77; reconquest of
  N.Y., 94, 95, 125-6; campaign
  for the south, 101; imprisonment, 114; local and domestic
  struggles in colonies, 107-8;
  resentment against, 109; property confiscation, 115-16; enlistment in royal regiment, 119-23;
  war of vengeance, 132-3; Savannah and Charleston abandoned
  by, 135; free blacks and slaves,
  136-40; in West Indies, 140-2;
  in Britain, 143-5; Loyalist Associations, 146; peace treaty,
  147-8; evacuation from N.Y.,
  151; preparations made in N.S.,

162-3; in Port Roseway, N.S.,
  165; in Shelburne, N.S., 166-7,
  203-12, 218-23; on St. John
  River, 167-8; in Saint John,
  N.B., 167, 168, 196-9; in Passamaquoddy Bay, 168, 196-7;
  creation of N.B., 169-70; P.E.I.,
  170; in Quebec, 172; Haldimand's plan for settlement,
  178-81; achievements of Haldimand and Parr, 182; reactions to
  wilderness, 183-5; social hierarchy in N.B., 189-91, 199; Kingston, N.B., 192-3; Fredericton,
  195; blacks in N.S., 207, 209,
  219-20; Annapolis Royal,
  212-13; Chedabucto Bay,
  214-16; interior of N.S., 216;
  Halifax, 219; Montreal, 227;
  title to lands in Upper Canada,
  229-30; Lower Canada, 227-31;
  exodus from Lower to Upper
  Canada, 232; Marysburgh, Ont.,
  234, 239-42, 244, 246; Kingston, Ont., 226, 227, 228, 231,
  235, 236-7; settlement prospects
  in Upper Canada, 243-4; self-
  government in Upper Canada,
  243, 245; returning to U.S.,
  248-51; adaptation to Canada,
  253-4

McCall, Archibald, 144
MacDonald, Capt. Alexander:
  background, 17-22; looks to
  Britain for victory, 85, 87, 88-9,
  93, 94; recruits regiments of loyalists, 22-3; objective of war,
  107; upset about rank, 121; view
  of N.S., 216
MacDonald, Allan, 20, 22, 79, 85,
  215
MacDonald, Donald, 79
MacDonald, Flora, 20, 79, 215

MacDonald, Suzanna, 110
MacDonell, Lt. Archibald, 75,
    232-4, 240-1, 242, 243, 246
Mackie, Richard, 149
McKnight, Thomas, 37, 138
Maclean, Allan, 78, 85, 90-1, 121,
    172, 224
MacLeod, Torquil, 79, 101
McMillan, Finlay, 216
McNutt, Alexander, 159, 162, 165
McPhee, Evan, 216
McRae, John, 79
Manchester, N.S., 214, 215
Marion, Gen., 104-5
Marston, Benjamin, 164-7, 168,
    186, 206, 207, 208-10, 218
Martin, Samuel, 113
Maryland, 27
Marysburgh, Ont., 234, 237,
    239-42, 244, 246-7
Massachusetts, 14-15, 58-60
Maugerville, N.B., 193-4
Maurer, Capt. Jacob, 232
May, John, 244
Mennonites, 73, 244
Michel, John, 149
Michilimackinac, 174
Millidge, Thomas, 212
Missisquoi, Que., 230-1
Mississauga Indians, 180
Mohawk Valley, 74-5, 78, 109, 176
Montgomery, Richard, 21, 91
Montreal, 61, 90, 91, 172, 174, 227
Mooney, William, 227
Moore, Samuel, 111
Moore, William, 141
Morris, Charles, 164
Murphy, Patrick, 150

Nase, Ensign Henry, 194
Nassau, 141
Nerepis River, 194
New Brunswick, 170, 189, 190,
    198, 200-1

New France, 160
New Jersey, 96
New Jersey Volunteers, 120
New Providence, Bahama Islands,
    62
New York (colony), 19-20, 53, 74,
    91, 93, 97, 172
New York City, 19-20, 79, 94, 95-6,
    99, 124-8, 130, 139-40, 141, 149
New York Volunteers, 120, 121, 122
Niagara-on-the-Lake (earlier
    Butlersbury, then Newark), 237
North Carolina, 35-6, 79, 101, 103
Nova Scotia, 62, 93-4, 145, 146,
    151, 157-70, 188, 203-23
Nova Scotia Gazette, 216

Oak Point, 184, 192, 194
Oliver, Ichabod, 96
Ontario. *See* Upper Canada
Out Islands, 141

Paine, Thomas, 62, 72-3
Paine, Dr. William, 186, 251
Paris peace talks, 142
Parr, Gov. John: background,
    161-4; Port Roseway, 164-5; set-
    tlement at St. John River, 167,
    168; separation of Saint John
    community from N.S., 170;
    achievements, 181-2; Shel-
    burne, 206, 207, 208, 209, 210,
    218, 221
Passamaquoddy Bay, 168, 186, 196
patriot, 49, 63
peace treaty (1783), 147-8, 177
Penn, John, 24
Penn, William, 45
Pennsylvania, 23, 26, 45, 72, 74,
    79, 117
Penobscot, Maine, 196
Pensacola, Fla., 89
Perkins, Isaac, 193
Peters, Thomas, 220

Philadelphia, 24, 59, 68, 73, 97, 98, 102
Pitt, William, 58
Pointe au Chêne. *See* Oak Point
Port Roseway, N.S., 146, 164-6
Port Roseway Associates, 165, 204, 206, 218, 221, 223
Portsmouth, N.H., 15-16, 69
Prenties, Samuel, 90
Prescott, Ont., 236
Prince Edward County (Ont.), 246
Prince Edward Island, 159, 163
provincial congresses, 58
Prussia, 87

Quakers, 73-4
Quebec (colony), 152, 157, 171-2, 178, 229, 243
Quebec Act (1774), 89-90
Quebec City, 61-2, 90
Queen's Rangers, 121, 122-3

Reid, Leonard, 108
religion, 40-1
Rivington, John, 128-9, 149-50
Robertson, James, 208
Rogers, Peter, 149
Roome, John Le Chevalier, 150
Ross, Maj. John, 250
Royal American Gazette, 208
Royal Gazette, 128, 149
Royal Highland Emigrants, 78, 79, 102, 121-2, 215, 224, 233-4
Royal Proclamation of 1763, 46
Royal Yorkers, 120
Ruggles, Timothy, 213

St. Andrews, N.B., 196
St. Anne, N.B., 195
St. Augustine, Fla., 80, 89, 135, 136
Saint John, N.B., 154, 169-70, 186, 188, 197-8, 200, 201
St. John River, 61-2, 147, 158, 160, 167-8, 183-4, 185-7

St. Lawrence River, 235
St. Lucia, 141
Salem, Mass., 65-6, 67, 248
Saratoga, N.Y., 98-9
Savage, Abraham, 78
Savannah, Ga., 135, 136
Scribens, George, 150
seigneurial tenure, 229-30, 243, 246
Sergent, Charlotte, 128
Seven Years War (1756-63), 45
Sewell, Jonathan, 70, 76, 251
Shelburne, Earl of, 161, 170
Shelburne, N.S., 166, 203-12, 218-23, 250, 252
Sherwood, Justus, 179
Shoemaker, John, 141
Sierra Leone, 220-1
Siger, John, 149
Simcoe, Lt.-Gov. John Graves, 245, 246
Simsbury Mines, 114, 115
Sissiboo River, N.S., 214, 217
Six Nations Confederacy, 91, 93, 175-6, 237-9
slavery, 136-8
Small, John, 22, 78, 216
Smith, John, 73
Smith, William, 53, 72, 133-4
"Sons of Liberty", 53
Sorel, Que., 227, 230
South Carolina, 35, 80, 101, 102-3, 104
Sower, Christopher, 74, 126, 250
Spain, 86, 100, 147
Stamp Act (1765), 46, 53
Stavers, Bartholomew, 15-16, 38, 69, 70, 143
Stearns, Samuel, 128
Stewart, Hugh, 73
Street, Lt. Samuel Denny, 168
Stuart, John, 235, 237, 239, 241
Studholme, Gilbert, 192
Sugar Act (1764), 46

Tarleton's Raiders, 103
tea, tax on imports, 55-6
Thayendanegea, 92-3, 175, 238
Thirteen Colonies: imperial theory, 39-41; religion and culture, 40-1; colonial assemblies, 42; imposition of new taxes, 46-7; freedom in, 48-50; cause of liberty, 54; Continental Congress, 59-60; armed resistance, 60; foreign adventures, 61-2; attempts at reconquest, 93-9; resentment against loyalists, 107-13; local committees of safety, 112-14; jails, 114-15; property confiscation, 115; slavery, 136; peace treaty, 147-8. *See also* United States
Thomson, Margaret and Thomas, 97
Thorne, Joseph, 126
tobacco plantations, 27-9
"tory", definition of, 68
Trenton, N.J., 97
Trumbull, Gov., 60
Two Sisters, 152-3

Union, 151
United States: peace treaty, 147-8; Iroquois land, 177, 237-8; returning loyalists, 248-51. *See also* Thirteen Colonies
Upper Canada, 178, 224, 228-9, 232-47, 252

Van Alstine, Peter, 227
Van Buskirk, Dr. Abraham, 96, 120, 203, 209, 221
Van Emburgh, James, 127
Van Norden, Gabriel, 96
Virginia, 27-33

voting rights, in colonial assemblies, 42-3, 54, 64

Wanton, Gov., 60
Washington, George: background, 29; command of Continental Army, 61; Curwen met, 68; siege in Boston, 77, 80-1; retreat from N.Y., 96-7; retreat from Philadelphia, 97-8; at Yorktown, 104; Cresswell's view of, 29; slaves from Mount Vernon, 137; enters N.Y., 152
Wentworth, Gov. John, 71, 170, 182, 221
West, Benjamin, 24
Westchester Refugees, 120, 122
Weymouth, N.S., 214
White, Gideon: background, 205-6; prospers in Shelburne, 209, 211-12, 219; exodus of blacks, 219-20; adapts to Shelburne, 222-3, 252, 254
Whitney, Sylvanus, 153
Whitworth, Nathaniel, 210, 212
Willett, John, 114
Williamstown, Ont., 235
Winslow, Edward: background, 185; settlement at St. John River, 185-9; petition for land, 189-92; chaos in Saint John, 198; colony of N.B., 199-202, 251-2; relative of White, 206; Marston's plight, 210; view of loyalists' efforts at Annapolis Royal, 217; "Niagara fever", 244
Wright, Daniel, 149

Yamachiche, Que., 226, 228
Yorktown, Va., 104